"H................................h of
hi....................................ook-
st..............................and
straight people." —*The Atlanta Journal-Constitution*

"A powerful memoir. . . . A universal story of triumph over agony and loss." —*Ebony*

"Harris is a great storyteller who knows how to tug on the heartstrings with wit and sensitivity."
—*USA Today*

"Harris's work exemplifies a command of the language and a skill at describing physical settings and mental states that elevate storytelling into the realm of literature." —*Austin American-Statesman*

"Harris's fans will embrace his fast-paced memoir eagerly, and then be caught up in this engaging writer's engagingly told life story." —*Booklist*

"Harris is a wonderful writer." —*San Francisco Chronicle*

"What's got audiences hooked? Harris's unique spin on the ever-fascinating topics of identity, class, intimacy, sexuality, and friendship." —*Vibe*

E. LYNN HARRIS

WHAT BECOMES
OF THE BROKENHEARTED

E. Lynn Harris is a former IBM computer sales executive and a graduate of the University of Arkansas at Fayetteville. He is the author of eight novels: *A Love of My Own*, *Any Way the Wind Blows*, *Not a Day Goes By*, *Abide with Me*, *If This World Were Mine*, *And This Too Shall Pass*, *Just as I Am*, and *Invisible Life*.

In January of 2004, *Not a Day Goes By* was made into a nationally touring theatrical production. In 1996, 2002, and 2003, *Just As I Am*, *Any Way the Wind Blows*, and *A Love of My Own* were named Novel of the Year by the Blackboard African American Bestsellers, Inc. *If This World Were Mine*, *Abide with Me*, *Any Way the Wind Blows*, and *A Love of My Own* were nominated for NAACP Image Awards. *If This World Were Mine* won the James Baldwin Award for Literary Excellence. Harris was named one of the fifty-five "Most Intriguing African Americans" by *Ebony* for four consecutive years, including 2003. In 2002, Harris was included in *Savoy* magazine's "100 Leaders and Heroes in Black America." He was inducted into the Arkansas Black Hall of Fame in 2000. Harris divides his time between Atlanta, Georgia, and Fayetteville, Arkansas, where he is currently Writer in Residence at the University of Arkansas and has served as advisor and cheer coach for the Razorback cheerleaders.

E. LYNN HARRIS

WHAT BECOMES OF THE OF THE BROKENHEARTED

A MEMOIR

ANCHOR BOOKS
A Division of Random House, Inc.
New York

For my mother, Etta W. Harris, for unconditional love and being the most remarkable woman I know

and

For Aunt Gee, for teaching me that love worth having was worth waiting for, and also for being my first true best friend

In Memory

Lawrence Allen Sr. (Uncle Lawrence)

Duane Bremond

Eric Gupton

Thelma Coleman

Work like you don't need the money

Dance like nobody is watching

and

Love like you've never been hurt

—Anonymous

ACKNOWLEDGMENTS

This author is grateful to God for waking me up each morning and allowing me to have a career that I love and have a great deal of passion for.

The author thanks his family and friends, old and new. (More on them later.)

This author is proud to be a part of a publishing company that cares more about people than publishing bestsellers.

The author thanks Stephen (still the great) Rubin for his leadership, friendship, and support. Also to the amazing team of Michael Palgon, Jackie Everly, Bill Thomas, Suzanne Herz, Jen Marshall, Pauline James, Gerry Triano, Dorothy Boyajy, Emma Bolton, Clare McMahon, Kim Cacho, Rebecca Holland, Meredith McGinnis, Jenny Frost, Kathy Trager, Judy Jacoby, John Fontana, Tracy Jacobs, Anne Messitte, LuAnn Walther.

The author thanks Chris Fortunato and his staff.

Special thanks and love to Alison Rich, my publicist, whom I will miss dearly this summer as she gets to know the new love of her life. Hurry back, Alison!

Thanks to Sherri Steinfield and Felicia Polk for picking up the publicity slack. Welcome back, Sherri.

The author expresses special thanks to Martha Levin for discovering me and encouraging me to write this book. Your support and friendship mean the world to me.

The author is thankful that he has the best editor in the world who also happens to be one of my most treasured friends, the amazing and talented Janet Hill.

Thanks also to my backup editors and wonderful friends Charles Flowers and Chandra Taylor.

Thanks so much to Carol Mackey of Black Expressions for all your support.

Thank you to Christine McNamara, Karen DiMattia, and the folks in audio.

The author thanks his support staff: my agents John Hawkins, Moses Cardona, and Irv Schwartz. My accountant, Bob Braunschweig, and banker, Renee Ruff. The author couldn't make it without his special and trusty attorney, Amy Goldson. How do I manage without Anthony Bell and Laura Gilmore? Thanks, guys!

A warm shout out and a load of thanks to Tony Hillery (of TZR) and crew.

Many, many thanks also to the staff of the Trump International Hotel and Tower, with special thanks to Elizabeth, Suzy, and Carlos for being amazing people and friends who have never said no. I will miss you guys next fall more than you know.

The author thanks the following organizations for their continued and wonderful support: Delta Sigma Theta, Zeta Phi Beta, Alpha Kappa Alpha, Sigma Gamma Rho, Kappa Alpha Psi, Alpha Phi Alpha, The Links, NAACP, and all the book club members who read my novels and then write me and tell me what they *really* think.

The author thanks many members of the media for continued support, but most especially Roy Johnson, Linda Johnson Rice, Susan Taylor, Patrik Henry Bass, Deborah Gregory, and

Essence, Ebony, and *Savoy* magazines. Black Radio continues to be the life-line between my fans and me. Heartfelt thanks to: *The Tom Joyner Morning Show,* Doug Banks and DeDe McGuire, Wendy (Got the Heat) Williams, Steve Harvey, Frank Ski and his team, with special kisses to Wanda, Ryan Cameron, Donnie Simpson (much love to his beautiful wife, Pamela), Skip Murphy and his crazy team, with kisses to Nannette, Cliff, and Jeanie on the left coast. Summer wouldn't be summer without you guys. Thank you, thank you!

The author expresses thanks and love to his many fans who buy all my books, spread the word, and show up in the heat to get their books signed. Your support means the world to me! Now you can stop asking me when the memoir's coming out and what the "E." in "E. Lynn" stands for.

e. lynn harris
Atlanta, Georgia
May 2003

What Becomes
of the
Brokenhearted

I wanted the first line of my memoir to be brilliant. Something poetic that would linger after the final page had been turned. But I have learned that life brings you only lightninglike bursts of brilliance, and they are rarely lyrical. There is no other way to say it: I tried to kill myself one humid summer evening. Thank God I failed.

It was August 1990. After the day's heat had broken, I wandered around my one-bedroom Washington, D.C., apartment hopelessly depressed. Even though it was the beginning of a new decade, I was wondering how I had survived the previous two.

I had been depressed before, but never to the extent I felt the days preceding that night. I drank a bottle of Korbel champagne, and then made a call of desperation to my favorite Aunt, Gee, and her son Kenny, a minister who lives right outside of Atlanta. I mumbled on for a few minutes about how bad my life was; they told me they loved me, but I already knew that. They told me to trust in God and pray. I told them I would try to feel better, even though I felt God wanted no part of me. In my state of sadness, nothing I could say could explain how I felt: that my family's love was not enough, and that I had no reason to believe in God, much less live another day. I was convinced that I would die one of the brokenhearted.

I moved slowly into my bathroom and took out a large bottle of sleeping pills that I had convinced a close doctor friend to prescribe because recently I had found drinking was the only way I could get a few hours of sleep. I emptied the jar and assembled the white capsules in a straight line on my glass coffee table and slowly and methodically began to take them. I took one at a time, and then two at a time. I chased them with naked gulps straight from a bottle of hundred-proof vodka.

Before the pills began to take effect, I turned off the lights, the television, and the stereo. It still wasn't quiet enough. The darkness and silence were compromised by the sounds of the busy city traffic outside the three-story brick walk-up. Directly next door was a twenty-four-hour service station, and I could faintly hear the *ding-ding* of cars driving over a hose that alerted the attendants to the need for service. I could also hear the distant slamming of car doors, and the faint sound of voices.

I crawled into my bed and decided to give God a final chance to perform one of the miracles I'd heard about in childhood Sunday school classes. I talked silently to God, telling Him that I was ready to leave this place called earth. I asked Him to forgive me for taking matters into my own hands, but I knew He understood my pain and knew my heart. I closed my eyes and believed I was closing them for the last time.

I AWOKE ON THE HARDWOOD FLOOR next to my bed, with my face in my own vomit. For a moment I didn't remember how I had ended up on the floor or how I'd vomited, something I had done only twice in my entire life. I was confused and disoriented, and I had a headache from hell. My stomach was beckoning my attention as well.

The bedroom was still dark, so I didn't know what time it was. The night before, the pills and vodka, came back to me. I realized that my suicide attempt had failed, that God was in control and not ready for me yet. For a few startled moments I did not move. I just lay there in a fetal position with my eyes wide open and my eyelashes still.

Finally, I crawled and stumbled into my bathroom, then stood up and attempted to wash my face. The medicine cabinet mirror would not allow me to forget the previous night. I knew I was in deep trouble. I went to pick up the phone and realized it was off the hook. Once I got a dial tone I started to dial 911, but ended up calling a taxi instead.

It was only later, at Howard University Hospital, seated in the busy emergency room among gunshot victims and drug addicts, that I realized I wanted to live. Why I wanted to live was not quite clear, but I knew that I must live. My suicide attempt the night before had been unsuccessful for a reason.

Some of my recollections of the days preceding my attempt are a blur. I remember being overwhelmed by hopelessness and the feeling of how badly I wanted to die and be forgotten. I wanted to join my several close friends who had gone on before me. I wanted to be released from all the loneliness, feelings of shame and despair. The pain I felt but couldn't describe. I wondered how I, once described by a college professor as "a young man of unlimited promise," could end up trying to take my own life. Was it because I was a black man living in America? Was it because I was gay? Or was it because I was a gay black man who was living in a world that had a problem with both?

I've never had a problem being black, and on most of my days have taken great pride in that fact. I know that being light-skinned has given me a few advantages not enjoyed by every African American. But at the same time, I have to admit that I've sometimes felt a little disconnected from other African Americans, like I didn't quite belong, that I hadn't suffered in the same ways of many who had come before me and therefore wasn't "black" enough.

Once, when I was about nine years old, I asked my mother if my cousin Charles Jr., who shares the same skin color as mine, and I were white. She gave me a *Boy, you must be crazy!* look and suddenly burst out laughing and said, "Naw, boy, you and Charles Jr. ain't white." It wasn't that I wanted to be white, but I could look and see that our skin color was different from my sisters' and most of my cousins'. For some reason I still felt different, and as a young boy I had no way of explaining why. As a child I only knew that if it wasn't my color, then what could it be?

I don't recall the exact day I discovered I was gay or different. When I was young I always felt that it was something that only God and I knew. That it was our little secret and made me feel closer to Him. Still, being gay was the one thing about me that I prayed constantly that God would change. He didn't.

I am a black gay man.

Years ago, it would have caused me great pain to even write the word *gay* on paper to describe myself. I have cried more tears than the rivers can hold because of the word "gay." Early in my career as a novelist, no matter the subject matter that I was writing about, I would dodge questions about my sexuality. Maybe because there is so much more to describe me.

Still, each day that I'm alive, I become a little more self-assured and comfortable in my body. My healing process has been aided by saying what I know to be true. Writing has allowed me to change my self-hatred and doubt into true self-esteem and self-love. My prayers have changed out of absolute necessity so that I could fully enjoy the second half of my life.

After several months of intensive daily therapy, I returned to Little Rock, Arkansas, the city in which I was raised. My doctor thought it would be helpful in assisting with my recovery from my illness. At first I was afraid the trip might cause my depression to deepen, but I traveled back home despite my reservations.

On that trip I visited my grandmother, Bessie Harvey, the rock of my family, who was living in a high-rise retirement home. When I was young, I called it the old folks' home, but my grandma didn't appear old to me despite the fact that she was in her eighties. Neither she nor my mother knew of my suicide attempt, and when I told them I had been sick, I think they naturally assumed I had AIDS. I quickly volunteered the fact that I didn't. They had reason to be concerned, especially since in the previous two years I had repeatedly informed them that another one of my friends under thirty had died. I told them I was taking medication and seeing a doctor regularly, and that with prayer (something they both believed in) I would be well soon. I didn't think they would understand if I told them I had been diagnosed as clinically depressed.

I began to wonder if depression ran in my family. Did my mother and grandmother do what many other blacks with depression do—simply ignore it? Were their statements of "being down in the dumps" or "feeling blue" a form of depression?

During the visit, a table in the corner of Grandma's tiny studio apartment captured my attention. Covered with various knickknacks and a faux crystal candy dish, the table hosted pictures of all her children, grandchild, and great-grands—a pictorial history of our family. One picture stood out: In the middle of the table in a dusty silver frame, there was a sepia-colored photo of a little boy.

He looked about two years old. Smiling with tiny teeth, he had lively teddy-bear brown eyes and dark sandy-colored hair, neatly parted. He looked happy, like he didn't have a care in the world.

"Grandma, who is this?" I asked as I picked up the picture to inspect it closer.

"Let me see, baby," she said, as she reached for her glasses.

But before I showed the picture to her, it dawned on me that the little boy in the photo was me. I stood transfixed, looking at the picture and wondering if I was ever really that happy, and if so, whether I could ever be that happy again.

IT HAS BEEN MORE THAN twelve years since that afternoon. My grandma has since gone on to glory and her rewards. My success as a novelist has allowed me to experience the happiness I saw in the eyes of my childhood photo. There have been amazing days and nights in my life that I couldn't have even dreamed of myself.

I've also experienced disappointments. I realize that I live in a world that constantly reminds me that being black can sometimes be unacceptable and that I am a member of a race many of whom consider my sexuality inappropriate. I understand that no matter how much I have accomplished since that night in Washington, D.C., filmmakers and movie studios aren't rushing to make my life story a feature film or even a movie of the week.

In many ways writing saved my life. It's my hope that sharing my experience will give hope to others who are learning to deal with their "difference." I want them to know that they don't have to live their lives in a permanent "don't ask, don't tell" existence. Truth is a powerful healing tool.

But my hope for this book doesn't stop there. I think there is a message here for anyone who has ever suffered from a lack of self-esteem, felt the pain of loneliness, or sought love in all the wrong places. The lessons I have learned are not limited to race, gender, or sexual orientation. Anyone can learn from my journey. Anyone can overcome a broken heart.

This story—my story—is a voyage of seeking joy in simply being human. And unlike my novels, in which I can always craft a happy ending, here in the real world happy endings can't be plotted and penned with colorful words packaged inside covers with beautiful people adorning them. In sharing my story, it is my hope that readers will see glimpses of their own life and then bring about their own happy endings by living one day at a time, discovering their true passions, and realizing that every life is a story worth telling.

This is my story.

CHAPTER 1

"Easter day is near . . .
Easter day is . . ."

Beverly Smith, a chubby ten-year-old, paused. She had forgotten the words again. I wanted to shout out *Easter day is here*. Why couldn't she remember her speech? Even I knew her six-line speech.

Instead of saying *here*, Beverly stuck her fingers in her mouth and twirled her thick, uncombed plaits with her free hand. She looked as though she was going to cry, but suddenly she began to giggle, much to the dismay of our Sunday School teacher, Miss Whitfield, and myself. Beverly's completion of her speech was the only thing that stood in the way of my practicing my Easter speech and then joining my friends for a quick game of kickball before twilight covered the colored section of the east side of Little Rock, Arkansas.

It was the early 1960s and we were the only three people left in the Metropolitan Baptist Church, an ash-gray building as big as its name, and the centerpiece of our community of forty-plus families.

I was frustrated. All the other children had practiced their speeches and darted out of the church onto the streets to play before their parents called them in. It was not the kind of neighborhood where whole families sat down for dinner together, like

Leave It to Beaver, because in the 1960s, many of the black adults worked two jobs. In my neighborhood, if your own parents didn't tell you to come in, then some other adult would, and you had better obey.

I got tired of looking at Beverly, so my eyes moved to the wooden boards with black slip-in numbers listing the hymns from the previous week and the total attendance of Sunday School. I could hear the laughter and shouts filter in through the open windows of the church. From the voices I could tell my peers were playing the popular game of hide-and-seek, where the seeker sang, "Honey . . . honey . . . b . . . bar . . . b . . . bar . . . b. I can't see you see . . . see you see. Last night, night before, twenty-four robbers were at my door. I got up, let them in, hit 'em in the head with a rolling pin."

Miss Whitfield had saved me for last, because I had the longest speech: twenty-two lines. A speech that long was usually given to kids in the sixth grade, and never to an eight-year-old. I had memorized each line the first day I received the typewritten speech.

As Beverly started over and once again struggled for the words to her speech, my thoughts wandered to the upcoming Sunday. As my eyes left the wooden boards and moved toward the empty pulpit, I thought how proud my mama and daddy would be when I stood before the congregation and said my speech in my new Easter coat. Easter Sunday was the one time during the year I could count on Daddy being at church alongside my mother.

In my fantasy, church members would marvel not only at my presentation but at my new coat as well. They would question where the coat had come from and how my parents could afford such extravagance with three children. Little colored boys from my neighborhood were lucky to get a new shirt and possibly a clip-on tie for Easter or Christmas.

With a little coaxing from Miss Whitfield, Beverly finally finished her speech. I quickly jumped from the pew, raced to the front of the church, and said my speech in record time, every word perfectly clear and correct.

"That's wonderful, Lynn, but slow down a little on Sunday. Nobody's going anywhere until you finish." Miss Whitfield smiled. I nodded and smiled back, taking note that my accuracy had removed the anguish her face had shown during Beverly's struggle.

Easter Sunday 1964 finally arrived. After my bath, I raced into the tiny room I shared with my two younger sisters and saw the coat laid out on my twin bed. It was red, black, and green plaid with gold buttons. Daddy and I had picked the coat out together at Dundee's Men's Store. The coat had been on layaway since the day President Kennedy was shot in 1963. It's strange how vividly I remember that rainy and dreary day and how I tried to contain my excitement about getting out of school early while all the teachers at Bush Elementary were in tears over the news they'd heard over the intercom system.

After I got home that day, Daddy and I walked in the cold to the edge of downtown Little Rock. At first I thought that maybe I was going to the President's funeral when Daddy said he and his little man "Mike" were going to Dundee's to buy new suit coats. I realized that this was not the case when Daddy handed over five one-dollar bills and the elderly white man gave him a gray payment book. The coat was the first piece of clothing that I could remember that hadn't come from JCPenney's or Kent Dollar Store and was the first piece of clothing I had picked out. Now Easter was here and I could wear my new jacket. Mama had assembled it alongside a pair of black pants, white shirt, and red and black clip-on bow tie, and the shoes my daddy had polished to perfection sat under my bed.

I quickly put on my new clothes, and I could see my sisters, Anita and Zettoria, who were five and three, slip on new dresses over their freshly pressed hair. Anita had on a blue taffeta dress, and Shane (our nickname for Zettoria, since her name was so hard to pronounce) had on an identical one in pink. Their dresses were pretty but didn't compare to my coat.

From the bathroom, Mama urged us to hurry, while Daddy called from the living room for us to gather for a final inspection before we left for Sunday School. My sisters grabbed their new black patent-leather pocketbooks and raced to the living room to greet Daddy. I peeked from the corner of our room to watch Daddy's reaction.

"Look, Daddy. Don't we look pretty?" Anita said as she twirled around. Shane giggled as she put her pocketbook strap to her mouth.

"You sure do look good. Look at my little girls. Shane, take the purse out of your mouth, baby," Daddy said.

After Anita and Shane had accepted their compliments from Daddy, he called me in for inspection.

"Where is my little man? Come out here and let Daddy see that new coat," he said.

I quickly buttoned up each of the three gold buttons and dashed to the living room for Daddy's endorsement of my outfit.

"Look, Daddy. Look at me," I said with excitement as I twirled around like my sisters had moments before. Suddenly Daddy's bright smile turned into a disgusted frown. What was wrong? Didn't he like my new coat? Had Easter been canceled?

"Come here. Stop that damn twirling around," Daddy yelled.

I stopped and moved toward Daddy. He was seated on the armless aqua vinyl sofa. Before I reached him, he grabbed me and shouted, "Look at you. You fuckin' little sissy with this coat all buttoned up like a little girl. Don't you know better? Men don't button up their coats all the way." Before I could respond or clearly realize what I had done wrong, I saw Daddy's powerful hands moving toward me. His grip was so quick and powerful that I felt the back of my prized coat come apart. A panic filled my tiny body when I saw his hands clutching the fabric. I began to cry as my sisters looked on in horror. I could hear Mama's high heels clicking swiftly as she raced to the living room from the kitchen.

"Ben, what are you doing?" Mama asked.

"Shut up, Etta Mae. I'm taking care of this. Stop all that damn crying. Stop it now!" Daddy said to me.

I couldn't stop crying as I saw one of the gold buttons roll under the metal television stand into the corner of room.

"If you don't stop that crying, I'm gonna whip your little narrow ass," Daddy warned as he released me.

Now I was crying harder than before. Snot dripped from my nose to the top of my lip as my mother inspected my badly torn coat.

"Come here, baby. Stop crying," she said as she pulled me close to her chest.

"Let him go. Stop babying him," Daddy said as he pulled me from my mother's embrace. "How is he ever gonna become a man with you babying him all the time!" he yelled.

Mama didn't answer. She never did when he talked in this tone. She knew this routine too well.

"Stop that sniffling and clean your face, you little sissy," he said to me. "What are you going to wear to church now?"

I didn't answer, and I wiped my nose with the arm of my prized jacket and began crying once again.

"If you don't stop that damn crying, I'm going to make you wear one of your sister's dresses to church."

I caught myself and stopped crying. Daddy meant what he said. I would be the laughingstock of the entire neighborhood. It wouldn't matter that I had the longest and most difficult speech. I could see all my friends pointing and laughing at me.

I looked at the anger in Daddy's eyes and the fear on my

mother's face as I blinked back tears. The small four-room clap-board house was silent with the exception of my sniffles. The liv-ing room suddenly felt too small, the ceiling too low. I looked around the room at my mother and sisters and then out the win-dow, and watched the cars race past our house on East Twenty-first Street.

I don't remember much after my mother pulled me back into the bedroom. I remember standing before the packed church that Easter Sunday and hearing my name being called and the older ladies of the church adorned in their Easter Sunday finery saying, "Go 'head, baby. Preach the word."

I said my speech, each word of the twenty-two lines. I could hear the polite applause and "amens" that followed, as I, with my head held low, took my appointed seat on the pew with the other children from my Sunday School class, dressed perfectly in their finest clothes. I don't remember what I wore that Easter Sunday or many Easters that followed. All I recall is that I wasn't wear-ing a dress, and I remember what my daddy had said to me. I didn't know what a sissy was and why Daddy despised them so. All I knew was that I was determined never to be one.

MY NAME IS NOT MIKE. Not Michael. It is Everette Lynn Harris, but my daddy called me Mike when he was proud of me. I often wondered why I wasn't named Mike, but since he was the only one in my family who called me that, I figured Mama had won the battle of names when I was born during the early sum-mer of 1955, two years before my hometown would become famous not for the state's natural beauty, but rather for trying to keep nine colored students out of their prized Little Rock Central High.

The more I thought about it, I figured Daddy called me Mike because he thought Lynn was a girl's name, and Everette, a name my Great-Aunt Mary had made up, didn't sound tough either. But I loved my middle name, and that's what my mother, sisters, and cousins always called me. When friends at school would ask why I spelled Lynn like a girl, I would reply, "Because that's the way my mama spelled it."

Maybe Daddy called me Mike because of Michael Stewart, one of my childhood friends whose father was one of Daddy's running buddies. Whenever Daddy called me Mike, he would always have a look of pride on his face, so I didn't really mind.

My daddy, Ben Odis Harris, was a towering, slightly over-weight red-boned man with a talent for painting signs and drink-ing, which was when his other talent showed, beating up people smaller than he was. His favorite punching bags were my mother and me.

He was loved and adored by most of the kids in our tight-knit neighborhood of working-class colored people, and was affectionately called Uncle Ben by neighborhood children who shared no lineage with my sisters and me. Maybe it was because Daddy always appeared good-natured when he walked or drove around the streets of East Twenty-first, Rock, and Commerce. Daddy would often gather up children for trips to the Sweden Crème on Main Street for ice cream during sticky summer months. Maybe they liked him so much because sometimes when Daddy drank he was funny, and acted like a big child himself before he became violent.

Daddy filled my own life with fear for as long as I could remember. Fear that I talked too much, read too much, and couldn't perform simple tasks like getting his water cold enough, or that I would forget to wake him when he went to sleep in front of the black-and-white television. After all, as he often reminded me, I was a poor excuse for a son.

During the first twelve years of my life, I found very few ways to please my father. It didn't matter that most of my teachers loved me and that I made straight A's and only got B's in citizenship because I talked too much at school, partly because I was afraid to talk at home. Daddy did seem proud when I came home dirty and bloody from street football games. It didn't matter that I was usually the last one picked for a team.

His moods would change in a positive way when he had steady work painting signs or driving the local sanitation truck or when he wasn't drinking his syrup-colored liquor. When there was no work and he was drinking, a storm would settle down upon my mother and me and we would wait, in terror, for it to pass.

Sometimes I felt he loved me. Once he took me fishing at a small pond behind the Arkansas state capitol. Another time he took me with him when he was driving a truckload of bananas to St. Louis. My sisters wanted to go, but Daddy said no, "Just me and my little man." We slept in the truck's private compartment, and ate cheeseburgers with ice-cold milk at the many truck stops along the highway between Little Rock and St. Louis. I could tell Daddy was having fun on the trip because he called me Mike the whole time and he would have the biggest smile on his face when other truckers asked him if I was his son. I remember the sleeping compartment of the truck smelled bad and was uncomfortable, but I didn't mind. I was with my daddy.

Times like that trip were short-lived, and most of the time I felt he hated me. Sometimes even horrible memories play over and over in my mind, evoked by things I read or see in movies or on talk shows.

As a child I loved to read, but I had no desire to be a writer. I wanted to be a teacher. Once, when I was eleven, I was playing school with the neighborhood kids on our front porch. Daddy came storming out of the house and shouted in front of all the children assembled, "Only sissy boys want to be schoolteachers." Then he kicked all my books and fake report cards off the porch and gave me an *I dare you to go get them* look. He didn't know that even at that young age I knew that education was going to get me away from him.

School and the Little Rock Public Library became my refuge. There I could numb the pain and fear I felt every time I entered our house and knew that he was there. Even when I'd forgotten the whippings he'd give me for just looking at him the wrong way, I would still worry about the late-night beatings he would give my mother.

One night I was awakened from a deep sleep by my mother's screams and crying. He was beating her, and when I tried to call out her name, nothing would come from my mouth. I thought he was killing her, the screams were so loud. I felt I had to do something, but every time I tried to call out her name or move, nothing happened. I was paralyzed.

Finally the beating stopped. I could hear my mother's quiet sobs and Daddy's loud snoring, but I still couldn't speak. Soon I felt my body could move once again, and I got out of bed, fell to my knees, and prayed silently that God would protect Mama, return my voice, and allow me to sleep.

I did sleep, and by the next morning my voice had returned. When I washed up and entered the kitchen, my mother was cooking breakfast as though the previous night had never happened. Looking at her, I realized that what Grandma always said about the power of prayer was indeed true. Since that night I have rarely missed a single night of getting on my knees and praying for my mama's safety and a restful sleep.

My mother, Etta Mae, is a strong-willed woman who during most of my youth worked two jobs, went to Business College, and still found time to serve as president of the Bush Elementary PTA and den mother to my Cub Scout troop. Mama is a stoutly built woman with no grand notion of her beauty, sable-brown skin, and sleepy eyes that sparkle when she smiles.

Even when I look at her today, and though time has passed

for the both of us, she looks the same. She was the second child, and the first daughter, born to Robert and Bessie Allen Williams. A few years after her birth, my grandmother and grandfather divorced and my grandmother remarried Teroy Gaines, whom we called Paw-Pa and who was the only grandfather I would know. Paw-Pa, also a divorcé, brought to the marriage a son, Roy, and a daughter, Jessie Lee. Soon after my grandparents' marriage, they had a child together, Arthur Lee, the baby of the family. Theirs was a close-knit family, from what I could see. Today my mother will not hesitate to call her big brother when a problem arises, and her sister—and my cherished Aunt Gee (aka Jessie Lee)—are not only sisters but best friends and traveling companions.

My mother is a gentle and kind woman, the most humble and noble woman I've ever known. I remember how she would gently rub the hurt from my body when it was covered with welts from Daddy's switch or belt. Getting sick was something I looked forward to as a child. Mama would love me back to health by rubbing my body with Vick's Vaporub and making me lemon-laced tea. I felt so loved and special that I didn't even mind the spoon filled with castor oil I had to take before bedtime. When my sisters and I were ill, Mama didn't care what Daddy had to say and would allow us to sleep in their queen-size bed and hold us tight like we were still babies.

On countless nights she woke my sisters and me and led us from our house, two blocks around the corner to my grand-mother's house, when Daddy's beatings and drinking became too much for even her to bear. But she loved Daddy deeply despite his many faults.

My family was poor, though not welfare poor, and there were times when I thought I was the only one who knew. Our house was four small rooms, and it wasn't as nice as some of the homes on neighboring streets or the large white mansion that our landlords the Pettyways owned. I'd catch a glimpse of the beautiful home with the marble foyer and polished hardwood floors when Daddy would sometimes allow me to take the fifty-dollar monthly rent to Mrs. Pettyway. Though very high yellow, the Pettyways were colored, and it helped me to realize that being colored didn't necessarily mean poor.

But if it hadn't been for Mama's hard work, we would have been on welfare and would most likely have lived in the projects. We had some cousins on Daddy's side that lived in the projects, and to me it wasn't so bad. They had playgrounds, recreation centers, and all their houses were made of brick. As a child I always dreamed of living in a brick house, and it didn't matter where it was.

Daddy's beatings caused me to retreat into my own silent world, which was probably worse than the physical scars. Sure I spoke, but only when I wasn't worried about how I should act or what I should say.

In my silence I lived in a make-believe world that provided me great comfort. In this world I lived in a brick house and had a mommy and daddy who loved each other and me deeply and dearly. It was a home where I got a hug and kiss from both of my parents as I headed off to school carrying a leather book satchel, a Jetsons lunchbox filled with my grandma's German chocolate cake, fried chicken tucked neatly between two pieces of light bread, and a thermos filled with ice-cold chocolate milk.

Inside my head, I had a life filled with friends who took pride in our friendship and who would pick me first for sandlot football and dodgeball despite my size.

I retreated as often as possible, because I knew what was waiting when I returned to the real world. Daddy's abuse sent me the chilling warning that the world wouldn't take too kindly to a sissy boy whom even a father couldn't love. When I look back, I realize my childhood was stolen just as it was getting started.

The dual beatings of my mother and me became common-place, with lapses occurring if we stayed away at Grandma's for a couple of days. Daddy would come to Grandma's and beg both her and Mama to change their minds and give him one more chance. When we would return, Daddy would become briefly what he should have been all along—a good husband and a good father.

When he was being responsible and generous, he would pile us all in the family station wagon and take us out for a drive to the Dairy Freeze in Granite Mountain for hamburgers and chocolate ice-cream cones. The hamburgers were five for a dol-lar, and sometimes Daddy would buy an order of french fries for my sisters and me to share. We would leave the drive-in and go to the Little Rock Airport and watch the planes take off and land. He could also be generous around the holidays, especially Christmas. My sisters and I would really clean up with toys and clothes. Of course, his kindness never lasted long. Looking back, I realize his generosity was dependent on how much he was working or how much he was drinking.

GROWING UP I LOVED THE HOLIDAYS, which meant family gatherings at my Grandma's, where I knew I would get an extra dose of love, like an extra Christmas present under the tree. My extended family knew what I was going through with Daddy and wanted to make sure I knew I was loved.

Even though she had over twenty grandkids, my Grandma always managed to put a silver dollar in my hand when nobody was looking. A deeply religious woman, Grandma made the best German chocolate cake in the world. Grandma's house was the place the family would also gather to greet our relatives from Michigan who often drove for days to see us during the summer. Those visits were cause for Grandma and Mama to cook big meals for everyone, and top it all off with watermelon and homemade ice cream. Grandma would allow my sisters, cousins, and me to take turns cranking the ingredients together in a wooden bucket. Grandma convinced us that our help made the ice cream taste better than store-bought ice cream any day.

During the holidays I knew there'd be a chance I would get a chance to spend some time with my Aunt Gee. She always made me feel like she was so happy to see me. Aunt Gee made me feel like I was the only little boy in the world and would smother me with hugs and kisses just like Grandma would smother her chicken with rich gravy. In many ways, Aunt Gee was and has remained a second mother to me. One of my few childhood memories before entering the first grade is of a toy doctor's set that Aunt Gee bought me when I was about fours years old. She'd given it to me one Christmas and I paraded around my Grandma's house with the black bag like I was on my way to perform surgery. Aunt Gee's husband, my Uncle Charles, was in the Air Force, and so she didn't always live in Little Rock or nearby where I could visit them often. When I was in the sixth grade, Uncle Charles was stationed in Spain for three years. I thought I was going to die and cried for days when I found out it would be a long time before I could see my favorite aunt, uncle, and cousins. Aunt Gee had four boys, and I always felt like Kennie, Charles Jr., Tony, and Carlos were more like brothers than cousins to me. Of course, we argued and teased each other, but never for long.

My mother's older brother, Uncle James, also treated me like I was one of his boys. He's a handsome man with a contagious smile and an infectious laugh. When he walked into Grandma's house he was like fireworks exploding on a summer night, and that made me very happy. Uncle James would look at me, smile, and say, "Come here, boy," and I would race into his large arms, where he would pick me up and twirl me around until I was so dizzy I couldn't stand up. I knew Uncle James was different from my daddy because I never saw him hit or talk ugly to his wife, Aunt Hattie. He always went to church with his family, and to his children's sporting events. At times he was just like a big kid who loved his mother and sisters dearly.

There was one thing I hated about the holidays: They ended, and I knew I would have to return home to Daddy.

AROUND AGE TWELVE, most of the boys I knew were interested in liking girls and making the junior high football team. Football and girls were on my mind too, but so were death and going to heaven. I had heard, and Lord only knows where, that if a child died before age twelve, he or she would go straight to heaven. No questions asked. And even though I didn't know much about heaven, I knew it had to be better than the terror I faced daily at 520 East Twenty-first Street.

My main concern about heaven was that my mother and grandmother might not be there right away. Somebody had to stay and look after my sisters, which now included the addition of my new baby sister, Jan. When Mama was pregnant, I prayed for a little brother who might make life easier, and I would no longer be the only boy in a house full of women. I didn't count Daddy, since he was now staying away from home more than usual. I wasn't completely disappointed that I had a new baby sister, though, because I felt a special bond with Jan.

I had another fear about going to heaven, which was never having the chance to go out with Rose Crater, the first girl who made my heart rattle with adolescent romantic thoughts every time I saw her. Rose was a beautiful, butter-colored girl. One spring day I saw her crossing the street in front of Booker Junior High, and I could feel excitement swell inside my stomach. I knew who she was because she was the daughter of A. C. Crater Sr., the head football coach at Booker. Her mother was a secretary at Carver Elementary, and the Crater family was considered middle class. She had an older brother, A. C. Jr., who was smart *and* an athlete. Rose was one of two seventh-graders on the varsity cheerleading squad, and she had no earthly idea that I existed. But I thought maybe if I died it would be big news because I was so young, and she might wonder who I was. On the other hand, I'd never get to see her again. It was my first love affair, and I was in conflict.

My fascination with death had begun around age eight, with the deaths of President Kennedy; Miss Whitfield, my favorite Sunday School teacher, who had died of breast cancer before she turned thirty; and Mr. Joseph P. Nunn, a family friend with a beautiful singing voice who lived next door to Grandma with his wife and three children—Joe Jr., Rita, and Gary, who was one of my first childhood friends. I couldn't understand why three people who were loved by so many could die so young.

I had strange notions about life and God. One of the strangest had to do with the power of words. I was convinced that at the beginning of your life you were given a set number of words to utter and when you used them up you died.

I figured that the President, Miss Whitfield, and Mr. Nunn had died so young because they had used all their words. I knew Miss Whitfield talked a lot in Sunday School and also sometimes did the announcements and the welcome at church. The times I had seen the President on television he was always talking, and Mr. Nunn loved to talk not only to adults but to children as well, and he sang solos almost every Sunday at church. Words were powerful, I thought, and must be used wisely.

I remember weeks after Mr. Nunn's sudden death from a heart attack, I was silent, speaking only when I absolutely had to. Even when I had to speak, I would count the number of words in my head and eliminate those words that were not necessary. I would look at my mother and sisters in disbelief when they would talk needlessly. Didn't they know what I knew? I didn't want to tell them, because they might tell Daddy. The more he talked, the better. I silently wished he was close to his limit. I hoped that his cussing and name-calling counted double or maybe even triple against his limit.

A few months before my twelfth birthday, I decided death was better than my life with Daddy, and I began to talk excessively. I would read books out loud, even though I was so proud of the fact that I had learned to read silently before anyone in my class. My constant jabbering got me in trouble not only at home but at school as well.

On my twelfth birthday, I was terribly sad when the day ended and I was still in the land of the living. My family didn't understand why I was so sad, since birthdays in our home had always been joyous events. I didn't tell anyone why I was brokenhearted; I felt empowered by my secret knowledge about God, words, and death.

A couple of weeks later, something happened that made me happy I'd stayed around. God gave me a miracle.

Daddy was out of work, and his drinking had increased so much that Mama had to hire a baby-sitter even when he was home. She was still working two jobs and taking classes at Capital City Business College, and was unaware that I was now getting a daily beating for no apparent reason. Sometimes Daddy would look at me in disgust and say, "Go in there and get my belt, you little sissy," or "Go get a switch so I can tear your ass up. Make sure you get a strong one." Outside of the family no one really knew the degree of the abuse except our baby-sitter, Marilyn Jean Morris, whom we called Jean.

Jean was our "play" cousin. Our families had known each other since the first day we moved into the neighborhood in 1962. Her family lived upstairs from the neighborhood grocery store, right across the street from my grandmother's house on

Twentieth and Commerce. Jean and her sisters, Gail, Terrie, and Rose, along with her brothers, Richard and Winston, became so close to our family that we just started telling everybody that we were cousins.

Jean was a beautiful chocolate-brown girl with thick long black hair. She was in the tenth grade and was one of the first girls from our neighborhood to make the Bear Kitten Drill Team at Horace Mann High School. Most of the girls on the drill team and the cheerleaders at Horace Mann came from Granite Heights, a middle-class enclave where my crush Rose Crater lived.

Some evenings I would sit on the front steps of our house and wait for Jean to walk past after drill team practice in blue gym shorts, a white blouse, and white majorette boots, with purple and gold pom-poms bouncing as she strutted down the block like she was leading a parade.

One evening while Jean was in the kitchen cleaning, with me close underfoot, Daddy called from the living room for me to bring him some cold water. Jean silently reached into the high cabinet and pulled down a purple aluminum tumbler Mama had gotten with Top Value stamps saved from her weekly trips to Safeway Grocery.

We looked in the freezer for ice, but the trays had not been filled, so Jean and I ran the tap water for several minutes until it turned ice cold, or at least it felt ice cold to me. With the tumbler filled to the top, and fully aware I had already taken too long, I raced from the kitchen to Daddy's permanent spot on the sofa.

After a few gulps, that look I had seen more times than I wanted to remember crossed his face.

"This water isn't cold," he said. "Didn't I tell your dumb ass that I wanted cold water?"

I nodded in dismay and told Daddy how Jean and I had made sure the water was cold. Then I wondered, *What did I say that for?*

"What did I say, you little sissy?" he yelled.

"Huh?" I responded.

"Huh . . . hell. Don't you think I know the difference between cold water and shit from the tap? The water isn't cold," he said as he dumped the remaining water on me and my white undershirt. The water certainly felt cold to me.

"You are going to do what I say if it kills you. Your little narrow ass thinks you so goddamn smart. Go get my strap," he demanded.

I didn't move fast enough for Daddy, and he suddenly grabbed me and started hitting me with his huge bare hands. When I started to cry, his hands seemed to strike with a more powerful force. He was beating me like he was fighting for his life with someone his own size. When he got tired of using his hands, he reached for an old extension cord he'd always used to threaten me with but had never used in the past. Mama didn't even know he had the extension cord and thought he used only switches or his belt when he whipped me.

He then told me to drop my pants. I was screaming, because I knew the extension cord would hurt more than his regular belt or a switch.

"And take off that underwear, too," he yelled.

When I had followed his orders, he grabbed me by my head and forced my small head between his huge thighs, tightened them like a vise so that I couldn't move and could barely breathe as he beat my naked bottom with the electrical cord. When he tired, he howled at me to stop crying and to pull up my pants and take my ass to bed. I raced toward my bedroom, nearly falling on my face as I struggled to get away from Daddy and pull up my pants and underwear.

Moments later, as I sat on my bed holding tight to a pillow like it could protect me, I heard the front door slam. I looked out the window and saw Daddy jump into his car and drive off in the direction of his favorite liquor store on Main Street.

Jean walked into the room with a towel and rubbing alcohol. She told me to lie on my stomach and she would make me feel better. When she saw my backside, she said, "Oh my God!"

I jumped up and raced into the bathroom, and Jean followed. I gazed into the mirror and saw my battered behind looking a raw pink color, and I started to cry again.

"Come here, Lynn. Let me put some of this on you," Jean said.

I asked Jean if the alcohol would make the welts and pink color go away, and she smiled sweetly and nodded. When she swabbed the cold liquid on my fresh wounds, I started to cry uncontrollably. I could hear my sisters, Anita and Shane, outside the bathroom urging me to stop crying. They always surrounded me with a tender protectiveness when I got a whipping for no reason. Jean promised to make Kool-Aid popsicles, one of my favorite treats, if I stopped crying, but I didn't want any kind of popsicles, homemade or store-bought.

I wanted my mother to come home and hug me and tell me everything would be all right, that it would be okay for me to use up all my words and die. I wanted her to tell me that she and my sisters would be just fine, that God in all His grace would understand that I was a little bit over the age limit but he would still allow me a place in heaven. I wondered what I could have possibly done to deserve the constant beatings.

When Jean finished putting the alcohol on my bottom, she instructed me to go and put on clean underwear. That's when I noticed my underwear was covered with several spots of blood. As I gazed at my stained underwear, thinking I needed to hide them from Mama, Jean said something that would change my life; words that would release Daddy's power over me.

"Lynn, don't worry about Uncle Ben. He will get his someday," she said. "You know, maybe he's not even your real daddy," she added, looking directly into my eyes like she was trying to convey some special secret to me.

What was Jean talking about? Of course he was my real daddy. He was the only daddy I'd ever known. I couldn't remember a day of my young life when he hadn't been there. Besides, if he wasn't my real daddy, then who was? Was it somebody I knew?

Through my sniffles I asked Jean what she meant. Jean said confidently that no father would treat a son the way Ben treated me, and that she had a cousin whose stepfather treated him the same way.

Such a thought had never crossed my mind. It was simply too incredible to be true. I was wondering how I could find out if Jean was right without asking my mother and risking another whipping, when the picture of Mama's gray cardboard box entered my mind. The box housed all of our family's important papers and was hidden in Mama's closet.

I told Jean about the box, and minutes later I found myself on her narrow shoulders, reaching for it amid Mama's shoes and hatboxes. My sisters were on lookout, instructed by Jean and me to holler if they saw Daddy's car or Mama coming home. When I located the box I grabbed it too quickly, and in my nervous excitement I fell from Jean's shoulder to the floor. The box flew from my hands and crashed down beside me.

I quickly started rummaging through the stack of papers, looking for my birth certificate, a piece of paper that I'd never seen. Whenever our school requested birth certificates, Mama always delivered them personally. I didn't know what the record of my birth looked like.

I asked Jean if she knew, and she told me she thought it was on black paper. Jean grabbed a stack of papers and was opening them up one by one and then carefully closing them back. All I saw were papers with names of insurance companies printed on them and layaway receipts, but nothing on black paper. When we reached the bottom of the box, I suddenly saw a black piece of paper covered with white ink.

I saw my name, "Everette Lynn," and then my eyes scanned over the rest of my document. In the place where it said "Last name," I saw "Williams." I thought, *That's not my last name*. I knew it was my mother's maiden name and the last name of my Uncle James, my mother's older brother, and my cousins. I continued to look over the document, when suddenly Jean said, "Look here."

"Look where?"

"Where it says 'father's name,'" Jean instructed as she pointed to a box on the document.

My eyes followed her slender finger to the spot labeled "Father's last name," and I saw the name "Jeter." My eyes moved in amazement to the "First name" slot and saw "James." My father was James Jeter and not Ben Harris. But who was James Jeter? I wanted to cry, but I felt a happiness inside that I had never known. The man I called Daddy was not responsible for my birth.

"He's not your daddy," I heard Jean say as I stared in silence at the document. I read that my father was born in Union, South Carolina, and that I had actually been born in Michigan, and not Arkansas as I'd always thought.

"Uncle Ben's not your daddy. Now we know why he treats you the way he does."

Yes, I thought in the stillness that covered our house. I continued to sit cross-legged on the floor, not worrying anymore about Daddy returning as the later afternoon gave way to early evening. I sat for a long time holding the document tight, and then studying it and thinking, *Yes, now we know*.

My discovery that Ben Harris wasn't my biological father didn't stop the beatings and verbal abuse. But with my newfound knowledge, neither Ben's words nor his hands had the same power over me. When he did whip me, it was as if I magically detached myself from my body. My secret information provided me with an omnipotent shield that protected me.

In early 1969, when I was thirteen, my mother divorced Ben. The beatings had finally become too much to bear even for someone as strong-willed as my mother. Maybe she realized the beatings could eventually become fatal. After a lengthy separation during which Ben spent time in Los Angeles, California, he returned one afternoon and pulled a butcher knife on her as she hung up clothes in our backyard. My mother's screams had brought not only me, but many of our neighbors, to her rescue as Ben ran away in fear of the police.

Looking back, I realize how brave my mother was in deciding in the 1960s to live without a man in her life to help raise four children. Divorce was a rare occurrence in our community and was considered grown folks' business. There were separations, but most times the husbands came back. I couldn't count the number of times Ben would leave for days and sometimes for weeks after he and Mama had serious knock-down-drag-out fights. Still, I never heard either one of them mention the word *divorce*.

All I knew about divorce was what I had seen on the '60s version of the television show *Divorce Court*, but all the people on the show were white and had what sounded like all sorts of crazy antics going on in their families behind the scenes. It seemed very different from the beatings that occurred in our house.

The only way I knew for certain that Mama was divorcing Ben was by eavesdropping on her phone conversations with my grandma, whom she was always very close to, or her best friend at the time, Mrs. Bertha Vault, who lived directly across the street from us.

My suspicions were confirmed when I saw "Etta Mae Harris versus Ben Odis Harris" listed under divorce proceedings in the *Arkansas Gazette*. I was probably the only child in my age group who regularly read the court proceedings and the obituaries, checking to see if any young children had gotten a free ride to heaven. I read them immediately after the comics and sports.

The day the divorce became final was a strange one for me and Mama. I was filled with tremendous relief, but I knew it was the beginning of a difficult time for her and my sisters. I would be just fine spending my days dreaming about my perfect father who loved me and lived in Michigan. Still, I realized that, despite Ben's many faults, my mother and sisters loved him. I had to admit that even I loved him and in some way would even miss him, since he was the only Daddy I had ever known.

When Mama came home after the court proceeding, she didn't come into the house like she normally did after a long day's work. She sat on the front porch in a rusty metal chair in silence for hours.

I sat close by on the concrete porch as my mother gently rubbed the top of my head. There was a threat of tears in her eyes, but she didn't cry. I looked away at the pumpkin-colored sun, half hidden by a heavy silhouette of clouds, until I suddenly felt my mama's body move. As she stood and let out a sigh, I looked up at her and said, "Don't worry, Mommy. I'll take care of you."

"I know, baby," she murmured softly as she walked into the house for the first time as a single mother of four. I sat on the porch until darkness covered our block, thinking of ways I was going to keep my promise.

WITH BEN OUT OF MY LIFE FOR GOOD, I naturally assumed my life would become better, and for the most part it did. I became the man of the house, helping my mother take care of our home and my sisters.

I got a paper route to earn extra money. Perhaps I should say that Mama and I got a paper route, since it was she who woke me up every morning at five to drive me around our neighborhood delivering the *Arkansas Gazette*. Most of the other carriers I knew delivered the paper on foot in the early darkness of the morning.

As the man of the house, I experienced several unexpected emotions and a set of new problems. The biggest fear was that Ben would return in the middle of the night and hurt Mama and me. I was never worried about him doing anything to my sisters, because I knew how much he loved them. This fear was lifted when I heard Mama tell someone on the phone that Ben had moved to Los Angeles, California.

I also felt a sense of guilt, because I felt Mama had divorced Ben not because she had fallen out of love with him but because she had finally become aware of his treatment of me. I felt it was my fault that my mother didn't have a man in her life while all her close friends and my Aunt Gee had the support and love of a husband. Several times I overheard my mother's friends ask her when she was going to marry again, and Mama would always reply, "Honey, I'm married to my kids."

Junior high was more challenging than I had ever imagined. The challenge didn't come from academics. Even though my grades started to slip, I was still scoring at the top on standardized tests. In the seventh grade, I was told I was reading on a twelfth-grade level.

It was my socialization as a young black man that suffered, and the realization that maybe Ben was right about me, that I was a sissy. I was a small child physically, all legs and teeth. All the boys at the modern, split-level Booker Junior High seemed bigger and more manly than me. It didn't matter that most of the boys who made me feel that way were in the eighth and ninth grades.

I tried out for football as Ben would have wanted. I was cut the first day. I will never forget how small I felt the first time I was in the locker room with the other boys and how they looked at me as though I didn't belong. I didn't even know how to put on a jockstrap. At first I tried to blame it on being bookish, but deep down I knew that was not the reason for their smirks. It was most likely in that locker room that I realized I was different from other boys.

So instead of becoming a star football player, I became the class clown to get in with the cool crowd. Sometimes when my talking got me put out of class, I would stand in the hallway and recite word for word the television special *Charlie Brown's Christmas*. I loved that show as much as *The Wizard of Oz*.

While my popularity soared, my grades plummeted. Besides, tough, cool black boys weren't supposed to make only A's and B's unless it was in gym or industrial arts. I even became good friends with my secret crush, Rose Crater, because she thought I was so funny and made her laugh. My bad grades didn't really bother me, because I knew I could do the work if I took the time.

I stole one of the pens the teachers used for report cards and learned how to change F's to B's and C's to fancy A's. When I lost my prized pen, I simply forged my mother's signature when report cards went out. Mama was too busy working two jobs and trying to keep food on the table and a roof over our heads to notice.

It was while I was at Booker that I became aware of the class difference among black people in Little Rock and the importance of your family's background and skin color. There were several students at Booker Junior High who lived in Granite Heights, a middle-class housing development north of the lower-class housing project called Granite Mountain. Kids from Granite Heights were dropped off in fancy cars, while students from Granite Mountain took the bus. I lived within walking distance of both neighborhoods. The most popular girls, including Rose, were light-skinned and had the most handsome members of the football team vying for their attention.

In my view, the children from the Heights had it made. They dressed nicely every day, never brought their lunch from home, and always seemed to have money in their blue jean pockets or leather purses. And they all seemed to have both a mother and a father.

I envied my classmates and secretly desired to be not only close friends with them but a member of their families as well. I suddenly longed to be a part of a family that included two parents. Even if one of the parents was Ben.

The following year I chose not to return to Booker Junior High for my eighth-grade year. Instead I transferred to the integrated West Side Junior High, located about thirteen miles from my home. The reason was simple: At a new school I could start my journey toward manhood over. I would make new friends and forget the way I was beginning to feel about myself.

There was also another reason: I was curious about white people. West Side reportedly was one of the few schools that was about half white and half black in its racial composition. The only white people I knew were the ones I saw on television and the owners of the neighborhood drug and grocery stores.

When I enrolled at West Side, I was surprised to learn that the school was now about 70 percent black. White students had begun to transfer in big numbers to Pulaski Heights and Southwest Junior High. The remaining white students didn't seem any better off than the black ones. In fact, the blacks appeared to come from the better families. I was shocked when I found out that one of my classmates, Tammie, a beautiful blond girl, actually lived in a mobile home. At West Side, one thing was different: All my teachers were white, which was a first for me.

Mama didn't understand why I wanted to go to another school when there was a practically new school only six blocks from our house, so I didn't have her full support. Busing had not started in 1968, so it was my responsibility to get to school the best way I knew how, which meant walking. Each morning around seven o'clock, I would start my trek from the east side to the more thriving west end, where nobody knew the real Lynn Harris.

My solitary walks were great, and may have marked my beginnings as a writer. My walks were a time for thinking and dreaming about how my life would be once I left Little Rock. I felt that my hometown was too small for my grand dreams of living in a high-rise apartment, like the kids from the television show *Family Affair*, or becoming a *Soul Train* dancer. On a more realistic level, I dreamed of having my own room and having pen pals from different states and countries.

Every day I'd feel a rush of anticipation when I would cross Main Street and walk past the Governor's Mansion. I always wondered what it was like to live in a house that big. The Stewart family home marked the halfway point of my trip. They had recently moved from our neighborhood to a nice brick-front between West Side and Dunbar Junior High, the other black junior high school.

For the most part, I enjoyed West Side and my new teachers and friends. Still there were problems. As it was at Booker, the boys at West Side seemed so much bigger than I was, so much more self-assured when it came to girls. But I still made friends by using my smarts and quick wit. At West Side, being a little smarter than the other kids had its advantages. But that was not always enough to become firmly entrenched with the cool kids.

To prove yourself, you either had to bully other kids or challenge authority—which at West Side meant testing the mostly white teaching staff. I welcomed it. In my adolescent insecurity I needed people to know who I was, or who I wanted them to think I was—a cool boy without fear.

I had become such a terror in the school's library that the librarian, Miss Lowery, had me permanently banned for always talking too loud and then ignoring her when she asked me to be quiet. Somehow I avoided getting into fights with my classmates.

One day in math class, I was reading an *Archie* comic book that was neatly tucked in my math book. The teacher, Mr. Ask, was explaining new math problems on the board. I was bored and thought I knew everything there was to know about math. Besides, the adventures of my favorite comic-book characters, Archie, Betty, Veronica, and Jughead, were far more interesting. More so than any of my school books, *Archie* and *Richie Rich* comic books had become my windows to the white world I was so curious about.

Mr. Ask, a young-looking, lanky white man, evidently called my name to answer a question, but since I was so deep in my comic book, I didn't hear him. I did hear him when he screamed my name, obviously annoyed. Startled by the increased volume in his voice, I jerked upright and my comic book fell from inside the aqua-colored math book onto the maple plywood floor. When I reached down to retrieve it, I spotted shiny black shoes.

"Lynn, put away the comic book," Mr. Ask barked. All of my classmates' eyes were on me. I could hear giggles. My time had come to prove how tough I was. Mr. Ask had called me out and embarrassed me in front of my peers, so I had to respond in an aggressive manner. If I didn't, my popularity, such as it was, would be sacrificed, and it would take more than letting the cool people cheat off my exams to restore it. I knew what I had to do.

"I will when I finish," I said with a smart-assed tone.

"Now!" Mr. Ask shouted at the top of his lungs. His narrow face turned beet red. The class giggles turned to loud laughter. Without taking his eyes off me, Mr. Ask ordered the class to return to their math books.

"Put the comic book away," he repeated.

When I was slow to respond, he grabbed the comic book. Now I was pissed. My sisters often played games like this with me, and if I couldn't stand them doing it, I certainly wasn't going to let Mr. Ask get away with it.

Without thinking, I took my heavy math book and fired it at Mr. Ask, hitting him right above the left eye. I couldn't believe what I had done. Neither could my classmates. They started to laugh and clap, and several were banging their desks with balled fists.

"Did you see that shit? Lynn popped Mr. Ask," Billy Ray, one of the school's tough boys, said. I felt powerful. Other than my sisters and a cousin here and there, I had never hit anyone, and now I had hit a grown man—and a white man at that.

As I sat at my desk with a cocky smirk on my face, Mr. Ask became so enraged that he grabbed me by my shirt collar and literally dragged me to the principal's office. Not only was I promptly suspended for three days, I was also informed that I would be reinstated only when my mother or father returned with me. My troubles had only just begun.

Since my mother left home for her new factory job before dawn each morning, she had no idea if my sisters and I ever went to school. She assumed we did, which was usually correct, but she never checked up on us because we never gave her a reason. My suspension initially didn't seem that bad. I figured I would take my three-day vacation and then figure out some way to get back into school without my mother knowing what I had done.

My first step was to convince the principal that my mother

couldn't come back to school with me. I thought of disguising my voice, which hadn't changed and was still soft and girllike, and coming up with some dreaded illness that would prevent my mother from escorting me back to school. But the day I mustered up the courage to try, the principal's secretary started asking lots of questions, so I quickly hung up. I think she realized it was me.

I easily fell into the routine of staying at home all day watching soap operas, daydreaming, and planning adventures. Since all the grown folks in my neighborhood worked, I didn't worry about being seen going in and out of the house during the time when children were supposed to be in school. The only adults I saw were the white store owners when I would go to the store to spend my lunch money on candy and gum. On the rare occasion when they would question why I wasn't in school, I would tell them my baby sister was sick and I was the only one big enough to take care of her while my mother worked. Since I had the reputation of being a pretty good kid, everyone in the neighborhood bought my story.

I was having a great time at home all by myself. The tiny house was suddenly like having my own big room. I didn't miss going to school all that much. I realized that the only reason I had liked school in the past was that it got me away from Ben. Even though I loved to read, now that he was gone, there was no need for school.

I imagined I had become quite a legend at school since I was kicked out for hitting a teacher. If anybody ever doubted my toughness, they couldn't possibly now. Since none of my classmates lived near me, I didn't have to worry about someone opening their big mouth and telling my sisters—or even worse, my mama—what I had done.

Everything was going fine until day forty-four, when my vacation came to an abrupt end. My mother came home one day at her usual six o'clock hour. Everything appeared normal until she casually asked me if I had been to school. I knew something was wrong by the tone of her voice, but I said "Yes" anyway. My mother went into a screaming rage, telling me that I was lying, that she knew I had been suspended. She told me about a white man (a truant officer) showing up at her job wanting to know why I hadn't been to school for weeks and weeks.

That evening I got one of the worst whippings my mama's ever given me. The next day, Mama missed work and took me back to West Side Junior High. While waiting for the principal, I studied Mama's stoic face. Her worried and tired eyes didn't seem to blink, and she sat there as still as a statue. She seemed afraid, too, which I couldn't understand since I was the one in trouble.

Weldon Faulk, the principal, was stern but polite. He was a handsome, middle-aged white man with onyx hair sprinkled with gray around the edges. When he explained to my mother the seriousness of my offense, I started to pay attention.

Mr. Faulk had a list of examples of my being a little too smart for my own good, and told her about my ban from the library. Mama said nothing. She didn't show any emotion until he brought up my grades from Booker and the straight F's I had received during my extended vacation. Suddenly my mama's face scrunched up as if she were in pain. I knew she must have felt embarrassed and humiliated, but she continued to sit there in silence.

The principal explained that several of my teachers didn't quite know what to do with me since my classroom performance prior to the suspension could best be described as erratic. He pointed out that my standardized test scores indicated that I was capable of making straight A's, a theory supported by my brief moments of brilliance on some classroom tests and some English book reports. He indicated that something was seriously wrong with me, and he seemed to be placing the blame on my mama. I wanted to shout at Mr. Faulk to stop attacking her, that none of this was her fault. She was the best mama in the world, but he had broken her down.

I stopped looking at my mama and gazed out the open window. The office suddenly filled with Mama's sniffles. I looked at the woman whom I loved more than anyone, as nickel-sized tears rolled down her face. She pulled a handkerchief from her black pocketbook and wiped away the tears. I used to think Ben was the only one who could make her cry, and now here I was causing her so much pain.

When she composed herself, Mr. Faulk asked if she had any questions about my reinstatement. She shook her head and then quietly asked him if he knew how hard it was to raise four children completely alone. Mr. Faulk looked down at his desk and tapped a pen on the folder that held my permanent records and politely said, "No, Mrs. Harris, I don't."

When Mama left my school to return to work, Mr. Faulk told me to remain in his office. After he walked my mother out, he came back and made me feel even worse, telling me how sorry he felt for my mother. He warned me that I had better get my act together unless I wanted to end up in reform school, a threat I thought only black parents used.

He asked me what I planned to do with my life; I choked back tears and sullenly told him, "I'm going to college."

Mr. Faulk lifted a piece of paper from the folder on his desk and said, "Not with these grades you aren't."

He went on to explain that my dream was not impossible, but that it would be difficult if my tough-guy and class-clown actions continued. He told me colleges wanted only top students, but fortunately for me they wouldn't see the horrible grades I had made since only grades beginning with the ninth grade were considered. He said my little vacation would probably mean that I would have to repeat the eighth grade, but that would give me a chance to get back on the right track.

Did he say repeat the eighth grade? Fail? I couldn't do that. If I couldn't pretend to be tough or funny, then being smart was the only thing I had left. If I failed the eighth grade I would be the laughingstock of my sisters and cousins, not to mention my former classmates from Booker Junior High, who probably believed that I thought I was too good for my neighborhood school. I still considered them friends, but I rarely saw them when I started going to West Side, because I left home so early and got home late.

I begged Mr. Faulk to suggest ways I could avoid repeating the eighth grade. He looked at me with dismay and told me I had gotten myself into a terrible mess, but said he would see what he could do because he felt I had potential. He warned me that if he heard I was giving any of my teachers any trouble whatsoever, I would be expelled so fast I would feel the door hitting my back on my way out. I promised to be the best student at West Side Junior High, and then I raced to the scene of my crime: math class with Mr. Ask.

MR. FAULK KEPT HIS PROMISE, and I was promoted to the ninth grade without summer school. I managed to pull up my grades during the last marking period, and I entered the ninth grade with excitement. I surprised myself and some of my classmates when I was selected to be on *The Bear Chat*, the school newspaper. I loved writing and wanted to be a sportswriter. I really didn't think I had a chance, because the newspaper staff was always filled with Honor Society students, but I submitted a sample story anyway. It was rare when someone without those qualifications even applied.

My reputation had preceded me, and Mrs. Adams, a petite

blonde, told me the first sign of trouble (she'd obviously heard of the Mr. Ask book incident) and I was off the newspaper staff. She then told me that my writing sample was one of the best she had seen in all of her years teaching. I was one of two black students selected for the usually all-white staff.

Things were getting better at home, as well. During the summer, Mama purchased our first home. How she saved the money was amazing to me, and I couldn't wait to get out of the house of horror that 520 East Twenty-first represented to me. We moved to a large white frame house with a huge porch and yard, located on the corner of Sixteenth and Johnson Streets in the heart of the west end and about fifteen minutes' walking distance to West Side. I was excited about living in the same neighborhood as the majority of my classmates, but I was even more excited about having my own room for the first time.

I couldn't sleep the first night I spent in the twin bed in my own room. It didn't matter a single bit that the furniture in my room was purchased from a secondhand furniture store. The only thing that mattered was that it was mine. And though I wasn't known for my neatness, I was determined to keep my room spotless.

Besides moving and being on the newspaper staff, something else special happened before the school year began: I had my first real girlfriend. Beverly Rice was the younger sister of my classmate and good friend Valerie Rice. The Rices were a large family with nine children who lived on Allis Street, which was two blocks from my house.

NaNa, as everyone called Beverly, was a cute, big-legged, pigtailed girl with enchanting brown eyes. The first time she smiled at me I felt the hairs on my skinny arms lift like they were going to take my body to the sky. A couple of days later, Valerie told me NaNa liked me. About a week later, I finally got the courage to call her, and the first thing I said after she said hello was, "Will you go with me?"

"Yes," she replied.

"Okay. Bye," I said as I hung up the phone with a huge smile on my face. I was thinking how everything was going my way and maybe I didn't need a father to show me how to become a man. I could figure it out on my own.

Our relationship lasted only about a month. One day, out of the blue, NaNa called me and said, "I'm quitting you."

"Okay," I replied. The circumstances of our breakup are no longer clear to me, and I don't think I even understood back then. In our brief month together I had become a permanent fixture in the Rice household, showing up the first thing in the morning to walk to school with my girlfriend. After school we would sit on their porch until Mrs. Rice would tell me it was time for me to go home.

I didn't have a clue what girlfriends and boyfriends did besides walk to school together and occasionally hold hands. I think this made NaNa's mother and father very happy. Mrs. Rice especially loved me because I was always polite and wouldn't look for a silver coin when I ran errands for her. They were like family, a second home, and this didn't change after NaNa ended our relationship.

I share this story of my brief romance because NaNa and her family gave me something I desperately needed. Her affection for me made me feel like other boys in my peer group for the first time. They all had girlfriends long before I did. NaNa was like a booster shot for my self-esteem. Living in the same neighborhood with the middle-class Rices made me feel like I was their equal, entitled to date their daughter.

I ENTERED THE NINTH GRADE determined not to let my mother or Mr. Faulk down. What he had told me about college and grades stuck. Even though I didn't know anyone besides my teachers who had gone to college, I knew a post-high-school education was my ticket out of Little Rock.

I applied myself and my grades soared during the first grading period of the ninth grade, but because of my academic performance the prior year the school placed me in all remedial classes, one step above special education. But after my grades were reviewed, and I took another schoolwide standardized test, I was transferred into regular classes. Sometimes the classes were full. In the case of algebra, my remedial math teacher, Mrs. Ann Young, set up a desk in the back of the classroom and taught me what the honor students were learning. Mrs. Young, who was so beautiful with her silk chocolate skin, treated me at times like I was the only student she had.

My classroom accomplishments didn't go unnoticed by Mr. Faulk. He was so impressed with my turnaround that he asked me to introduce a speaker to the student body at the Career Day Assembly. This was an honor usually reserved for the Student Council president and top students. Most of my friends who knew me as a cutup were shocked when I stepped to the podium to introduce Mr. Moise Seligman, president of Arkansas Paper Company, a former West Side student when the school was all white.

Mr. Seligman was a tall, distinguished-looking man with a bald head, who favored the actor Yul Brynner. I liked him immediately. He was very nice to me and really seemed interested in me. White people were still a big mystery to me. Most of the white people I came in contact with didn't treat me with any disrespect but always maintained a superior air, like they knew they were better and felt sorry for me. Mr. Seligman didn't act that way at all.

A couple of weeks after the assembly, I wrote Mr. Seligman a letter thanking him for the personal interest he took in me and then in a bold move asked him for a summer job. Three days after mailing the letter, I was called into the principal's office to take a call from Mr. Seligman's secretary, who informed me that Mr. Seligman wanted me to come and work at his company during the summer. I was so excited, I let out a loud scream. The school secretary smiled, and Mr. Faulk beamed like a proud father.

All my family and friends were impressed when I told them about my exciting new office position at Arkansas Paper Company. The majority of my friends would spend their summers competing for cleaning jobs at fast-food restaurants (very few blacks were offered service or cashier jobs in these establishments), and passed the summer either cutting grass or praying the government had a summer jobs program. Prior to my job at Arkansas Paper, all of my jobs had been manual labor, like washing dishes or cutting grass. The summer before, when I was thirteen, I had even worked as a houseboy for a brothel in North Little Rock.

One of my favorite cousins, Jacquelyn, helped me get the job, but she had no idea it was a brothel. She worked at the owner's resale shop in downtown Little Rock and knew the owner was looking for someone to help take care of her yard and garden. The first couple of days I spent under the beat of the summer heat, but when I arrived on the third day I was told I was needed to help out in the house.

I was washing down the baseboards in the dining room, and so I was under the table when I saw one of the several white men who came to the house during the day rest his hand on the crotch of one of the attractive blond ladies who came to the house in the mornings and left each day when the news came on. All of the ladies wore lots of makeup and short-shorts with midriff blouses.

I didn't know much about sex, yet I knew something was going on when after a few drinks the men would retire to one of the several bedrooms. I didn't say anything to anyone and did what my mother often told me: "Mind your own business and leave grown folks' business alone." Some years later, my hunch proved correct when I saw on television the lady who paid me in cash daily being led out of her house in handcuffs, while the reporter spoke of the prostitution bust in North Little Rock. I never said anything to my mother or my cousin Jacquelyn about what I knew about that house.

My position at Arkansas Paper Company didn't turn out to be the glamorous office job I had dreamed of, but it was better than the brothel or cutting grass all day. I was put into a huge warehouse, where I spent most of the time trying to keep out of the way of people with real jobs. It turned out Mr. Seligman really didn't have a position for someone so young and small, so I ran errands for the secretaries and for the men who worked in the warehouse. Otherwise my eight-hour days were spent reading and attempting to look busy and stay out of trouble.

It seemed like everything was just too good to be true, and I set out in what now appears to have been a deliberate act of sabotage, or maybe my old book-throwing self was just rearing his dumb head one more time.

After my first two weeks at the paper company, I received my first paycheck—eighty-eight dollars after taxes. I decided I needed a wallet to protect my money from strangers, so I cashed my check at the downtown branch of Worthern Bank and walked a few doors to Woolworth's.

Woolworth's was one of my favorite stores. It wasn't as expensive as most of the stores downtown, and the lunch counter sold fried chicken, cheeseburgers, and thick malted shakes. My plan was to buy the wallet first, then sit down at the lunch counter and treat myself to a fried chicken dinner or a cheeseburger—or maybe both, since I felt like a rich man.

A white saleslady with thick bifocals directed me to the aisle where the wallets were located, and my eyes immediately spotted a beautiful black imitation leather wallet. I picked it up and looked at the $5.95 price tag. I subtracted the money in my head from the amount that was bulging in my pocket and realized that almost ten dollars of my money would be depleted with the purchase of the wallet and lunch.

I looked around and noticed that the long aisle was completely empty, with the exception of an elderly black man pushing a broom in the opposite direction. I quickly removed the price tag from the wallet, balled it up, and put it into my front pants pocket. I placed the shiny wallet in my back pocket. I decided to abandon my lunch treat and walked briskly out the revolving doors near the bus stop. No sooner had I smelled the fresh summer air than a huge hand grabbed my arm so tight that I could feel fingernails digging into my flesh.

"You're under arrest for shoplifting," a deep male voice said. I turned around to face one of the meanest-looking white men I had ever seen. In one motion he lifted the wallet from my back pocket, pulled my arms behind my back, and placed silver handcuffs around my wrists. I was scared to death, and when he asked my name, who my folks were, and where I lived, I became mute. Three days would pass before I uttered another word.

My two-night stay in the Pulaski County Juvenile Detention Center taught me one crucial lesson: Jail was not for me. After being arrested, I was hauled off to the Little Rock police station, where I was photographed and fingerprinted and treated like all the other criminals, despite being only fourteen years old. My silence continued throughout this process. I decided that if I was going to be sent to reform school, then nobody would know, and that included my mother and sisters. If the policemen didn't know who I was, then how could they tell anyone what I'd done?

When the officers continued their questioning, I just stared passively, as if I didn't hear them, as if I were both mute and deaf. The officers talked among themselves about what they should do to me. After some debate, I was put in a police car and taken to Juvenile Hall.

Juvenile Hall was located in a huge redbrick building with barbed-wire fences all around it and a security guard posted in a tiny booth. On Sunday outings my family would sometimes pass this place, and Mama would remind my sisters and me that this was the place bad kids were sent and sometimes they threw away the keys. I felt like I was doomed to hell for yet again embarrassing my mother.

I was given a used pair of pajamas and placed in a small cell that looked just like the ones in prison movies on television. The space included an iron cot with dingy white sheets and a pancake-thin pillow. In the corner was a small washbowl and a steel bucket that I assumed was my toilet. The only illumination in the room was from the car headlights on the streets below and a single shaft of light from the hallway directly outside the cell.

Members of the staff tried to talk to me, asking me if I was hungry or if I was scared. Of course I was scared, but I didn't know if I was more frightened of spending the rest of my life in jail, or the whipping Mama would give me once she found out what I had done. I figured I'd starve to death before I told them anything.

In my silence, I would scheme ways to escape and move to Michigan and search for my real father. I figured he lived in Flint, since that's where I was born and we had a lot of relatives who lived there. I knew if I could just get out of the cell, adventures galore awaited me outside Arkansas.

My thoughts were constantly interrupted by guards who would bring food to my room on a steel tray and look at me and ask, "The cat still got your tongue?"

When the guards would leave, some of the other detainees tried to engage me in conversation by hollering out, "Hey, you in the middle cell. What did you do?" When I wouldn't answer, they speculated on what crime I had committed and whether I was really deaf and dumb.

Early Saturday morning, I awoke and knew immediately that I wasn't having a bad dream. To make matters worse, it was ridiculously hot for early June, even for Arkansas, making the cell feel like an oven.

I could hear birds twitter softly outside as I wiped summer sweat from my forehead and wrote my first story in my head—a script that I prayed would release me.

I would tell the officials that I was from Michigan and I had stopped at the Woolworth's while my bus took a brief rest stop in Little Rock. If they released me I would promise never to show my face in Little Rock ever again. I would tell them that my parents were wealthy funeral home owners. But what if they wanted to call my parents before sending me home? I didn't even know the area code for Michigan. During the time that I was there, when I became bored thinking of how I was going to secure my release, I created stories about my adult life when I would leave Arkansas for good. I wanted to go to New York and move to Harlem and live like the character John from my favorite novel, James Baldwin's *Go Tell It on the Mountain*.

I managed a second day and night without speaking, but when Sunday morning came, I thought of my mama and sisters getting ready for church and I suddenly became very sad. I would have given anything to be at home preparing for Sunday School. I missed my family. I wondered if they missed me too, and if they were frightened that something terrible had happened to me.

As the day passed, I became angry at myself. I had wanted to secure a good job to help my mother, since she no longer had a husband because of me. I wanted to be the man of the house, but here I was stuck in Juvenile Hall. I began to worry about my job. What if Mr. Seligman found out? He would fire me immediately, and then I wouldn't have a summer job, which meant no new school clothes. I knew I would have to leave Little Rock when word got out that I had been in jail. This was a humiliation I would never live down.

Then I did something I always did when I was really afraid: I got down on my knees on the hard concrete floor, and I prayed to God that He would rescue me and take me away from the jail and Arkansas forever. Almost immediately I felt better, knowing something would happen.

Sure enough, Monday morning it appeared that my prayers were answered. It was still dark outside, but I knew daybreak was close because the sounds of cars had increased. I stood and looked out the window, feeling sorry for myself and wishing I were on a bus heading to work after a weekend rest, when I heard the key to my cell turn. It was too early for breakfast, and I wondered what was happening. Were they going to beat the truth out of me?

When the door opened, the guard led in a regal-looking black lady with beautiful brown skin and black and gray hair, fashionably styled. She started to ask me questions, which I still didn't answer. She seemed nice and looked vaguely familiar. She put her index finger to her polished lips, turned and faced the guard, then suddenly positioned herself directly in front of me and said, "You're Bessie's grandson, aren't you?" I didn't answer, but my face gave me away. She looked at the guard and said, "I thought so. His family has been looking for him all weekend."

A couple of hours later, the guard reappeared and escorted me to the communal rest room, where he instructed me to shower and returned my clothes without giving me any indication what was going on. Once I was dressed he led me to the lobby of the building, where I saw my mama standing with her arms folded tightly. I was so excited to see her that I raced into her arms and hugged her. Tears formed in my eyes, but they didn't slide down my face. Mama hugged me back while she whispered in my ear, "I'm going to tear your butt up when I get home from work."

My silence continued as I got into Mama's car and she took me to a nearby bus stand and told me to carry my behind home and not to leave the house. When I asked if I could go to work, she said "Yes" but instructed me to come home right after I clocked out.

When I walked into the Arkansas Paper Company almost two hours late, I saw Mr. Seligman with a coffee cup in his hand and a bright smile.

"How was your weekend, Lynn?" he asked.

"It was fine, sir, but I couldn't wait to get back to work," I said, happy to once again hear my own voice.

I was hoping that a day at work would cool Mama off and she would forget her jailhouse promise, but she didn't. I got the whipping I deserved.

Still, a whipping from Mama was different from one of Ben's, because she always felt bad afterward, so lots of reassuring hugs and love followed. A couple of hours later, as I lay on my bed convinced that I wouldn't steal another thing in life, and would never ever spend another night in jail, Mama served me chocolate ice cream and pound cake in bed and gave me advice I would always try and follow the rest of my life: "You're smart, baby. Don't use that gift for bad. Use it for good."

IT WAS DURING MY NINTH-GRADE YEAR that I had my first sexual encounter. It was with a girl from the neighborhood who'd made advances toward me. One evening when her parents were still at work, she invited me up to her bedroom. I remember feeling both excited and nervous, wondering if I was doing it right, and for days I couldn't get the intoxicating smell of sex out of my mind. We had sex a couple more times before I surrendered to the other sexual thoughts I'd tried to suppress since seventh grade. I would learn that other young men were thinking the same things I was. I wasn't the only one.

One morning while I was walking to West Side Junior High I passed by the massive Central High, as I did every day, and spotted the object of my first bout of lust: a boy two grades ahead of me. I knew who he was because he was a track and football player for the Central High Tigers. That morning our eyes met briefly, and I felt tiny sparks dance through my body. This was something that hadn't happened when I'd been with a girl.

A couple of days later I was headed home, and as I passed Quigley Stadium, which was adjacent to Central, I saw him again. This time he was wearing a sleeveless T-shirt that was cut right above his navel and gray running shorts, and he was carrying a football helmet. I couldn't help but stare at his honey-amber skin and marvel at his body, one that was perfect and usually reserved for Greek statues. He caught me staring at him and walked toward me. I expected him to angrily demand what I was looking at, but instead in a wordless command he motioned for me to follow him to an empty corner of the stadium into the sun-pulled shades of twilight, and I had my first physical contact with a boy—a boy who looked and carried himself like a man.

The sexual contact went on for more than a semester—usually at my mother's house in the early morning after my sisters had left for school—even though he would barely talk to me. Still, I loved the way he smelled and how my heart would race when I would see him silently take off his skintight jeans to reveal white Jockey underwear that always looked new. It ended one morning when I spotted him and several other Central High football players, both black and white, sitting on cars whistling at girls as they strolled toward the high school. Our eyes met briefly, and while I continued looking in his direction for some sort of recognition, he turned to a friend and whispered into his ear and started laughing so hard that he rolled off the car. I figured he had said something about me, and I increased my pace as I began to perspire with embarrassment.

We would never again meet at my mother's house or in our private spot in the stadium, as he started dating and later married one of Little Rock's most notable beauties after she got pregnant.

CHAPTER 4

When the time came for me to enter high school, I again left my neighborhood and ventured into the unknown and unfamiliar. Instead of attending the historic Little Rock Central High, which was within walking distance of my house and which all my classmates from West Side would be attending, I decided to attend Hall High.

Hall High opened and closed in 1957. It was closed by order of then–Arkansas Governor Orville Fabus after the National Guard came to Little Rock to protect the brave nine black students who entered Central in 1957. Rather than allow "The Little Rock Nine," as they came to be known, to attend Central, Governor Fabus ordered all the schools in the capital city closed.

Hall High was a modern orange brick building located in a wealthy section of west Little Rock, a neighborhood of beautiful mansions in the shadows of gently rolling hills. With an enrollment of more than fifteen hundred in 1970, Hall was one of the largest schools in the state, though its minority enrollment was less than 5 percent.

For the first time, I was surrounded by the white folks I saw on television, the ones I had expected at West Side. I was able to attend Hall because of a program implemented by the school board called Freedom of Choice, which allowed black students to attend a school where they were a minority. This meant all of the city's high schools were open to black students. The one all-black high school, the much-loved Horace Mann High, was being phased out and didn't enroll a sophomore class in the fall of 1970.

When I entered Hall for the first day of classes, I didn't know what to expect. Filled with a mixture of joy and self-conscious-ness, I wondered whether I had on the right kind of clothes and shoes. Would I fit in? I didn't ever remember seeing so many white people in one place and being so close to them.

On those first couple of days, my new classmates appeared friendly, pointing me toward classes when it was obvious I was lost. The first day I did see a familiar face, Mr. Faulk, my princi-pal from West Side, who had been promoted to principal at Hall. He nodded politely when he saw me, but he didn't speak—maybe because he looked as lost as I was.

There were about thirty other black students in the class of '73. About ten of them lived in the University Park section of town, an enclave of the city's few black professionals. The rest came from the east side and were bused to Hall against their will. I knew some of them from my seventh-grade year at Booker. Needless to say, they were not nearly as happy to be at Hall as I was. The closing of Horace Mann was controversial within the black community. The school board wanted to close it perma-nently in 1970, but protests prevented it, and in a compromise the school board allowed the existing students at Horace Mann to finish there.

The majority of the students who lived near Hall walked to school, though many had fancy new cars parked in the student parking lot and spent many lunch periods in the cars, smoking and eating McDonald's. Hall High had a reputation for being a school for rich kids. Little Rock did have two private schools, Catholic High for Boys and Mount Saint Mary's, which were both located close to Hall. Still, the majority of the city's elite attended Hall.

I remember how proud I was to attend Hall. I spent some of the money I had earned during the summer on pumpkin-orange-colored sweatshirts with "Hall High Warriors" emblazoned across my chest. I loved getting off the bus and walking in my neighborhood, the heart of Central territory, wearing my sweatshirt and bragging to my friends how Hall was the best school in the whole world. Of course, they would tease me and tell me how they couldn't wait until Thanksgiving morning, when Central and Hall played the biggest football game of the year for the victory bell. It didn't matter if one of the schools had lost all its games and the other was undefeated. All that mattered was who came out victorious on Thanksgiving Day.

I wanted to feel a part of Hall High immediately and make new friends, so in a very bold move I decided to run for sophomore class representative on the student council, the equivalent of sophomore class president since it was the only elected office a sophomore could hold. I don't think many people thought I had a chance of winning, but I thought if I met every single person in my class, I could prove them wrong. At least people would know who I was and I might make some new friends. At that time in my life I thought I might one day run for Congress, but now I realize it was the beginning of a period in my life where I attempted to overachieve so people wouldn't notice the differences about me that I was beginning to hear loud and clear in my heart. Even though I wasn't having sex with anyone, I thought about it all the time, and most of my thoughts were about men.

Eleven people vied for the position of class representative, and most of them had been student council presidents or officers of their junior high or were the star football players and cheerleaders, the very people I was anxious to meet. All the candidates gave brief speeches to the sophomore class, and I felt proud when I ended my speech by saying, "Put the little X in the little box that will help put Lynn in the top spot." The applause that followed was loud and comforting. I felt like a part of Hall High.

Election Day arrived and I was feeling good because a lot of my new classmates had told me how much they loved my speech, how it was one of the best. When I asked a few of them if they were going to vote for me, many were noncommittal. One classmate, Ronnie Selle, told me flat out that he loved my speech but wasn't going to vote for me because his girlfriend, Sherrie Kaufman, was running. I remembered Sherrie, a raven-haired beauty who was very nice to me at a candidates' meeting. She is the one I would have voted for had I not been running.

At the end of the day, Principal Faulk called all the candidates into his office and congratulated each of us on wonderful speeches and a well-run contest. I took a deep breath and clenched my fists as I looked around his office at the nervous faces of my competition. I prayed a silent prayer that I didn't come in last.

"There will be a runoff between the top two," Mr. Faulk said. "Brian Sudderth received 112 votes." That wasn't a big surprise, since Brian was the favorite mainly because he had been president of Forest Heights Junior High, the feeder school down the hill from Hall.

"And Lynn Harris received 156 votes. The runoff between Brian and Lynn will take place tomorrow morning in homeroom," Mr. Faulk said.

My heart was beating a mile a minute as everyone turned toward me with smiles and congratulations. I was on top of the world, like I had just won the presidency of the United States. I couldn't remember being happier. A bespectacled Brian came over and gave me a hearty handshake, wishing me good luck. I thanked him and expressed a similar sentiment, though I really wanted to win.

In one brief day, I became one of the most popular people at Hall High. I was on the verge of accomplishing something no black student had ever achieved there, or at any of the other majority white Arkansas schools, by winning a student government position.

The night before the runoff, I was so excited I couldn't sleep. I left home at six-thirty the next morning so I wouldn't be late. I wanted to shake the hands of as many of my classmates as humanly possible as they entered the building.

In my homeroom, my teacher asked everyone to give me a round of applause for doing so well in the election so far, but I detected the sound of impending doom in her voice, like I had done all I was going to do.

As I prepared to mark my ballot, I looked around the classroom and noticed I was the only black student present. The other three black students in my homeroom were nowhere to be found. I naturally assumed they would be voting for me, even though they didn't know me any better than Brian. I wondered if they were out in the student parking lot smoking, or skipping homeroom altogether.

Around third period, which was usually at 11:00 A.M., my name and Brian's were called over the intercom to report to the principal's office. As I was heading toward the office, I saw one of the black girls from my homeroom walking into the building. She came over and asked me if it was too late to vote. When I asked where she had been, she told me that their regular bus had broken down. I told her I didn't know if it was too late to vote but that she should ask our homeroom teacher.

When I walked into the principal's office, Brian was already sitting and having a friendly conversation. Mr. Faulk instructed me to take the seat next to Brian. When I sat down he began to study a piece of paper, which he held directly in front of his face like a shield.

Mr. Faulk told us again how proud we should be and that it was a very close race. My stomach was dancing with nervous energy.

"Lynn, you received 323 votes, and Brian, you received 326. Congratulations, Brian," he said as he came from behind his desk to shake Brian's hand. I fell into a daze as I looked at Brian and Mr. Faulk. I stared at every wrinkle on Weldon Faulk's deeply lined face, and at Brian's teeth, flashing like perfect rows of Chiclets gum. I started thinking: *Three votes.* I couldn't believe it. Three lousy votes. Suddenly the face of the black girl from my homeroom came into my mind and I started to recall how many black students rode that same bus. My thoughts were interrupted as Brian extended his hand to congratulate me on a good race.

"You should be really proud," he said.

Proud . . . proud of losing? Mr. Faulk did say I had lost.

"Thanks, and congratulations, Brian," I said softly. I felt like crying, but I didn't.

Mr. Faulk told us to go back to our classes, and that he would announce the results over the loudspeaker during fourth period. He told Brian he could use his phone and call his parents and tell them the good news. He then looked at me and asked if I wanted to call my parents. Of course, parents meant two, and Mr. Faulk knew that I was being raised by my mother, alone.

What would I tell my mother if I could call her? That I had lost an election that she didn't even know I was running in? In fact, I hadn't told anyone outside the confines of Hall High, not my mother, my sisters, or my neighborhood friends, because I didn't want to be discouraged. How could I call my mother, who worked in a factory where no phone calls were allowed unless it was a matter of life or death?

I told Mr. Faulk I didn't want to call my mother but I would like to talk to him in private as Brian called his parents. When Brian left, Mr. Faulk again congratulated me on how well I had done and mentioned what a long way I had come since my suspension at West Side.

The implication in his comments was clear—that I should be happy that so many white students had voted for me. When I told him that I thought at least twenty black students were late because of a broken-down bus and didn't have a chance to vote in the election, he looked at me with a puzzled expression and asked me what I thought he should do.

"I think they should be allowed to vote," I said.

My statement caught Mr. Faulk off guard, and he stood up from his chair and dismissively said that wouldn't be fair. Brian had won, and besides, he had called and told his parents. Furthermore, if he allowed the colored students to vote now, I would win—and he simply couldn't allow that.

Colored students, I thought. I couldn't believe what I'd heard. I was shocked by the use of the word *colored* from a man whom I had known to be fair and had been a popular figure with black students at West Side.

But I knew he was right about one thing: I would win if he allowed the students who rode the bus to vote. I remained silent and stared at him in disbelief as he once again congratulated me on my efforts and assured me that there would be other opportunities for me during my junior and senior years.

I left the principal's office and headed to my fourth-period World History class. When I walked into the room, everyone was smiling at me. Several white girls who sat near me whispered that they had voted for me and they thought I was going to win. I gave them a half-smile, but their enthusiasm didn't make me feel any better. Before taking my seat, I realized I had left my books in my previous class. As I was getting ready to ask Mrs. Crosby, our teacher, if I could be excused, a frail female voice came over the intercom: "The results of the election of sophomore class representative are as follows: Lynn Harris, 323 votes, and Brian Sudderth, 326 votes. Your new sophomore class representative is Brian Sudderth."

The room fell silent. *Don't cry*, I told myself. But I could feel warm tears streaming down my face. Mrs. Crosby noticed this and asked me if I wanted to be excused. I didn't need to answer. I raced out of the room, down the hallway, and out the door into the student parking lot. The dam of anger and sorrow broke, and the tears rushed down my face with a cleansing freedom. My career as a politician looked as if it was going to end as quickly as it had begun.

THE WEEKS FOLLOWING THE ELECTION, I began to understand that I'd lost only a small battle. Running for sophomore class representative won me a lot of new friends and admirers, so I wasn't disappointed very long, since popularity was what I really wanted and craved. Sure I wanted to win, but losing gave me the time to capitalize on my newfound popularity. I felt that my white classmates viewed me as their equal, and I had never enjoyed this type of popularity at Booker or West Side, even when I was acting a fool. But did these people like me for me, or for the impostor I was slowly becoming?

Two beautiful white girls, Becka Henry and Karen Krenz, offered me friendship by inviting me to dinner at the newly opened Farrell's Ice Cream parlor in McCain Mall. I went even though I was a little bit concerned riding in a car with two white girls. But Becka and Karen never seemed uncomfortable around me and became my first white female friends.

Most of my white classmates and some of my black ones naturally assumed that I lived in University Park, since they knew I didn't ride the school bus. I refused rides home by making up excuses, like I was waiting for my mother to pick me up. Once their cars were out of sight, I would start my trek down the hill to the public bus stop.

When my classmates asked what my parents did for a living, I lied. I told them my mother was a supervisor at Teletype, a respected Little Rock company where she actually worked but wasn't in management. The stories about my father were grander, because since I didn't know anything about him, making him a family court judge in Michigan didn't seem like a stretch. How could anyone prove it wasn't the truth?

Sometimes my deception caused problems. During the spring semester one of our basketball games went into double overtime. I accepted a ride from a white classmate, since I knew the last public bus had left the area minutes earlier. The young lady drove me straight to University Park, and I didn't bother to correct her. Once we arrived at the fashionable neighborhood, I asked her to let me out on the corner of Sherry Drive, pointing to a huge brick house at the top of the cul-de-sac as the place where I lived.

When she asked me if I wanted her to drive me all the way home, I told her I was going to stop and visit a neighbor. She smiled at me, and I thanked her for the ride. After her royal blue Camaro faded from sight, I waited a few more minutes and then started my twelve-mile walk home. My mother and sisters were sound asleep when I finally got home around 2:00 A.M., tired and drenched in my own sweat.

CHAPTER 5

At the end my sophomore year, Mama sent me to Flint, Michigan, for the summer, to stay with my Uncle Clarence and his five children. I think she thought it would be good for me to be around boys my own age and experience the fatherly influence my uncle could provide.

Uncle Clarence really wasn't my uncle but my mother's first cousin. We always called him uncle because all adult male relatives were uncles and he was too old to be a cousin. He had three brothers, Lawrence, Roy, and Jesse, whom I called uncle as well.

This was not my first time visiting Flint during the summer, but it would be the first time I would spend the entire summer. I had never been away from my mother and sisters for such a long time, and I was excited. After the last day of school, I boarded a Greyhound bus and took the twenty-six-hour bus trip, armed with a yellow vinyl suitcase full of new summer clothes and the money I had saved from after-school jobs pinned on the inside of my pants. I couldn't wait to see Uncle Clarence and his children, Clarence Jr., Carolyn, Rickey, Wayne, and Janette.

Uncle Clarence was a widower who never seemed to lack female company. A big, bearlike, high-yellow man with a bald head and hearty laugh, he always seemed to have a cigar or pipe hanging from his mouth. He worked for one of the big automobile companies, like almost everyone else in Flint. He was also a part-time mechanic, so it wasn't unusual for him to have strangers visit his two-story house, which sat on the corner of Thirty-fifth and Alexander.

I seemed to fit right in with the Allen household. With an attic and a basement, the place was big enough so that you could have some privacy if you wanted. Two of my cousins, Rickey and Wayne, were close in age to me and treated me like a real brother and introduced me to all their friends, both male and female.

Rickey was light-skinned, smart, and was only a couple of months older. Rickey had just completed his sophomore year at Flint Northern High School. Wayne was a year younger than I was. He was chocolate brown and handsome, with thick curly black hair, thick eyelashes, and hair over the majority of his body, even though he was only fourteen years old.

I loved hanging out with Wayne, who already had a large female fan club. Wayne carried himself like he was older, always telling me what we were going to do, whether it was swimming or playing stickball. I think he got a big kick out of the fact that I enjoyed spending more time with him than my other cousins. The truth of the matter was that some of my other cousins teased me about being so skinny and "talking country," but Wayne rarely teased me.

One day I was alone in the normally busy house washing dishes. The house was quiet, with the exception of my hands going in and out of the soapy dish water. It was a rule in the Allen household that everyone had to wash dishes and help out with the cleaning. This was different for me, because my mother had never assigned me chores that were considered women's work. At home I was responsible for taking out the garbage and cutting the grass. But I didn't complain, since none of the Allen boys seemed to think there was anything wrong with doing housework.

Just as I was rinsing out one of the last glasses, I glanced out of the kitchen window and saw my uncle get out of the passenger side of a blue car. At first, I thought that maybe the driver was my Uncle Lawrence or Uncle Roy, but when I saw him get out, I immediately knew he wasn't one of them. The stranger locked his car door and started to walk across the street toward the house with my uncle. As the two got closer, an eerie feeling washed over me. I couldn't take my eyes off the stranger. He looked familiar, but I couldn't place where I knew him from.

Before the two of them reached the garage, I noticed how much the stranger looked like me. I immediately thought, *Could this man be my father?* When I dreamed of him, I never had a physical image of him; I just prayed he wouldn't treat me like Ben had. My fantasy for my real father was that he was somebody important, like a judge or a lawyer, or at the very least a teacher, preferably a college professor. I hoped that he was loving and stern. I dreamed he would take me to football games and play catch with me in the backyard of his mansion.

When I heard the back screen door open, I had a sudden urge to hide. I wanted to run upstairs to my bedroom or downstairs to the always dimly lit basement. But I was frozen harder than my Grandma's homemade ice cream. The position of the kitchen prevented me from leaving without being in full view of the back screen door or the front porch. Maybe if I didn't say anything they wouldn't know I was in the house. I heard my uncle's footsteps coming up the small flight of stairs as he called out my name: "Lynn? Is Lynn here?"

I didn't answer as I rubbed my damp hands on my khaki shorts.

"Lynn," Uncle Clarence's booming voice called out again. My heart was pounding, and I felt sweat form on my nose and forehead. I moved slowly to the hallway and was suddenly standing face-to-face with my uncle and the stranger. When I looked at him, it was like looking into a mirror. His skin was the same caramel color as mine, his nose and lips larger versions of my own. The only noticeable difference was that his hair was black and curly like Wayne's. Maybe he wasn't my father, I thought. Not with such beautiful hair.

"I got somebody I want you to meet," my uncle said.

"How are you doing, young man?" the stranger asked.

"Fine," I muttered.

"Lynn, this is James," Uncle Clarence said. *James.* That was the name on my birth certificate.

"Do you know who I am?" he asked.

"No, sir," I lied.

"I'm your daddy," he said. "Didn't your mama tell you 'bout me?"

"No, sir," I said. As far as I knew, my mother didn't know that I knew the secret she kept hidden in the gray box. Maybe she had planned this meeting so we would talk about it once I returned home. I knew my Aunt Gee had to know about my father, but I never asked her direct questions about him. Maybe I was afraid if I ever met my father, I would have to give up my fantasies.

For a moment, the three of us stood close together in the small hallway. Then, without warning, I suddenly darted between them like an elusive running back and bolted down the short flight of stairs and burst through the screen door. Once I got outside I was running so fast that I slipped and fell, scraping my arms and knees. I quickly got up and ran toward Pasadena Street and the community basketball court and playground in search of my cousin Wayne.

Once I reached the playground, I didn't see him or anyone else I knew. I was heading toward the swimming pool inside Northern High gym when I noticed an empty set of swings, which looked inviting and safe.

I had dreamed so many nights about my father and what it

would be like to meet him. I fantasized that he would take me away from Little Rock and allow me to live with him, that he would teach me how to be a man. Now that the time had come, it wasn't at all like my dreams. I wanted to be happy, but I felt a sadness shadowing me. Why had I run away from him? What was I afraid of?

I don't know how long I sat on the swings. The summer sun set peacefully. My mind was eased by the incredible evening colors—yellow, orange, and a hazy purple, the type of colors that made you believe in the mystical power of nature. I swayed in the swing until the playground became pitch black. I didn't return home until I was certain the stranger was no longer there.

AFTER HAVING GONE SO MANY YEARS without my father ever seeing me, I would have been disappointed if he had given up so easily. But I was still afraid of him. I feared that he couldn't live up to my dreams and that he wouldn't like me. Maybe he would think I was a sissy, as Ben had. So I was a bit surprised by the flash of joy I experienced the next day when my father returned with a look of determination on his handsome face. He was leaning against his car when I came out of the house headed for the grocery store.

The night before I had been unable to sleep, consumed with thoughts of how my life would change now that I had met my father. Wayne and Rickey thought it was exciting to meet a father I never knew. They filled my head with thoughts of all the gifts I could expect. "Think of all the holidays and birthdays he missed," Wayne had pointed out.

"How are you doing, young man?" he asked.

"Fine," I whispered.

"Where you headed?"

"Nowhere," I lied.

He walked toward me and asked if we could talk. My heart was pounding with fear and excitement: I feared that I would say something dumb, but I was excited that my father wanted to talk to me.

He told me he was sorry he didn't get to talk to me that much the night before. He then told me some very exciting news. I had some brothers and sisters anxious to meet me. *Brothers?* Had he said brothers? This was too good to be true. I had always wanted a brother. Were they older? What were they like? Suddenly I wanted to know more. Suddenly I wasn't afraid.

"Where are they?" I asked.

He told me they were at home and they wanted me to come and spend the night. I told him I couldn't do that without my Uncle Clarence's permission, and he was at work. But I told him I really wanted to meet them.

My father suggested I ride home with him and he would bring me back whenever I was ready. That sounded fair to me. I had already made up my mind that I wasn't going to spend the night. In Flint, the Allen household was the only place I really felt safe. I just wanted to meet my brothers. I wasn't that concerned about my new sisters, since I had three perfectly good ones back in Little Rock.

As I got into my father's car, I was still a little uneasy. After all, I had just met the man. What if he didn't bring me back? I would never see my mother and sisters again. I remained silent as he turned off Saginaw Street and drove through downtown Flint. Once on the freeway, my father turned down the radio, rolled up his window, and turned on the air conditioner.

"Roll your window up," my father ordered. Without hesitation, I complied. He started asking me questions about my mother. I told her she was fine. Then he asked me about school, and I told him I had just finished the tenth grade. He told me James Jr. was going into the seventh grade. That meant he was younger than I was. I wondered why he had my father's name. For a moment I wished I had been named after him, since I was his firstborn. At least I assumed I was his first child. Maybe it was he who had named me Everette Lynn. Maybe, unlike Ben, he liked my name and didn't think I had a sissy name.

I couldn't believe what was happening. Occasionally we spied each other from the corners of our almost identical eyes. I think he was as nervous as I was.

A few minutes later his car exited from the freeway, and after a few stoplights he pulled into a nice-looking neighborhood of neat two-story homes with brick fronts. Black children scurried from the streets at the sight of my father's car, while others rode bicycles on the sidewalks in front of manicured lawns. Most of the houses looked brand-new. They all looked the same, but they were better-looking than any house I had seen black folks living in in my neighborhood. I was impressed.

A couple of blocks later, we turned into the driveway of one of the identical homes and out ran two boys and two young girls. They were smiling and seemed excited to see my father and me.

"This is Lynn, your big brother," my father said proudly. I liked the way he said my name.

"I'm glad to meet you," the younger of the two boys said. He hugged me at my waist.

"I'm James Jr.," he said.

"I'm David," the older one said quietly.

The two girls, Tamela and Pamela, came over to introduce themselves. They were identical twins. I didn't have twin sisters back home!

"I'm Lynn," I said. I felt like I was coming out of a trance. My littlest brother was holding my hand tight.

My father instructed him to let me go and suggested we go inside. James Jr. ignored my father's order and held tightly to my hand as we went through the screen door into a large living area.

I noticed a petite, attractive woman come from a dining area, smiling as she approached me.

"You must be Lynn," she said. "I'm Jean Jeter, your daddy's wife." Her smile was warm and engaging.

"Yes, ma'am," I said.

"Come over here and give me a hug. James Jr., let his hands go," she said. As we hugged, she whispered in my ear, "I'm glad you came."

I was glad I had come also. The fear and tension suddenly left my body while my littlest brother looked at me with a comforting smile. They all made me feel welcome, like I belonged. David seemed a little distant and ill at ease. Maybe he was upset because he was no longer the big brother.

One of the twins came downstairs carrying a small infant.

"This is your other little brother," she said, handing me a beautiful copper-colored baby.

"What's his name?" I asked as I took him in my arms carefully.

"Andre."

I looked down at him, and his big brown eyes stared up at me. With the exception of my little sister Jan, Andre was the most beautiful baby I had ever seen. His head was covered with dark curly hair. He looked like a combination of my father and Jean. I smiled at him, and his small mouth released tiny bubbles.

"I think he likes you," Jean said.

Andre fell asleep in my arms, and James Jr. encouraged me to put him down so that he could take me outside where a group of neighborhood children had gathered. I felt like a celebrity.

James Jr. introduced me to everyone in sight as his "big brother from down south." While we were walking back, I asked James Jr. why David was so quiet and he told me he wasn't my father's blood son and he might be a little bit jealous of me. He told me David's father lived in Saginaw. Now his silence made sense.

James Jr. suggested I ask our father to take us to the drive-in. When I asked him why, he replied, "I know he'll take us if you ask." Sure enough, after a fried chicken dinner, my father asked me what I wanted to do. James Jr.'s instinct had been right, and I even scored points with David, who seemed to loosen up while we were at the drive-in.

After the movie, and much to the dismay of my new family, I returned to my uncle's house, using the excuse that I didn't bring clothes to spend the night. They were all disappointed, but James Jr. took it harder than anyone. His tears almost made me change my mind.

When I got back to my uncle's house, Wayne and I talked all night about my father's house and my new brothers and sisters. I was tempted to call Mama and tell her about my evening, but I didn't.

BEFORE THE SUMMER ENDED and I returned to Little Rock for my junior year, I visited my father's house several times. I never spent the night or felt totally relaxed around him. I loved my brothers and sisters and David and Jean. My father's wife was easy to talk to and told me it was okay for me not to feel totally comfortable with my father, that our relationship would come with time. I told her that now that my father was no longer a fantasy but human flesh, I was afraid that he might disappoint me or I would disappoint him. Jean gave me solid advice by telling me to just be myself. I didn't have the courage to tell her that I felt being myself had never been good enough.

On those rare occasions when my father and I talked alone, he tried hard to make up for all the lost years. He shared how when I was a baby my mother would leave me with him for long weekends while she worked. He told me he would make a pallet on the floor and play with me until we both became exhausted.

My father told me how much his parents (when they were alive) had spoiled me as well. When he talked, his face would brighten, but I couldn't relax and return his smiles.

I learned from my father that my mama and I had left Flint when I was about three years old. He told me how sad he was, and I wanted to ask him why he didn't come and get me. Didn't he know all the torture I was going through with Ben? Weren't daddies supposed to protect their children?

My mind was filled with so many questions that I didn't ask him. Like why didn't he marry my mother? Why didn't he come to visit my mother and me in Little Rock? Why had he waited until I was almost an adult to show up?

I thought maybe once I felt more comfortable with him and was able to distinguish my dream father from my real father, I could really talk to him. This was, after all, really the beginning for us, and we had next summer and so many summers to come.

MY QUESTIONS FOR MY FATHER were never answered. I never had the opportunity to ask them. The father I never really knew was killed before I could return to Flint the following summer. The victim of a drunk driver, my father was killed instantly when a car in which he was a passenger collided with a parked eighteen-wheel truck.

It was April and I was in Jacksonville, Arkansas, spending the weekend with my Aunt Gee and her family, who were now living on the Little Rock Air Force Base. My older cousin Kennie and I had gone to see *The Odd Couple* at the base theater.

It was a dreary Friday, and when we returned my aunt asked me to come into the dining room alone. Her beautiful face was covered with a look I had never seen. I could tell something was wrong. My first thought was that something had happened to my mother, grandmother, or sisters. She told me there had been an accident in Michigan and that my father had been killed instantly. At first I was relieved it was my father and not my mother. Things could be tense at times between my mother and me, but life without my mother was something I couldn't imagine.

My aunt hugged me, as she often did whenever I saw her, but this time she held me longer, and the hug was tighter than usual, as if she were really trying to assure me that everything would be fine.

When I went into the room where I slept, I was confused about how I was supposed to feel. I really didn't feel sad, and that bothered me. I had known friends who had lost their fathers, and recalled how sad they'd been. Where were my tears? My stomach was full of nervous energy, and I couldn't fall asleep. But there were no tears.

In the pitch-dark room my eyes remained open the entire night. I tried to remember what my father looked like, but his face wouldn't come to mind. I suddenly wished I had a photo of him.

As I lay there in silence, I hoped that I would get some kind of sign from my father or God on how I was supposed to feel, or that I would hear some voice that would tell me it was all right if I didn't feel like crying. But there was only silence.

MY FATHER'S DEATH WAS the first time Mama acknowledged him. When I returned home from the weekend, she asked me if I wanted to go to the funeral. I didn't know where she would get the money to fly me to Michigan, because times were still hard for us. I told her no, because I didn't like funerals and I had never flown on a plane.

She didn't pressure me to go, nor did she volunteer any more information about my father. I started to call Jean and my brothers and sisters, but I didn't. Months later when I tried, the phone had been disconnected.

What I did after my father's death was what I had done before I met him: I depended on my fantasy father, who could be whatever I wanted him to be. My father now could be my best friend. He would be a kind and loving man who would understand that I was different from most boys my age.

My fantasy father would provide me a shoulder to cry on when people disappointed me. My father would assure me that I could do anything I dreamed of, as long as I treated people the way I wanted to be treated. But mostly, my fantasy father would just be proud of me.

I never saw my brothers and sisters again after that summer. I heard from my Uncle Clarence that Jean had died from complications of alcoholism a year after my father had been killed. I wondered if my brothers and sister were sent to live with relatives or if they were shifted around to different foster homes. It was horrible for them to lose both parents, and I was thankful I still had my mother. I have always regretted that our lives never crossed again. Maybe someday they will.

CHAPTER 6

T he summer of '72 was a time when I finally had to acknowledge to myself that my feelings toward men were not like those of most boys my age.

My selection to Arkansas Boys State marked the starting point for my summer of discovery. Boys State was a one-week program sponsored by the American Legion to prepare young men for leadership roles in government. Some of its graduates include former president William Jefferson Clinton and current Arkansas governor Mike Huckbee, and being selected was an honor I had coveted since ninth grade, when I saw a neighbor, Mike Price, who attended Central, wearing the white with navy blue trim Boys State T-shirt. I was impressed.

Despite the sophomore-year election, I still hadn't given up on a career in politics, and Boys State was a place to test those aspirations. I didn't run for junior class representative, because Brian had done a good job and seemed more popular than when he had first come to Hall. I decided against challenging him for student body president, because I was contemplating applying to several colleges for early admission after scoring high on the ACT I took during my junior year. My score was so impressive that my counselors wondered why I wasn't on the honors track at

Hall. An after-school job and trying to combat my sexual emotions became much more than I could handle, so school work didn't always get my full attention.

My urge to leave Little Rock was stronger than ever. I was convinced that the city was too small for my dreams and differences. I looked to Boys State as a chance to receive leadership recognition on a state level. Privately, I was beginning to realize that my interest in politics and the support of others was a search for self-esteem. If I could win an office at Boys State, white people at Hall would view me as an equal, while black students would respect me and look up to me. In my sixteen-year-old mind, respect would become very important if people ever learned of my difference.

Boys State was held at Camp Robinson, a former military base outside of North Little Rock. The size of each school in Arkansas determined how many delegates it sent. Hall had eleven, and I was one of three black students selected, a first at Hall.

All the representatives were assigned to barracks named after different cities and counties in the state. There were so many delegates that it was rare to be in the same county as someone from your school. The entire week I caught only glimpses of the boys from Hall, the majority of whom were star athletes, and, of course, Brian, who had been elected student body president for the upcoming school year.

The first night, I was elected mayor of my city, which was ironically named Hall County, but I had my eye on the lieutenant governor spot. No black had ever held that position, and it was crazy to think a black could be elected governor of Boys State in 1972, since blacks made up less than 4 percent of the thousand-plus participants. Dexter Reed, someone I knew from Booker Junior High and a star basketball player at Parkview, did run for governor that year and lost badly to Mike Huckbee, the same Huckbee who would become the real governor of Arkansas in 1997.

To win a state office, you had to have the support of your city and the political party to which you were assigned. The parties were not the standard Democrat or Republican but instead were represented by the colors green and gray. I was a member of the Green party.

I was not elected lieutenant governor at Boys State in 1972. In fact, I wasn't even nominated, but I received something I had dreamed of my whole life: my first best friend.

John Carl Gessler slept in the bunk below me. I don't recall the first time I saw him or how we became such fast friends. He blended in with all the other white boys in the crowded barracks. I do remember his coming up to me, extending his hand, and saying, "Hi, I'm Carl Gessler and I'm running for the gate, trying to get out of here. Will you vote for me?" He joked about how most every guy he met was running for something, and it didn't seem to bother anyone but Gessler that we were locked behind Camp Robinson's massive gate.

Carl had beautiful olive-colored skin, with angular features and full lips, and dark black hair that fell boyishly over his forehead. His smile revealed perfect rows of white teeth. His physique was slight and unremarkable when compared to the hundreds of high school football players around us.

We would talk while marching alongside each other as we traveled to the mess hall and classroom sessions. He was always cracking jokes. Carl had this smile of infinite kindness that I had never known from a white person or any boy my own age.

I became so enamored with Gessler, as I would come to call him, that I gave up my dreams of running for a major office (which would use up a lot of time) so that I could spend all of my free moments with him. Luckily, we both were elected to the office of state senator. The win ensured us a trip to the state capitol on the Friday before the camp ended. In the real Arkansas senate chambers I would nominate my new friend for senate president, an office he won easily.

Looking back, I know my attraction to Gessler was not sexual. But our friendship was special and intense. I had never met anyone who thought so highly of me, and who didn't mind telling me and showing me with boyish hugs of affection and kind words.

Gessler was from Hot Springs, a city fifty-five miles southwest of Little Rock. The city of about 35,000 was known for its hot mineral baths, the Miss Arkansas pageant, and Oaklawn Racetrack. In the fifties the city was known as a little Las Vegas because of gambling and rumors of the mafia coming in and out of town.

At the end of Boys State, Gessler made me promise I would come and spend the weekend with him. I had been to a white person's house for the first time during my junior year when I had attended a Key Club meeting at the home of Connie Blass, one of the most popular and wealthy young ladies at Hall. I was nervous, but Connie and her mother both went out of their way to make me feel comfortable.

I told Gessler I would try, but I was on my way to Washington, D.C., for a government program the week after Boys State ended. I was so looking forward to going to D.C. and visiting the campus at Howard University, one of the schools I was considering attending. But my friendship with Gessler made me wish I hadn't been selected for this exclusive program that was bringing low-income African American students from around the country to work in a government agency. I wanted to spend the summer in Hot Springs. In fact, I wanted to move there.

With Gessler, I shared many long-held secrets except for my sexual interest in men. Gessler was sympathetic when I told him about Ben and losing my father so soon after meeting him.

I even shared with him the fact that I hadn't cried since my real father's death.

"That's understandable. You really didn't know him," Gessler said to me.

The night before camp ended, while most guys were celebrating their return home, Gessler and I escaped from the crowd. On the concrete steps of an empty barracks we talked about how much we would miss each other and promised to write every week of the summer. On this beautiful moonlit night, Gessler tossed his hair back from his eyes and looked at me and said, "You know what?"

"What?" I responded.

"I just realized something," Gessler said.

"What's that?"

"You're black."

"Yeah, and you know what else?" I said.

"What?"

"You're white."

We both broke out into joyous laughter as we reached for each other and gently butted our heads together, briefly holding tight to each other's neck. It was also on that night when we discovered we were born the same day, only hours apart. From that moment on, we became known to mutual friends as the salt-and-pepper twins. I left Boys State without the office I thought I needed to feel good about myself, but with a friendship that made me feel even better.

WHEN I THINK BACK ON THAT SUMMER, I remember Stevie Wonder's beautiful ballad from his album, *Music of My Mind*. "Super Woman (Where Were You When I Needed You)" expresses the loneliness one feels when he's lost someone special, not to death, but distance. And even though neither a lover nor a friend had died, I felt lonely for most of the summer and my senior year. Maybe it was the first time I realized that my feelings toward men meant the only love I could expect was the love I already had—from my mother and people required by convention to at least try to love me, like my sisters and other relatives.

I REMEMBER THE NERVOUS ENERGY I felt as I boarded my first flight to Washington, D.C. Actually it was more than being nervous; I was scared, so fearful that the plane would fall out of the sky that I called the program director a couple of days before I was due in Washington to see if they could provide me with a bus ticket. Although she convinced me that the plane would be safe, I still had reservations until my grandma shared a little prayer with me. She told me to say it before I got on the plane. Today I travel constantly, but I don't get on a plane without her prayer: *Dear God, I'm going on a little trip today. Please keep me safe all the way.*

I arrived safely in Washington, D.C., and caught a cab to Calhoun Hall at George Washington University, where the participants would be staying for the six-week program. We would work half-days at government agencies and spend the rest of our time attending classes on things like etiquette, and sightseeing in the nation's capital and surrounding areas.

During the first day of orientation, one of the counselors warned boys in the program to be careful because Washington had a huge gay problem. *Gay problem?* Curious, I raised my hand, and when the program's director recognized me, I asked, "What is gay?"

The room roared with laughter. Here I was, this hick from Arkansas who had already been singled out as the one who wanted to ride the Greyhound bus to D.C., asking what gay was.

Maybe the students were laughing at my heavy southern accent, which most of the kids from larger urban areas called "country." The director had a puzzled look on her face as she glanced toward one of the male counselors for help.

A participant from Omaha, Nebraska, a big football player type, stopped his laughter long enough to look at me and say, "Punks, sissies. Boys who want to be girls. I know y'all got them down south."

"Oh," I said, embarrassed. So that's what I was. *Gay.* Part of a problem. From that moment on, Washington seemed determined to teach me things about myself.

I noticed how at times I became uncomfortable with my own kind. By this I mean black male teenagers from low-income homes. Of course, I gravitated toward the girls in the program. I formed few close friendships with the boys, because I felt I had little in common with them. They teased me about the way I talked, because I had a body that resembled a young girl's, and because, they said, I dressed like a white boy with my Izod shirt and penny loafers. I was proud of the fact that my after-school jobs allowed me to dress like most of the kids at Hall. The boys seemed to receive great joy inflicting pain in tearing one another down. I learned how racism becomes internalized and self-destructive. For a teenager already lacking self-esteem, the words hurt.

I missed Gessler desperately—so much so that when I didn't receive a letter from him, I became depressed. I called him and explained how important his letters were. I guess he got the message, because practically every day for the rest of my time in Washington I got a letter from Gessler. So what if it was a copy of his first letter. A rerun wasn't what I wanted, but it helped ease some of the loneliness I felt. I knew he had to be thinking about me every time he put the letter in the mailbox. I also got letters from some of my classmates at Hall, like Connie Blass and Karen, and Becca, who was attending Central.

Not all my experiences with the guys were bad. When some of them realized I knew a lot about sports, they actually talked to me. I got along great with all the girls in the program, including the director, a beautiful schoolteacher from Detroit who allowed me to come to her apartment in the dorm when I was feeling lonely and needed someone to talk to. I told Ms. Jefferies all about Gessler and what a special friend he was. One day when I was down in the dumps, she looked at me and asked, "You miss that white boy, don't you?"

"Yes, I do."

WASHINGTON, D.C., BECAME the first place where I actually saw two men holding hands, being openly affectionate, and dancing together. Every Saturday night the George Washington University student union was the home of Gay Pride in the Summertime dances.

On Saturdays our curfew wasn't until midnight, and with nothing else better to do, several of the program participants decided to go to the dance because the people always seemed happy entering the student union. The first time I resisted, but I sat on one of the concrete banisters surrounding the union and watched with a curious excitement as I saw men walk in as couples. I knew then that if the opportunity to see what gay pride meant presented itself again, I was going to take it.

That chance occurred the following weekend. It was a steamy summer night, and pulsating lights and strains of the Billy Preston hit "Outer Space" drew several of us to the huge room that during the day served as the cafeteria. We paid our fifty cents and went into the dark crowd to join the festive dancing. The music was fantastic and blaring. The immense floor was dark, with the exception of strobe lights circling the crowd as they moved in frenzy.

I danced with several of the girls from the group until I was dripping wet. When the lights came on, I was surprised but pleased to see so many good-looking men, black and white, hugging and kissing.

A few of the kids from the program looked like they were going to throw up, which I thought was kind of funny. Here they were acting as though this was the first time they had seen such behavior, the very same macho boys who had laughed at me when I asked what gay meant. I thought they knew.

As we started to make our dash from the party back to the dormitory before curfew, Pam, a street-smart young lady from St. Louis and one of the few people I felt comfortable with, spotted a very attractive black man who could have been a movie star, or at the very least a model. He had beautiful hazel-green eyes and dark, curly black hair that matched his equally hairy chest. He was shirtless, like many of the men in the room. Pam, who called me "Little Rock" (my first nickname since Ben called me Mike), grabbed my hand and pulled me toward him.

She was ranting about how could this fine *"mutherfucker"* be gay. With me holding her hand, Pam walked right up to the guy and tapped him on his naked shoulders and said, "Hey, can I ask you something?"

"Sure," he said as he turned toward us and smiled.

"Are you gay?" Pam blurted. I waited nervously for his answer.

"Yes, I am," he said.

"But why?" Pam asked with disbelief.

"Are you and your friend straight?" he asked.

"Yes, we are," Pam said, speaking for both of us. I was just standing there staring at him. The fact that he looked so perfect and shared my desires and appeared proud of it just blew me away.

"Why are you straight?" he asked.

"What do you mean?" Pam asked.

"Why are you straight?" he repeated.

"Because that's the way I am. That's just me," Pam said.

"Then that's why I'm gay. It's just me," he said, smiling.

The man introduced himself as Michael and told us that he was from Washington, D.C. He said that maybe he would see us next weekend. Pam was disappointed that Michael was convinced that he would be gay the rest of his life. I remember how sure of himself he was, how happy he looked.

When we got back to the dorm, Pam told all the girls in the program about Michael and how fine and nice he was. She was certain she could change his ways.

Pam didn't get a chance, because we didn't see Michael again that summer. The director of the program found out about our outing and forbade us from ever going back. Of course, I obeyed. I didn't want to get sent back home for attending parties where men danced only with men.

For the remaining Saturdays that summer, while the rest of the students were coupling up with each other, I would sit near the window of my dorm room and watch the beautiful men of all colors walk hand in hand into the GWU student union.

I learned two things from that experience: The director taught me the fear people have about the unknown, and Michael showed me the pride conveyed in knowing who you are.

I RETURNED TO LITTLE ROCK and Hall anxious to get on with my senior year. I hoped it would be the swiftest of my life. Washington, D.C., had piqued my curiosity about the pleasures of big-city living, and I knew I would eventually return for good. I spent so many times daydreaming about living in a city like Washington, D.C., or New York City, which I got the chance to visit for the first time that year as well.

One of our field trips was a bus ride to New York City, where we saw the Broadway show *Don't Play Us Cheap*, which I thought was the best thing I had ever seen since I saw *The Nutcracker* when I was in the fourth grade at Bush Elementary. We also enjoyed a soul food dinner in Harlem. The bright lights and the beat of the city convinced me that this was a place where I belonged and I was going to find my way back, but first I had to finish my education.

Falling into the familiar high school routine wasn't easy after my summer experiences. I knew for sure that there was a big world waiting for me. I passed on running for senior class president despite the encouragement of some of my classmates, although I did serve as president of the Bi-Racial Council, a student group established to keep harmony between the races. I felt this was more important, since Hall was now about 30 percent black. Carolyn Higgins, someone I had known from Booker and was always in my homeroom, was elected secretary of the senior class, thus becoming the first minority to win a classwide election.

I talked with Gessler often and even got to visit his home. When I went to see him I experienced another sensation—namely, envy. At first this bothered me, but then I decided to use it for inspiration. I dreamed I'd one day live in a beautiful brick house, with a housekeeper and a two-car garage. I never let Gessler know how I felt, even though I'm sure he would have understood.

Gessler was making the most of his senior year at Hot Springs High School. He had a beautiful girlfriend, Megan, who was homecoming queen and a cheerleader. He was making straight A's and had been elected senior class president and talked of attending the University of Arkansas at Fayetteville and becoming a doctor. And he constantly told me I was his best friend, something I needed to hear.

There was nothing stellar about my senior year. My grades

were good but not great, but still schools like Vanderbilt, Princeton, and the University of Michigan, impressed with my college pre-entrance exams, wrote me letters as if I were a star football player. I eliminated Vanderbilt, because I had read somewhere that they had a high suicide rate, and I eliminated Princeton because I didn't consider myself Ivy League material.

I was intrigued by thoughts of attending the University of Michigan, because I knew Ann Arbor was close to Flint and I loved watching the football team with their maize and blue uniforms.

I had a cool job as a salesclerk in the boys' department at M. M. Cohns, the most exclusive store in Little Rock. When I wasn't working or in school, life was pretty boring. I looked forward to speaking with Gessler, watching college football and *Mary Tyler Moore*. I know it sounds crazy, but I identified with the Mary character, because it didn't seem like she had love in her life but she had good friends and seemed happy. She had the kind of apartment I thought I would have one day in New York City or Washington, D.C.

While other boys in my neighborhood spent time playing basketball or searched for private spots to have sex with girls, I spent countless evenings alone listening to the sounds of Smokey Robinson, Al Green, Marvin Gaye, and Stevie Wonder. This was a time when I convinced myself that true love existed only in songs, movies, or on TV. I'd never seen much romantic love in my own home, and if someone as special as Mama couldn't find it, how could I ever think it would happen to me?

It's not like I didn't try to have girlfriends. There were several young ladies, like Yolanda Wherry and Karen Curry, who made my heart beat rapidly, but they both lived in North Little Rock, which seemed so far away that romance was impossible.

They were both popular girls, the only black cheerleaders at Northeast and Ole Main, and certainly had better offers than one from a skinny boy from a single-parent home who still thought about a certain Central High football player when he slow-danced with girls at parties. Yet I don't remember ever feeling happier as a boy than I did when Karen let me wear her silver and blue cheerleader megaphone necklace for a week. If only I'd had a letterman's jacket to give her in return, Karen might have let me keep that necklace forever and help transfer my affection from football players to cheerleaders.

I had only two dates my entire time in high school. I went to school dances celebrating the beginning of the school term and homecoming, but I always went alone. One of my dates was with a young lady name Beverly Dean, a beautiful and smart girl whom I took to see the movie *Love Story*, and I ended up crying more than she did. My other date was a memorable one. Rose Crater, my first crush, went to my senior prom with me. She was still one of the most popular girls in Little Rock, having become the first black cheerleader at Parkview High. She also made history when she was elected the first black girl to be homecoming queen at a majority white school.

I remember how my heart started to beat at a rapid rate when I saw Rose in her beautiful aqua prom gown with matching turban. I felt like the luckiest guy in Little Rock, and that remains one of the most special nights in my life. Proms were not considered successful by most of my male peers unless they ended up in a hotel room or the backseat of a limo. In Little Rock there were a lot of prom babies who halted many a college career. My date with Rose ended sweetly, after a pancake breakfast a little after midnight at the International House of Pancakes.

Besides those two dates, I didn't allow myself to dream of a love life. I had one experience toward the end of the school year that made me realize that leaving my hometown for good would soon be an issue of survival.

I met him when I went downtown to pick up my senior ring.

I was at the Woolworth's lunch counter eating a banana split when he sat down next to me. A couple of minutes later, I realized he was staring at me as he played with his hamburger and fries.

He was older and quite handsome, with rich blue-black skin and snow-white teeth like the movie character Shaft. And just like the black movie detective, he turned out to be a "bad motherfucker."

Right before he left, he wrote his name and a phone number on a napkin and pushed it toward me. He never said a word. I called him later that evening, and he said he had been waiting to hear from me. We talked briefly, and he suggested we get together later that night. He told me his name was Donald and that he'd moved to Little Rock from Kansas City to be with his girlfriend, who was attending college at Philander Smith. There was no mention of why we were meeting, but I knew it wasn't to talk about his girlfriend. I told him it had to be late so I could be sure my mother and sisters were sound asleep.

We met behind a baseball field near my house. After small talk, we had sex in his car, a small Chevy Vega, which he had driven from the field into a nearby alley. When we finished, I felt excited, but Donald wore a look of disgust. I asked him if everything was all right.

He looked at me and shouted, "You goddamn faggot," then he started beating me unmercifully with his large fists. Every time I tried to escape his car, his fists pounded my face. It started raining and thundering and lightning, something that had caused me great fear when I was a child, and I was struggling to find the door handle. It seemed like the rain was falling with the force of Donald's fists, and I was afraid that he was going to kill me. All I could see were Donald's fists and Ben's face in a flashback of my 520 East Twenty-first terror. Suddenly this psycho stopped beating me, spit in my face, and then leaned over me, opened the door, and kicked me with the heel of his shoe out of his car into the cold rain. On the graveled alley I saw blood on my hands. My nose was bleeding. But I didn't think about the pain of his fists. All I could think about was Donald spitting in my face. It was devastating. No one had ever done that to me. It was like he was saying to me, "You don't deserve to be a human being. You're lower than low. You ain't shit."

Donald sped off as I lay on the concrete. When I saw that the car was out of sight, I pulled myself up and began to walk home in the rain. The lightning and thunder continued, but I had survived this encounter, and the weather was the least of my concerns. I cried as I walked home, and the rain kept coming, washing my tears away.

I snuck back into my house soaking wet. I knew I had to change my life before somebody killed me—or I killed myself.

CHAPTER 7

M y neighborhood street was covered in a stale gray dimness, like it was stuck between day and night. The only visible light was from the porch of the houses on Thayer Street. Our house was silent, with Mama and me up and my sisters still sound asleep, oblivious to the importance of the day.

Mama and I quietly loaded my cardboard boxes full of books, albums, and clothes into my new lemon-yellow Volkswagen. The car was a surprise graduation present from Mama. How she did some of the things she did amazed me. She had been saving money for me to go to college, but when I got a full scholarship, Mama bought me a car instead so I would go in style.

One funny thing about the car is that when Mama bought it, I couldn't drive. It took most of the summer, with lessons from Mama, family, and friends like Valerie Rice (NaNa's sister), before I felt comfortable behind the wheel. When I pulled out of the driveway that morning, I didn't realize that it would be one of the last times I would stay longer than seventy-two hours in either Little Rock or my mother's house.

The only differences between that day and any other were that I was leaving for college, and Mama's quiet tears. Maybe Mama realized that she was really releasing me to the world, or her tears may have been those of pride that I was the first one in my family to go to college.

"Now, baby, remember what I told you. When you get on the freeway, pick up speed, look to your left for cars, and watch out for those big trucks," she said. I think she was more nervous than I was about my first experience driving on the freeway. The image of her in a flowered cotton dress holding the screen door with one hand and caressing her collar with the other is an image fixed in my mind that I will never forget.

I assured her I would be careful and that I wouldn't go over fifty-five miles per hour. She made me check to be sure I had my Triple A motor card, and I promised to call the moment I arrived.

I repeated her instructions in a teasing voice. The situation needed humor, because I didn't want to cry. I was finally leaving Little Rock, and I didn't understand the sadness and fear I was feeling. I knew I would miss my mother and even my sisters, but this was the moment I had dreamed of. I was getting out of Little Rock. I was going to college. The University of Arkansas at Fayetteville awaited me, and I was scared.

Before I turned the key in the ignition, Mama once again told me to be careful and not to forget to find a church in Fayetteville and to pray. I smiled and nodded my head, and then I pulled out of the driveway and headed down the hill toward my big adventure.

In a lot of ways, I guess I was always meant for the University of Arkansas at Fayetteville. Gessler was going there, and despite a near-perfect academic record, he had always wanted to attend the university. I figured that since Gessler was white, rich, and smart, he could have gone to any college in the country.

There was no discussion of our being roommates, since Gessler knew he would pledge Phi Delta Theta like his older brother, Brad, and move into the fraternity house. The possibility of my pledging Phi Delta wasn't discussed either. I knew that not everything at the university was going to be integrated.

There was one reason I was excited to be attending the university. It was the home of the Arkansas Razorbacks. I had always been a Razorbacks fan, even though they had no black players on their teams during the sixties and early seventies. When I was younger, I'd fallen in love with them by listening to games on the radio with the voice of Bud Campbell, and by reading the words of Orville Henry, sports editor of the state's largest newspaper, *The Arkansas Gazette*. Mr. Henry was one of the writers I read religiously from seventh grade on. I had decided to study journalism and had hopes of one day writing about the Razorbacks under the tutelage of Mr. Henry.

The Razorbacks brought pride to the small state of Arkansas. I remember in 1969, when then President Nixon came to watch the national championship game between Texas and Arkansas. It seemed as though the entire nation was focused on Fayetteville, Arkansas, and I was so proud, even though the Razorbacks lost on that gloomy Saturday, 15–14. Despite that defeat, the Razorbacks were still my Dallas Cowboys, my Los Angeles Lakers.

My love of sports was the only thing that my stepfather Ben instilled in me as a little boy that I still hold dear today. In fact, I consider watching and attending sporting events one of my passions. I love college football, and win or lose, I love the Razorbacks. Ben would make me watch football games on Sunday, especially his favorite team, the St. Louis Cardinals, and even made me try out for Peewee football despite my tiny size. At first I hated being forced to watch sports, but it made Ben happy. I think he thought that if I was watching sports I would have less time to play house with my sisters and their friends. As I grew older, I developed my own appreciation for the games and for participating in sports when my body began to change and I could finally compete.

Back in the sixties and early seventies most of the black folks, including my mother, seemed to hate the Razorbacks. I assumed that for many, the lily-white team served as a reminder of the segregated South. My mother would get mad at me when I listened to Razorbacks football and basketball on the radio and sometimes would make me turn off the radio. Today we laugh about it, because my mother is almost as big a Razorbacks fan as I am.

A LITTLE MORE THAN FIVE hours later, I arrived at the U of A ready for a new start. I dreamed that it was going to be like those idyllic glimpses of college life I saw during halftime of football games on television. Everything looked peaceful and perfect, and the students looked happy. Every now and again there would be a couple of black students walking around the beautiful campus, carrying books and smiling.

A black student attending the U of A was a big deal in the early seventies. Top black students in the state usually shunned the school because of its isolated location in northwest Arkansas. The school had a reputation for being harder on black students, with tougher grading standards and social hostility. It clearly was no easy place to be black.

In 1973, Fayetteville was a sleepy town of about 30,000 whose population doubled when the school year started. Today it is one of the fastest-growing segments of the country, with headquarters for companies like Wal-Mart and Tyson Chicken nearby. The population now exceeds 50,000. A typical college town, Fayetteville has more restaurants and hotels than a town its size usually does, and on home football weekends, it magically becomes the second-largest city in Arkansas. It's a beautiful city that spreads out over a chain of rolling hills, which become washed in brilliant colors in the autumn. Today it's one of my favorite places in the world, but it didn't start out that way.

My first semester at the U of A, black students, as we were called then, made up less than 2 percent of the large student body. That didn't bother me, since the ratio at Hall had been similar my first year. If I hadn't attended Hall, I think I would have turned around and gone back home a few hours after arriving in Fayetteville. When I arrived at the campus, my heart skipped a beat of joy whenever I saw another person of color.

WITHOUT DIRECT ADULT SUPERVISION, I quickly learned the price of freedom. I went to every party I was invited to or heard about, and went to classes only when they didn't interfere with sleeping or watching *All My Children* and *One Life to Live.* So I shouldn't have been surprised when my first-semester grades were absolutely terrible. My GPA was 1.30 out of a possible 4.00.

My grades put my scholarships in jeopardy, and I was placed on academic probation. My mother threatened that I would come home and go to the local Philander Smith College if I didn't get my act together. She also told me I wouldn't be able to take my car back to campus. That was all I needed to hear. The second semester, I buckled down.

I took twenty-one hours and my GPA was a 3.88. My only B came in swimming. Even though I had made such terrible grades the first semester, I was not intimidated by my courses. As I had proven to myself before, all I needed to do was focus. Since I didn't have a romantic relationship, like most of the freshmen men and women I knew, it was very easy to do.

I did find something to keep me company on weekends. During my freshman year I discovered liquor and the instant self-esteem it brought with it. On Fridays some of my friends and I would find someone who was of legal age in front of a liquor store to buy beer and rum for us. I drank from Friday afternoon until late Sunday night. I was falling in love with drinking and the boldness it gave me. With the liquor plus starch—french fries and hash browns every day—I had put on about forty pounds by the end of my freshman year and I was starting to feel like a regular guy. No longer was I the skinny kid. Black women on campus were starting to look at me as a potential partner. I was smart, and now I had muscles to hold on to during those body-glued slow dances.

On the surface, life seemed more perfect than it had ever been. Being a college student gave me something I had desired for a long time: solid middle-class status. Attending the U of A turned out to be very lucrative from a financial standpoint. With my grants and scholarships, money was no longer a big issue for me. Tuition at the U of A was only two hundred dollars a semester for in-state students during the early seventies. In addition to the money I was receiving for my education, I was collecting Social Security benefits from my father's death by simply filling out some forms and presenting my birth certificate.

So I was able to afford designer clothes and a private dorm room, which I filled with albums, an elaborate stereo, a color television, and a portable icebox. With a new car and money in my pocket, most of the students I came in contact with assumed that I was from one of Little Rock's middle-class families, and I didn't bother to correct them.

THE THREE HUNDRED OR SO black students formed a community within the university community. Everybody knew everybody, which had its good and bad points. Like most groups, there was division. The black students from small towns didn't particularly care for the students from Little Rock. According to them, we were a bit arrogant. If you lived in a certain dorm, you were viewed a certain way. Reid Hall implied you were easy, and Humphreys Hall meant you were most likely a virgin looking for a husband. Of course, skin complexion and black fraternities and sororities offered more partitions. And then there were the jocks. During my first year at the U of A, thirty new black football players entered the university, a big jump from the previous year, when you could count the black players on one hand. Only a few were from Arkansas, with the majority coming from Texas. Still, on the weekend, everyone would manage to put aside their petty differences and party until the wee hours of the morning.

I loved to dance, and when I drank I became an even better dancer, Mr. Soul Train of the Ozarks. Usually after a few songs, more people would be watching me dance than dancing themselves, and I think it was then that the rumors started that I might be a little different. That I was a punk, which was the terminology used to describe gay people back then.

I first got wind of the rumor when a female friend told me what another woman had said after borrowing my car. I was now using my material possessions to gain friends. She told me a girl had said, "I don't mind riding and driving his car, but you know he likes to hug and kiss, and it's no telling where his lips have been." The innuendo hurt me a great deal, but I never confronted her, because my source had made me promise not to. To make matters worse, the lady was always smiling in my face and asking me if I could either take her to the mall or let her drive my car, and I always acquiesced. My self-esteem was very low and I was constantly looking for approval; I wanted everybody on campus to like me, including those who spread hurtful rumors.

Since the black population was so small, everybody knew who was sleeping with whom, unless you were like me and not sleeping with anyone. But after I dated a few campus beauties, the rumors seemed to stop.

Still, dating women could not stop the first serious college crush I had on a man. I noticed him the first day I was on campus. I was in Barnhill fieldhouse, taking a placement examination, when he walked in with several football players. He was wearing skintight jeans, a red and blue football jacket, and a gray railroad conductor–type cap; he was a beautiful cider-brown man with a thick mustache. At this point in my life I didn't have a single hair on my face, so I was impressed. Even though he was fully dressed, I thought he had one of the most beautiful bodies I had ever seen: broad shoulders, a small waist, and powerfully built bowlegs.

He didn't look in my direction and we didn't make eye contact, but I remembered him and found myself staring at him at some of the weekend dances. I didn't dare speak to him or inquire about his name.

One evening I was visiting a female friend at Reid Hall when I passed the open door of two good friends, Virlean Lofton and Rita Stitt, whose laugher was drifting out into the hall. A deep-voiced man was talking and laughing with them. I stuck my head in the door and there he was, sitting between Virlean's legs as she French-braided his short, coarse hair. Virlean invited me into the room. He looked up, smiled, but didn't speak.

I was exchanging campus chitchat with Virlean and Rita when suddenly Virlean said, "You know Elijah, don't you?"

"No, I don't," I said, fascinated by his thick black eyelashes and being so close to him. He gave me a black power handshake and said, "What's going on?" His hands were enormous and firm, so big that they swallowed my entire hand.

Elijah and I talked for a few minutes. I found out he wasn't from Arkansas or Texas like most of the football players, but from a place called Junction City, Kansas. When I asked him where that was, he told me near Kansas State University in Manhattan, Kansas. As I talked to Elijah, I became completely mesmerized by his unmistakable maleness. He didn't carry himself like an eighteen-year-old.

I tried not to stare at Elijah as Virlean put the finishing

touches on his braids. She had a small jar of Afro Sheen and was dabbing it on the rows in between Elijah's braids. To avoid staring at him, I began to make small talk with Rita, who was busy studying. I finally excused myself, and later that night in my dorm room I couldn't study or sleep because I was thinking about Elijah. My insides felt the way they did the first time I had seen Rose Crater. One big problem: Elijah wasn't a girl, and I knew I shouldn't be feeling this way.

ELIJAH AND I BECAME SOMEWHAT of an odd couple. On the surface there was no real reason for the two of us to become close friends. After my stellar academic performance during my second semester, I had developed a reputation as a brain. With Elijah's performance on the football field and in many of the dorm rooms of several good-looking girls, he was viewed as a stud and a dumb jock.

I looked at him differently. Elijah became my friend and protector. I became his friend and personal tutor, but secretly I wanted more. I never shared my true feelings, partly because I was consumed with fear and desire. The fear that if I told Elijah how I really felt I would lose his friendship, and become a laughingstock on campus, was balanced by the desire to have him protect me for the rest of my life. Still, I had a hard time understanding why this man made my palms sweat with his mere presence.

Whatever he asked me to do, I would do without even thinking about how it looked. I always told him where I could be reached. If he called, I would leave wherever I was. Once I even left the dorm room of one of the most beautiful women on campus, who was romantically interested in me. But Elijah was the same way with me. One night I had a flat tire on one of Fayetteville's darkest roads right outside of campus. I called Elijah, and he risked a curfew violation to come and change my tire.

Elijah and I were always rescuing each other from various situations. I would help him study for a test, or call him when he wanted to get away from his steady girlfriend for a booty call with another young lady who had captured his roving eye. When I moved into my first off-campus apartment, with three guys from Forrest City, Arkansas, I quickly decided I wanted to move out because every discussion about food and television viewing was a 3–1 vote, and I was always at a disadvantage. It didn't matter that most of the electronics were mine. I knew I never should have moved in with these guys, because I knew only one of them well. When I told them I was moving out, they told me I couldn't.

When I found a new apartment where I could live alone, Elijah showed up and stood by the front door with his massive arms folded, with a *Don't fuck with me* look as I moved my boxes and appliances into my car. The roommates didn't say a word. Elijah ended up spending the first night with me at my new apartment, sleeping at the foot of my bed because I expressed concern that my former roommates might retaliate. That wasn't really the truth, but nothing physical happened between us.

I had decided that if an advance was going to be made, Elijah would have to make it. I still had no idea of how to approach a man, and I wasn't comfortable with women either. Women in college were much more aggressive than those in high school.

There were so many things I loved and admired about Elijah. He had an air of toughness and street smarts about him, having practically raised himself with the help of his elderly grandfather. He also had a gentle side that sometimes revealed itself very easily. When I look back, I realize that he was the first black male who was as close a friend to me as Gessler.

And as with Gessler, our friendship remained strong and platonic throughout my college years, while my desire for men would find a new subject almost every semester. After my sophomore year, we didn't spend as much time with each other, because football and track took up a lot of his time and I was becoming involved in school activities and other crushes. Still, it was comforting to know Elijah was always only a phone call away.

I WAS LEARNING MORE THAN academics at the U of A. I was fine-tuning my skills of becoming a chameleon, or as my mother might say, "a very good liar." I lied because the truth about my background wasn't good enough. Attending Hall benefitted me in that I was able to move comfortably between the worlds of my white classmates at school and back home with my black peers. I lied about not only my sexuality but about almost everything else as well. I told so many mistruths that it became hard to remember what I'd said originally.

Was my father a lawyer, or a judge who had died tragically? Was my alleged girlfriend a student at the University of Missouri or Stephens College? Did I live in University Park or Pulaski Heights? None of my classmates ever questioned me extensively, and assumed I was telling the truth.

I was asked to be a part of some of the university's lily-white organizations, like Cardinal XX, an honorary society for the top twenty freshmen men, Phi Eta Sigma, and the *Arkansas Traveler* student newspaper and *Razorback* yearbook.

I was also following a pattern of falling for heterosexual men who befriended me and loved me like a brother. The only problem was that I was no longer looking for brotherly love. During my sophomore year, I had flipped for Hugh Perry Watson, a tall, good-looking, waffle-brown freshman from El Dorado, Arkansas. We met at one of the girls' dorms and later at Borough Commons, one of the huge cafeterias on campus, where a lot of black students would gather for meals.

Over lunch I discovered that Hugh was easy to talk to. We found we had a lot in common besides being the only boys in a family of girls. We both liked the Isley Brothers, and loved dancing and watching sports.

The one difference I took note of was our family makeup. Hugh's mother and father were still married, and his father, a high school principal, played an important part in all of his decisions. It seemed that Hugh didn't make a single decision without discussing it with his father. At first I admired their close relationship, but later I became envious of it.

With Hugh, and unlike with Elijah, I was in charge of the friendship. He was such a kind, gentle person and I was certain he would be the love of my life, because he seemed to need me. We became roommates and would spend nights in our dorm room with matching bedspreads, talking about life after Fayetteville. We planned to be in each other's wedding and there for the birth of our first children. I told Hugh about Gessler and how I wanted the two of them to meet. Despite my friendships with Hugh and Elijah, Gessler remained a close friend. We talked on the phone often, but the socialization of the campus prevented us from spending a great deal of time together. Gessler lived in the Phi Delta Theta house and was an officer, so he had a new set of friends and obligations. I understood, because there were times when I found comfort in being around my own kind. Besides, I didn't want anyone to call me an Uncle Tom any more than I wanted to be called a punk. Black students who had a lot of white friends were usually classified as Uncle Toms, though black men who dated white women were not.

I trusted Hugh, but I never told him that I might be gay or that I was harboring a romantic interest in him. I figured if it was supposed to happen, Hugh would know also. Our friendship was wonderful but confusing.

I told him about my true economic station in life, something I privately vowed to never tell anyone I met at the university. I was practically forced to do so halfway to Little Rock one weekend. Hugh had been bugging me to take him home with me. I guess he wanted to see what the big brick homes at University Park looked like on the inside.

Not surprisingly, my confession to Hugh didn't affect his feelings about me in any way. He had a great time at my house and didn't complain about having to share the small pullout sofa. My sisters and mother loved him.

Months later, I visited Hugh's home, and it seemed that every day we became closer. Neither of us made a move without talking it over with the other. We had become so close that I didn't mind that he was falling in love with the young lady he had taken to his high school prom, who also attended the university. I figured one day he would realize he was going to spend the rest of his life with me and drop her the moment we left Fayetteville.

I guess for someone looking in from the outside, the relationship might have appeared strange, though it was purely innocent. I couldn't admit to Hugh that I was gay or bisexual, because I hadn't completely admitted it to myself. Every time I thought about sex with a man, I recalled my encounter with the Shaft psycho and I knew being either gay or bisexual was not a consideration for a black man in Fayetteville or anywhere else in Arkansas.

One weekend we drove to El Dorado to get Hugh's winter clothes, and the plan was not to stay too long. We stayed only one night, a Saturday. His family, especially his father and mother, was extremely nice to me. I thought the trip and introduction had gone fine, but when I returned to school for the spring semester after the holiday break, all of Hugh's belongings were gone from our room. His top bunk had been stripped of the sheets. I looked in his closet and his clothes, books, and albums he'd left during the break were also gone. There was no indication that Hugh and I had ever shared a room.

I didn't know what had happened, and I was so stunned that I didn't know what to do. During the Christmas break, I had talked with Hugh almost daily from Atlanta, where I was staying with my Aunt Gee and Uncle Charles. There'd been no mention of his moving out or that he was having any problems with me or our friendship. Then I thought maybe something terrible had happened to him, that he'd been in a car accident.

I immediately picked up the phone and dialed Hugh's number in El Dorado. His father answered and told me that Hugh was back at school. He was very short with me, so I didn't quiz him on Hugh's whereabouts. When I hung up I thought maybe Hugh had gotten an off-campus apartment with his girlfriend and didn't know how to tell me. I knew they had spent a lot of time together over the holidays.

I went down to the head resident's apartment on the first floor to see if he could tell me anything. He informed me that Hugh's father had returned with him to campus the day before I arrived and demanded, without explanation, that Hugh move out of my room and be assigned a new roommate. I was stunned and deeply hurt. I was devastated. Why hadn't Hugh told me about his father's decision, and why had he made such a demand?

My stomach was tossing and turning, and I thought eating might help me think better, so I went to the dining hall. The first person I saw as I entered the hall was Hugh, who looked troubled. He reached into his coat pocket and pulled out the skullcap I had bought him for Christmas and put it on his head.

I confronted him, almost shouting, "What the fuck is going on?" He mumbled how he couldn't do anything about it and then stared at me in silence.

"Why?" I demanded. He didn't answer, as his big beautiful eyes wandered around the room in search of a response. "Hugh, you at least owe me an explanation. I thought we were best friends," I said.

"We are," he said softly.

"Then why can't we be roommates?" It was like I was pleading with him not to leave me after I had invested so much in our friendship. I could think only of all the plans I had imagined for us together after we left Fayetteville.

"My father says . . ." Hugh paused, and his eyes looked beyond me as his lower lip quivered.

"Your father says what?" I asked.

"My father said we're too close," he said quickly, almost whispering.

I didn't respond. His words hung between us as other students walked around us to enter the dining hall. Suddenly we realized we were blocking the entrance. We slowly moved toward a corner and just stared at each other. I looked down at a stack of old student newspapers on the floor, then back at Hugh. He was still staring at me.

Too close? What did his father mean? What was he trying to say? Had he read my mind? I was certain that I was the only person besides God who knew how I really felt about Hugh.

Suddenly I was furious. I felt like I wanted to hit Hugh or choke him. Instead I shook my head and walked up the stairs to another section of the dining hall. Hugh called my name, and when I looked back he asked if we could talk later. I didn't answer, and I didn't speak to Hugh Perry Watson again until almost two years later.

AS DIFFICULT AS IT WAS, I made the decision to cut off my friendship with Hugh. The distress of not being in his life or having him in mine was painful and brought on my first period of depression. I missed seeing his crooked smile when I came into our room from studying, or talking to him about the future as we lay in our beds, our voices weaving together like a chorus in the pitch-black room. But most of all, I missed the wonderful way I felt when I was in Hugh's presence.

My first thought was to leave school, and I considered transferring to Howard University. Howard sounded good because of D.C. and its large "gay problem." Maybe that's where I needed to be. I thought if Hugh's father could see through me, then maybe others could, too. It didn't matter how many girls I dated or how many lies I told. My infatuations with men were going to cause major problems for me. Yet I couldn't call myself gay. I felt a great deal of shame. I was convinced that if anyone found out about my feelings for men I would be laughed off campus by the other black students. I guess it would have been easier if I was just looking for sex, but I wanted love.

Whenever I caught a glimpse of Hugh on campus, walking hand in hand with his girlfriend, my misery became magnified, and the loneliness I felt before Gessler, Elijah, and Hugh closed in again. My pain was so intense, I couldn't imagine living another second.

I went to a drugstore on Dickson Street near campus and purchased a bottle of Sominex and took several pills and ended up spending the night in the student infirmary. I thought if I committed suicide Hugh would realize how much I was hurting. All that happened from the episode was that I got an upset stomach and I had to beg the university health officials not to call my mother. I agreed to see a campus counselor, a white female, but I went only a few times. I didn't think talking about my problems to a total stranger was going to change them.

I found solace in talking with a beautiful graduate student in the School of Architecture. Chris Hinton was a sophisticated woman who had earned a degree in drama at Jackson State University and then decided she wanted to be an architect. We had met in the same dining hall where I first talked with Hugh, and she had always been friendly toward me and was easy to talk to.

When I ended up in the infirmary, I asked them to call Chris. She reminded me so much of my Aunt Gee and my cousin Jackie, two women with whom I had always felt comfortable discussing my innermost thoughts, within reason. When I felt depressed and lonely, which was quite frequently, I would go to Chris's room and just talk to her about my feelings.

Despite my request, the infirmary called my mother. So I had to tell her what happened and why I wanted to die. I didn't tell her that I thought I was in love with Hugh, only that his friend-ship had become very important to me. My mother was a great comfort when I told her why Hugh had moved out. She assured me that Hugh's father didn't know what he was talking about and that he was the one with the problem. She asked me if I wanted to come home. I told her I would be all right. I appreciated her coming to my defense when someone had hurt me so deeply. I remember her soft and assuring voice telling me that I was her son and she loved me no matter what. Those words were reason enough to try and go on.

SLOWLY I TRIED TO BUILD UP my self-esteem by immersing myself in my studies, which had suffered during my depression and activities like the yearbook and the black student organiza-tion known as BAD (Black Americans for Democracy). The only social life I had was an occasional dinner with Gessler. He did recognize that I seemed distant, but of course I didn't tell him about Hugh or the sleeping pills.

Since Gessler's fraternity life seemed to make him so happy, I decided to pledge one of the three black fraternities on campus. I figured it was a way to make some new friends and a way to get the badge of manhood I so desperately needed.

Besides tales of hazing, I knew there was a deep homophobia that existed in some black men, especially in fraternities. Like

many all-male institutions, fraternity brothers were always terrified of the possibility of a gay member, so anyone who was suspect was raked over the coals about their sexuality during the
interviews before the pledge process started. I knew immediately
I was going to be in the suspect category. I wasn't dating anyone
seriously and I had tried out for the Razorback cheerleading
team during my freshman year, but dropped out before the finals
because I thought people might think I was gay. It didn't matter
that college cheerleading was considered a sport and that white
fraternities encouraged their members to try out.

I made line, I was invited to join the fraternity of my choice,
and was elected secretary of my pledge class. Nobody wanted to
be secretary. I wanted to decline the position, because to me secretary was a position likely to be considered soft. Besides, pledges
couldn't use the word "no."

One weekend while we were pledging, some big brothers
came to visit from UAPB (University of Arkansas at Pine Bluff),
the once-proud black college that had been forced to merge with
the U of A system. When big brothers from other universities
visited, they were given the same respect as members of the
chapters you were pledging. It didn't make a difference where
they came from if they were active, meaning paying dues. Each
brother was to receive the utmost adoration and reverence. Ass-
kissing was the norm.

When the brothers from UAPB came into our pledge meeting, one little sawed-off, four-eyed big brother was carrying a
big, thick paddle. In a booming voice, he called out my name the
minute he entered the room. His voice was so loud and forceful
that it gave me goose bumps. I was scared that some guy I had
never laid eyes on knew my name. How did he know me? My
pledge brothers all looked at me with fear in their eyes. This was
not a good sign.

I meekly stepped out of the line and looked straight ahead,

like I was a private in the Army. The guy was so short that I couldn't look him eye-to-eye without looking down, but looking down at him wasn't a consideration. Pledges never looked down on big brothers.

He joked and called me Miss Lynn Harris as he gently rubbed the paddle.

"My home girl told me you were a faggot. Are you a faggot?" he barked.

"No sir, big brother," I responded in a forceful voice.

He identified himself as big brother Taylor but didn't advise me where he was from, so I couldn't figure out who his home girl was. He went on to tell me that he didn't believe me and that his mission for his weekend visit was to make sure that my "high yellow, faggot ass" was no longer a pledge when he left. I wanted to cry, but I didn't dare. Memories of Ben flashed in my mind. I wanted to run out of the room and never return, but I didn't flinch. I wanted to be a fraternity man no matter what, and no little short runt of a man was going to stop me.

I knew what I was getting into, so I wasn't unprepared, just humiliated.

I survived the weekend and many nights of torture and was initiated into the fraternity. In a lot of respects, my initiation was a big step in my search for manhood. For the first time in my life, I had several black men I could honestly call my friends and my brothers. The extra punishment I received since they believed I was gay proved to advance my status in the eyes of many of my brothers. Despite the humiliation, I had taken the extra asskicking like a man, and it made me feel stronger.

In many ways, fraternities are like today's gangs. My fraternity wanted to be better than the other fraternities, especially the other black ones. We protected our territory, even though it was only a dorm floor. We were always looking for new members, trying to impress the top students before another fraternity did.

Like gang members, many of us were looking for a family. The only difference between fraternities and gangs was that we required a college transcript before the torture began.

At my first meeting after initiation, I was nominated for chapter president. I was sitting at the front of the room with my new fraternity T-shirt on, when I heard one of my line brothers nominate me. At first I was surprised. Then I was embarrassed, because I knew there was no way a neophyte member was going to be chapter president, especially one whose sexuality was still in question, although some of the suspicion had been put to rest by the way I'd handled myself during the pledge period.

The incumbent chapter president's name was also placed in nomination. He had been a good president, and I was certain he would win. When we voted, I lifted my hand for the other candidate and didn't turn to face my brothers when my name was called. Since we were all brothers there was no need for a secret ballot, but still I was afraid to look. I won by a margin of 22–6. I couldn't believe it. When I stood in front of the room, amid the cheers of my new brothers, I was nearly in tears. That moment was one of the most special feelings I'd ever experienced. I thanked my brothers for their faith in me and told them being their president would be the highlight of my life. And for a long time it was.

O n paper my senior year in college was one of the best in my life. It was a time when I finally got the feeling that life might be fair, when I would actually experience some of my youthful dreams of success and requited love.

At the end of my junior year I was selected as editor of the 1977 *Razorback*, the university's award-winning yearbook. I became the first black student to edit a publication at the university, and according to *Jet* magazine the first to head a yearbook at a major southern university. I was thrilled to see my name in a national magazine—especially *Jet*, because I had grown up with the magazine and was a big fan of its founder, John H. Johnson, who was also from Arkansas. I had been reading *Ebony* and *Jet* religiously since I was ten years old.

My selection also was featured on page two of the *Arkansas Gazette*, the state's largest newspaper at the time, and I got a note of congratulations from Mr. Seligman of Arkansas Paper Company. He told me he knew how proud my mother must be of me and that he was proud as well.

As editor of the yearbook, I was in charge of staff selection and had a budget of $300,000. I quickly hired my fraternity brother and line brother, Butch Carroll, as business manager and

Gessler as advertising manager. Butch and I had become really close after pledging together, and his friendship would later become one of my most treasured. I knew Butch would watch the money like it was his own, which was a good thing, and Gessler would bring in lots of advertising from local merchants and Greek organizations on campus.

During my junior year Butch had become a special friend, not only because he was my fraternity brother but because he had let me know that I wasn't the only black man in Fayetteville who had different feelings when it came to relationships between men. Yet Butch Carroll wanted all that life had to offer, like success and love.

One night Butch and another fraternity brother, Andy, were sitting in Butch's dorm room in Gregson Hall when out of the blue Butch posed a serious question. Thinking out loud, Butch looked at Andy and me and quizzed, "If being gay is so wrong, then why did God make so many gay people?" Andy and I were dumbfounded, and for several minutes silence hung over the room like towels on a clothesline. Butch's question started a dialogue and sparked a friendship that would become one of the most important in my life. For the first time, I had a friend who understood how I felt about being different from other guys and didn't feel bad about those feelings.

The funny thing was that I didn't like Butch when we met as freshmen, because one of my friends from North Little Rock had told me he had a friend attending the university that reminded him of me. At this time in my life, I had no interest in being friends with someone who was like me, because *I* didn't like me.

I also hired Butch's beautiful sister, Cindy, as my executive secretary. The rest of the staff members were hired with the promise that good work could lead to one of the more lucrative paid positions, like managing editor or production supervisor.

I spent half of the summer planning what I hoped would be

the best yearbook in the history of the university. I knew people would be watching closely since I was the first black to hold the position, so I laid out the book with lots of color photos, highlighting the campus I'd come to love.

I also hired a beautiful sorority girl, Kristie Kalder, as an entry-level staff person. Kristie reminded me of a young movie star, with her auburn-streaked hair and stunning olive skin. At first I thought she was a typical rich bitch girl trying to get an activity to pad her résumé. But Kristie was different and quickly moved up the ladder until she was second in command. The two of us worked long hours together, and another treasured friendship was formed. She was someone who not only had great ideas for the yearbook but who was also easy to talk to. My friendship with Kristie taught me not to judge people based on the way they looked.

When the school year began, I received another coveted honor. I was selected for *Who's Who in American Colleges and Universities* and was the only unanimous choice of the thirty-plus seniors picked by a secret student-faculty committee. I also became the first black male on the Razorbacks cheerleader squad, which I had summoned the courage to try out for when I was approached by several black football players who figured since I could dance well I could most likely do cheerleading. I had secretly wanted to be a cheerleader as much as I wanted to be editor of the yearbook, but my concern about what people might think had prevented me from trying out after I had quit the tryout process during my freshman year.

Male cheerleaders were a big deal at the U of A, as at most major southern universities. Most of the men on the squad had been high school football players, and I never thought any of the males the previous years showed outwardly gay characteristics. It was, in fact, similar to being a member of a sporting team because of the complicated partner stunts, and the entire squad worked hard to be perfect. Like the athletic teams, the U of A cheerleaders were nationally respected.

In addition to being a cheerleader, I was now rush chairman of my fraternity and was elected vice president of Black Americans for Democracy by a write-in vote when the person elected the previous spring didn't return to school. Everything was falling into place, but there was one piece missing. I was still looking for love.

BECOMING A CHEERLEADER was a catalyst that led to my first serious relationship with a man who would come to return my love and affection with equal measure. It was an experience I would later use in my first novel, *Invisible Life*, mixing in a little fact with fiction.

On the first Friday in October, as I was leaving the athletic complex from cheerleader practice, I literally bumped into a rock-hard body. I looked up at a handsome syrup-brown man, about 6'3" and 210 pounds. He had intense hazel-brown eyes, with long thick eyelashes, perfectly curled at the end, which gave him a permanent sleepy, sexy look.

When I apologized, he smiled, and I tried to remain calm and will my heartbeat to return to its normal pace. I was preparing to continue my journey home, but the stranger struck up a conversation about the game the next day and my being a cheerleader. When I looked at him, I realized that I had seen him at a dance the first week of the fall term at my fraternity house. I had noticed him because he was so handsome and he danced with masculine grace. He had worn tight blue jeans and a white T-shirt that didn't disguise his sculpted body. I remember that several young ladies I danced with had commented on how fine he was.

"My name is Mason Walker," he said as he extended his large hand.

"Nice meeting you. I'm Lynn Harris," I said.

Then he asked me something that I thought was odd: "Do you have a comb?"

"What?"

"Do you have a comb?" he repeated as he took his hand and rubbed it over his closely cropped hair.

I nervously looked in my gym bag, despite the fact that I never let anyone use my comb, which I felt was like a toothbrush. But he was a handsome man, and there were always exceptions. I searched but couldn't find my comb, and I began to apologize.

"That's okay," he said with a smile. His manner was different from that of any man I've ever met. He had a supreme self-confidence. When he spoke, he looked at me with a penetrating gaze, and I barely heard what he was saying because I was staring at his sensual lips.

We both stared at each other for a couple of nervous moments, and when we started to go our separate ways, I suddenly turned and asked him if he had any plans that evening.

"No, I don't. What's going on?"

Fridays in Fayetteville usually meant a beer run to Oklahoma with one of my fraternity brothers. They didn't sell Coors beer in Fayetteville, which made it seem like it was some expensive champagne. I asked Mason if he felt like riding the thirty miles to Oklahoma, and he quickly said yes. My stomach was filled with nervous energy as we walked to my car, which was now a royal blue Mustang.

It was a crisp, cool evening, and the autumn leaves were at their most brilliant; the campus trees appeared on fire with colors of gold and red. I felt like I was driving though an autumn postcard.

During the drive, I learned that Mason was from northern California, right outside of Oakland, and was a highly recruited athlete. We talked about sports and cheerleading, as well as who was screwing whom on campus. Of course, we covered male-female liaisons only.

It was around eight when we arrived back in Fayetteville. We had actually stopped the car to take a leak in opposite directions while viewing the gathering dusk. In a bold move on my part, I invited him back to my apartment to drink the beer, and he smiled and said, "I was hoping you'd ask."

When we got back to my apartment, I put on Elton John's "Bennie and the Jets," and then Norman Connors's "You Are My Starship" as we sat on my pale green sofa drinking beer.

I got up to use the rest room once again, then stopped in my tiny kitchen to get a couple more beers for Mason and me. When I closed the refrigerator door, Mason was standing directly in front of me. He smiled as I gave him a beer, and I was starting to feel nervous.

"Do you consider yourself open-minded?" Mason asked as we walked back to the living room. I could feel his body heat shadowing me as I walked a few steps in front of him. I felt like heat was being applied to a sore muscle.

"Sure." I smiled as I plopped down on the sofa.

"Are you certain?" he asked as he sat down next to me. This time he was sitting so close that our knees were almost touching.

"Yes, of course I'm certain. Why do you ask?"

Without responding, he grabbed my face, gently cupping it, and then he kissed me. It was a warm, wet kiss, and I realized that this was the first time I had ever kissed a man. It felt right, like the most natural thing in the world; what I had been waiting for all my life. Aided by the juicy fullness of his lips, Mason continued to kiss me, moving his tongue down my throat with authority.

When we stopped for a few moments, Mason pulled me close to his well-muscled body and whispered, "I think I'm in big trouble" with a wicked smile. His voice was soft, in strong contrast with the deep-voiced way he had previously been speaking. I didn't say anything, but I was smiling all over. For a brief moment, I closed my eyes as the music took control of me, then suddenly realized that there was no music playing in my apartment.

THE NEXT MORNING, I was awakened by the sounds of the Razorback marching band and a shattering band of light seeping through my bedroom window. As I rubbed my eyes, I suddenly remembered crawling into bed with Mason the night before and that I had to be on campus for an alumni pep rally before the football game.

I wondered what had happened to Mason, and if I had dreamed the entire wonderful and unbelievable encounter. I looked around my bedroom for a note with maybe his phone number and couldn't remember if I had given him mine.

I showered and headed to campus, where hours later I was leading cheers amid a sea of red-clad, hog-hat-wearing Razorbacks fans. But I wasn't thinking about the cheers or the game—the only thought my head had room for was Mason Walker.

After the game, a young lady I had been casually dating, Cherri Jones, met me down on the field all ready to spend the rest of the weekend with me. I had decided that I would never be seen in the stadium wearing my cardinal and white cheerleader uniform without a beautiful young lady holding my hand.

But on this day I didn't want to be with Cherri; as nice and beautiful as she was, she was starting to get on my nerves with her constant need for touching and kissing.

When we got back to my apartment, she laid her head on my shoulder as she gently stroked my face and I gazed at the television, half listening to it, half listening to her, thinking of Mason, when I heard a knock on my door. I jumped up from the sofa to open the door. I figured it might be one of my fraternity brothers who lived in the same complex, but it wasn't. It was Mason, standing there with a huge smile on his face. He was preparing to walk in and hopefully give me a hug and kiss, when he noticed Cherri sitting on the sofa.

Mason stopped and asked me if I knew where some guy whose name I didn't recognize lived. I asked him if he knew the apartment number. I guess I made up a number and told him to check the directory on the front of the building. He smiled and left.

Now I *really* wanted Cherri out of my apartment and back in her dorm, especially when she commented on how fine Mason was and how he acted like he knew me. I told her she was crazy and that I wasn't feeling well and maybe I should take her back to campus.

When I got back to my apartment, I prayed Mason would come back, but there was no knock at the door. All night I kept playing "You Are My Starship" and LTD's "Love Ballad" as I drank beer and thought of Mason.

The next morning I went to St. James Baptist Church, the only black church in town, with hopes of seeing Mason. I had seen athletes there several times, and he had mentioned that his father was a minister back in California. I didn't see Mason or any other athletes, but I did see the back of Cherri's head and I left immediately.

I spent the day wandering around my apartment, my body filled with nervous energy, hoping that Mason would again knock at my door. Just before dusk arrived, I went to the stadium to run and work off my anxiety. After running a few laps, I noticed some guys at the end of the field playing catch. One of them from the back looked like Mason. I stopped running and just stared down the field. A few seconds later, as if my hope had willed him to, Mason turned around. When he saw me, he smiled but didn't come toward me. Instead, he turned and kept tossing the ball to a white guy.

I decided I wasn't going to leave without speaking to him, so I ran a few more laps. Sweat was sliding into my eyes when I heard someone running up behind me and calling my name. I stopped and turned to see Mason standing directly in front of me with a huge smile.

"I thought I'd never see you," he said.

"I was beginning to feel the same way," I said nervously as I allowed my tired body to collapse onto the hard Astroturf field. Mason joined me, and in the empty stadium covered in a silver dusk, our eyes looking toward the sky, we talked and talked. I felt calm and certain that life had now decided to be fair. That I wouldn't have to spend my life looking for love only to end up brokenhearted. On that evening the full cycle of infatuation began and ended, and I started to fall in love with someone who would love me back for the first time in my life.

CHAPTER 9

On a sunny Saturday in May, I graduated with a degree in journalism from the University of Arkansas, and more than twenty of my family members were present. My mother, grandmother, and Aunt Gee and Uncle Charles from Atlanta were in the crowd of well-wishers. The only close family member missing was my middle sister, Zettoria, who was in a Little Rock hospital busy delivering my first nephew, Corey Lynn. I was not pleased when I found out that my sixteen-year-old sister was pregnant, but after I saw my nephew for the first time I couldn't be mad at her.

I was especially happy to have my mother at my graduation. She had experienced serious medical issues during my senior year but had instructed everyone in the family to keep it from me because she didn't want anything to affect my school work and pending graduation. It was not until after her successful surgery that Aunt Gee filled me in. Of course, I was extremely upset, because the thought of life without my mother was unbearable.

After seeing my family off the next Sunday morning, I loaded up my Mustang and followed Butch Carroll on a six-hour drive to Dallas and my new job as a sales trainee for IBM. Butch, who had received a new silver Camaro from his parents, had gotten a job with Foley's Department Store in Houston and had rented a small trailer and agreed to haul some of my junk.

I was mixed with joy and regret as I left Fayetteville. Joy because of the accomplishments I had achieved at the university, and regret because I was leaving behind the first man I had fallen in love with and who said he loved me.

Mason had stirred such strong, delicious feelings within me that I'd almost turned down my coveted position at IBM in order to remain close to him as he completed his education.

My relationship with Mason was a good, but not perfect, first love. It wasn't perfection because like many gay relationships, our time was shrouded in shame, secrecy, and stolen moments. He had become the first person in my life who displayed his love for me (though in private) not only emotionally, but physically as well. Our sex life was amazing. No longer did I have to leave a dance daydreaming about being with one of the handsome men on campus. I knew there would be a knock on my door before morning arrived.

After a glorious fall semester, Mason's girlfriend from California transferred to the university, and her presence caused enough friction to threaten our relationship. I never met her, and she didn't know that I existed, but I saw her hanging around the athletic complex and coming in and out of the jock dorm. I still saw a lot of Mason during the spring semester, but not as much as I had come to expect after we first met. Once again I had to become comfortable with the pain and disappointment of being alone, since now I was less interested in keeping up the pretense of being involved with a woman although I still took women to fraternity sporting events.

Mason, on the other hand, dated several women, both black and white, and was close friends with one of the most homophobic athletes on campus. When I look back on my relationship with Mason, I realize that his actions would prepare me for future loves.

I convinced myself that if I couldn't be with Mason totally, then Arkansas was the last place I wanted to be. It was time to move on, and perhaps absence would indeed make the heart grow fonder.

I HAD NEVER PLANNED A CAREER in sales, especially in the highly technical arena of computers. I thought about going to law school, mainly because I thought it would bring me the middle-class life I craved. I was pretty certain I could have my pick of law schools because of my grades and extracurricular activities. I even got calls from recruiters from several law schools urging me to apply, but I missed several important admission deadlines because of all my commitments. It was the late seventies and affirmative action was in full force, and I knew I was a prize catch. Today, I would have a hard time getting a lot of these schools to even look at my application, much less pressure me.

I had been lucky when it came to grades at the university. Several semesters, in many classes, my grades would hover between A's and B's, but because many professors knew who I was from my campus activities they would give me the benefit of the doubt; if I had an 88 or 89 average, say, which was usually a B, I would get an A–, which still translated to four points. One summer session, I was expecting to finish with a 3.00 average but ended up with a perfect 4.00. I had developed the gift of gab that would help me with my grades and would later help me with my sales career.

IBM had recruited me because of my grades and accomplishments, and because I had scored the highest of any minority student on their technical aptitude test. The white recruiter told me in disbelief, "In all my years of giving this test, I've never seen a Negro student score this high."

I think I scored high on the test because I didn't feel pressure to do well after the recruiter had told me during our initial interview that he didn't think I would do well because of my liberal arts background, but that I should take the test anyway. Before the test, he had told me he would recommend me to IBM Office Products, which sold typewriters and didn't require a technical aptitude. IBM salary offers were almost double what journalism graduates were being offered, and I thought I could work for a couple of years, save some money, and then go east for law school or journalism school.

Deep down I know I really took the job because of the reactions of my peers and professors when they found out I had been offered a job by IBM. They were all impressed, with many telling me I'd be foolish to turn down such an opportunity, and I, with my low self-esteem, was impressed that they were impressed.

Still, it amazes me when I think back on getting a job with IBM, a company very concerned with image. For my final interview with the branch manager, I wore a black open-collar shirt with a gold chain around my neck. My suit was a well-worn navy blue double-knit number with a matching vest. In addition, I had one of the largest Afros ever known to man, which I would braid nightly to ensure height and bounce.

On my first day at IBM, my fashion fiasco continued when I wore a modest Sears & Roebuck gray pin-striped suit that had a certain shine to it, with a pink shirt and a brown and blue clip-on tie. I didn't know how to tie a regular tie.

My first manager, Leon Creed, a well-dressed black man, called me into his office after our first lunch meeting. Leon was fair-skinned and had green eyes and straight auburn-colored hair, and I didn't realize he was African American until he told me he had attended Howard University. Then I took a closer look at him and realized that he was black.

"Lynn, have you ever heard of Brooks Brothers?" he asked.

"No sir, I haven't," I said.

Leon told me he was giving me an advance on my first month's salary and suggested I take the afternoon to go to a store called Brooks Brothers and see a man whose name he wrote down on a card. "Tell him I sent you, and don't leave until you've spent every penny," he instructed.

As I was leaving his office excited about my new wardrobe, Leon had one more piece of advice. "Lynn, when you leave Brooks Brothers, burn that suit," he said, and smiled.

On my first day at IBM, I had my first dress-for-success lesson. The first of many lessons I would learn.

"MY NAME IS LYNN HARRIS, Dallas branch, and I don't know what in the hell I'm doing here," I joked in a classroom designed like those found in many Ivy League law schools. My fellow classmates warmed me with their laughter, but I was serious. What had I gotten myself into?

I was in Endicott, New York, for my first IBM training class, and on the first morning we were instructed to give our name, the office where we worked, and our academic background. Everyone who preceded me proudly announced impressive educational résumés from some of the country's top universities. In addition, the majority had advanced degrees, and those who didn't had backgrounds in engineering. I was one of three African Americans in a class of forty-six.

One of the conditions of employment with IBM was the successful completion of a sixteen-month training program, which was considered tougher than most MBA programs. I was suddenly ashamed of my University of Arkansas degree and my family background once again. Failure loomed as a real possibility in a situation where I desperately wanted to succeed. Now it didn't matter what my college GPA had been or what I had scored on an aptitude test. IBM was not playing. A valuable lesson about competition in the real world was on tap for me in this quiet, upstate community.

A score of seventy-five was required to pass the course. I didn't think making a seventy-five would be difficult, even though the material was extremely difficult. The memorization skills I had acquired in college were not going to help here.

I studied with every free moment I had for the first test. I scored seventy-three. I made a lot of dumb mistakes, partly because I didn't know how to use a calculator correctly. In college I had had only one math course, something called Math for Liberal Arts Students. I think they just wanted to make sure students could add and subtract.

After my exam came back, I called my boss, and he already knew I had failed the test. He was supportive and told me he knew I could do it. Some of my classmates were actually afraid that their scores in the low nineties would disappoint their managers. All Leon, my manager, wanted me to do was pass the course, so all I needed was a seventy-seven on the next exam since they average the two scores. I assured Leon that I would make that and more. In many ways, I wanted to do well not only for myself, but for Leon. He was the first black sales manager in Dallas, and he and his wife Susan had quickly become my surrogate family and among the few friends I had in Dallas.

The next week I studied harder than I ever had in my life. I felt it was next to impossible for me to fail the second exam. Afterward I was so confident that I called Leon and assured him that I had passed with flying colors. He told me he was happy that I was so confident, but if I failed, it wasn't the end of the world. I ended the conversation by saying, "Don't worry. I aced the test!"

Leon responded, "Well, well, no matter what, you'll be just fine."

When my second exam came back, I was devastated by my

score: seventy-four. Again I had made dumb mistakes. I stared at my test paper and was stunned that I had failed a class I had worked so hard to pass. My classmates around me bragged about their scores, but no one asked me what I had made. I guess they could tell from my stone-faced daze. After everyone had left the classroom for a celebration, I remained seated at my desk as tears started to run down my face uncontrollably. Not only had I failed, but I had let Leon down and embarrassed my race in front of my white Ivy League–confident classmates. I felt lower than low.

Right before I left Endicott, my adviser told me they were recommending that I keep my position and suggested I repeat the two-week class. At first I said no. I had never failed at something for which I worked so hard. Besides, I knew the material. My adviser went on to tell me that I had an excellent attitude, was a hard worker, and got along well with others. She went on to say that one day I would look back on this class and laugh.

I was not in a jovial mood at the class going-away party or on the plane trip back to Dallas. When I got back to my new apartment on that Friday night, I collapsed on my rented bedroom furniture and didn't wake up until early Sunday morning. I was physically and emotionally drained. I wanted to quit and return to the safe haven of Fayetteville, but first I had to show all those rich white boys and girls I was just as smart as they were.

It would have been easy to walk away and look into law school, since I had just turned twenty-one years old. I felt lonely and I missed Mason. Then I thought about some of the people at the university who were surprised that IBM had offered me a job. I knew that a lot of people felt African Americans, as we were now calling ourselves, weren't qualified when we achieved certain positions. Maybe I wasn't qualified for this highly technical field, but I felt I had at least tried—if not for me, then at least for people, like my family, who thought I could do anything.

When I reported to work on Monday, everyone in the office

knew I had failed the class, and that included the garage attendant. I don't know this to be true, but it's how I felt when I
entered the building on Turtle Creek Drive. I walked meekly to
my desk in the sales pit area and awaited my review meeting with
Leon. One of the black service engineers told me that the first
black sales trainee in my office had flunked out of the program
and I was the first black trainee since he had been fired some five
years before. Like I needed to hear that, I thought. I held my
head down low as I walked into Leon's office right before noon.

I was surprised that Leon appeared to be in a very upbeat
mood. He asked me what I had learned in the class, and I started
spouting all the technical information I had learned. He looked
at me and said, "That's not what I'm talking about." He then
repeated his question. I was silent, because I didn't know what
Leon wanted me to say. I felt like a little boy desperately trying
to think of an excuse to avoid a whipping I knew I was due.

Leon then gave me a lecture on how I had not allowed any
room for failure, so when it happened I let it overwhelm me. He
told me that I had to allow room in my life for both failure and
success and treat them the same. What he said made sense. He
was not telling me I had to look for failure, but just to recognize
and prepare for it as a possibility. It was something I had never
considered.

LEON BECAME MORE THAN a manager to me. He was almost
like a father or a big brother. When I made mistakes, he would
point them out. Like how a black man hoping to make it in corporate America had to give up some things once considered
important.

I had cut my huge Afro that I had sported for several years
and was wearing my hair in what was called a short 'Fro. In the
South jheri curls were just appearing on the hair horizon. One

Friday when I jumped into my barber's chair to get a trim, she suggested I try a jheri curl. I was game, despite the fact that most of the women I knew hated jheri curls on men and called men who wore them "bamas," a term short for Alabamas, which meant real country. She convinced me that she could make my curls look natural and people would think it was my natural hair. Never mind the fact that they had never seen curls on my head before.

When she finished, I thought I looked good! Damn, I looked great. When I went to happy hour later that evening, some people whom I was familiar with were all asking me what I had done to my hair. I would pat it gently and smile as if to say, *It looks good, don't it?* I spent a great deal of the weekend looking in the mirror and spraying my special activator to keep my curls glistening.

On Monday I arrived at work still under the impression that I looked fabulous. My white coworkers knew something was different but seemed afraid to ask. I took my seat at my desk, which was located on the front row, directly in front of the branch manager's office.

The branch manager was a dead ringer for a young Ronald Reagan. He walked by my desk and did a double take when he spoke to me. A few minutes later my phone rang, and Leon asked me to come into his office for a minute. I walked into his office, and before I took my seat, Leon asked me, "Lynn, what did you do to your hair?"

"I got a jheri curl," I said proudly as I touched my greasy, saturated curls. Leon had a blank expression on his face. A few seconds later he said, "Lynn, the haircut has got to go." When I asked him why, he said that my haircut wouldn't work in this type of environment. When I demanded to know why, he told me he wasn't going to argue with me but that his supervisor had called him and asked what in the hell I had done to my hair. When I asked him if the branch manager told the white boys what to do with their hair, he said, "I'm not telling you that you have to get your hair cut. But I will say that this is one of your first big career decisions."

I looked at Leon with his naturally curly hair. He didn't understand, I thought. Was the IBM management trying to make me like them? I had changed my dress. I laughed at their corny jokes over lunch. I even answered some of my coworkers' dumb questions about what it was like being black when they had had a few drinks. Now they were trying to tell me what to do with my hair. I told Leon I wouldn't do it, and he suggested I take the rest of the day to think about it.

After I left the office, my anger continued and all I could think about was finding a good lawyer and suing IBM for discrimination. I called one of my new friends, Ken Baker, who worked for Southwestern Bell in a management position, and told him what had happened.

When he didn't take my side and agreed with Leon, I began to rethink my position. Maybe Ken and Leon had a point. If I was going to work in corporate America, then I was going to have to play by their rules. I had played by the rules of my fraternity and other organizations while I was in college, and this was pretty much the same thing, like some kind of uniform.

I thought about it for a couple more hours and then I ran to my car and returned to the scene of the hair crime. When I got there I discovered that my regular barber was taking the day off, and I was relieved. She had seemed so proud of her efforts. I jumped into the first empty chair and instructed the barber to cut it off. When I returned to work the next day, Leon gave me a pleasing smile, winked at me, and said, "I think your future at IBM is going to be just fine."

WHEN I MOVED TO DALLAS, I had never been to a gay bar. There were rumors that the mysterious place called George's in

Fayetteville was a gay bar, but I never went anywhere near there during my college days. I figured Dallas, a big city and all, had to have at least one gay bar. Still, I was afraid to find one and then go alone. All the people I had met in Dallas through work and church were straight—or at least I assumed they were.

Toward the end of my senior year, I found out that Mason, Butch, and I were not the only black men with secret desires. There were several, including members of my own fraternity, another black fraternity, and several grad and law students. We didn't interact a lot, because everyone was trying to protect their secrets. We used code words in our conversations with each other, like: *I'm game for anything* or *I know what time it is.*

I became friendly with a law student, Lance, who tried to seduce Mason the moment I left campus for good. One weekend he came to Dallas, and after a night of cruising several straight bars, he suggested we go to a gay bar.

Since I didn't know any, I turned to the yellow pages the next day. There were no listings under gay bars, so I tried to distinguish them from their names. Lance and I saw a listing called the Gay Paree, which we both agreed had to be a gay bar. When I called, a black woman answered the phone. I asked her where the bar was located, and she said South Dallas. I was thinking this was too good to be true: a gay bar right in the heart of the black community.

I had to be sure, so I asked the woman what their clientele was like. She responded, "What do you mean our clientele? We got a pool table."

I quickly realized this was not the place we were looking for. I told Lance the Gay Paree wasn't the spot and he suggested we call the gay information hotline, and sure enough they told us of a gay bar located downtown called the Old Plantation. The friendly voice from the hotline gave me directions, and at about ten o'clock on a humid August night, I was on my way to a gay bar.

During the drive to the club, I was nervous that I might run into someone I knew. I reassured myself by deciding that if they were in a gay bar then they were looking for the same thing I was. The only problem with that theory was that in the late seventies gay bars were considered quite chic because of the great music. I'd heard that a lot of straight men went to these bars to dance with their girlfriends.

When Lance and I entered the club after showing our three pieces of ID (I would later learn that multiple IDs were for black men only), we slowly followed the sounds of thumping music. Once we reached the main ballroom, my eyes became twice their normal size: men dancing with men, men kissing each other, and everybody just generally having a great time. Most of these men were white, with a few black guys sprinkled among the crowd on the dance floor. This was the era of Donna Summer and disco balls, and both were in full effect that night.

We had been in the bar for only about five minutes when my heart began to race. I thought I saw someone from Fayetteville— a tall, chocolate-colored man who I thought was on the baseball team at Arkansas. I pointed him out to Lance, and we both agreed we had seen him on campus. I wanted to leave immediately, but Lance said we should at least see if he was there with a woman or if he was "in."

Lance took a position on one side of the club and I stood at the opposite end, gazing at this vision of manhood whom I had remembered seeing once at the athletic complex, shirtless. Minutes later, I saw him move toward the packed dance floor with a short, blond man wearing pum-pum shorts. Lance and I met at the bar and decided that he was gay or bi and decided not to leave.

About thirty minutes later, we bumped into him on purpose and introduced ourselves to our former schoolmate, Roger, who told us he had left the university and was playing minor league baseball outside of Arlington, Texas.

I assumed he was into white guys from his previous dance partner, but when I came back from using the bathroom, Roger and Lance were in deep conversation and I felt like an intruder. My first night in a packed gay bar and I felt alone. No one asked me to dance, and I didn't have the courage to ask anyone. About two hours later, Lance told me he was ready to go and asked me if I minded if Roger came home with us. I told him I didn't mind, and I ended up sleeping on my sofa. The two of them slept in my bed. It would be the first of many nights when I would leave a gay bar feeling sad and lonely. It didn't matter that I now knew I wasn't the only one.

DESPITE FEELING FORLORN and the hard time I was given to gain entry, I would spend almost every Friday and Saturday night at the Old Plantation. It was even harder for darker-skinned brothers who didn't dress preppy, but there was no other place for black gay men to go and socialize.

This was not the extent of my social life. There was a place I frequented where I always felt welcome. Rascals was a black straight bar located near Love Field, the airport where President Kennedy arrived on that fateful day. It was the place for Dallas's up-and-coming buppies.

My first blind date was arranged by my manager Leon and convinced me that some women knew what time it was and could deal with men who were confused about their sexuality.

Deborah Long was a good-looking woman, a graduate of Hampton Institute, and when I met her I immediately knew I was going to like her. We agreed to meet at the Dallas Playboy club, which at the time was *the* hot spot in Dallas.

Deborah strolled through the Playboy Club as if she had a stack of invisible books on her head and carried herself like she knew what it meant to be sexy despite being only twenty-one years old. She had big, bright brown eyes with narrow brows accenting them and flashed a wide smile of victory between sips of her drinks.

After a few hours of engaging conversation, Deborah leaned over to me and whispered, "Every man I've met since I've moved to Dallas has been trying to get in my pants, but I don't mind if you want to. . . ."

I became a bit nervous and took a long gulp of my drink. A voice inside me urged me to give truth a chance. I liked Deborah a lot and didn't want to lose her friendship before it began, so I took a chance.

I whispered back, "Deborah, sweetheart, I'm sure that would be wonderful, but I think I might be gay." It was the first time I had said that to a woman who was romantically interested in me.

Deborah remained as calm as a puddle after the rain had stopped and said, "I know. You're gay, but that doesn't bother me."

In the middle of Dallas, Texas, I'd met my first fag hag girl-friend, even though at the time I didn't know that such a friend existed, or how wonderful they could be.

My employment with IBM was like an entry card with the A crowd, and I quickly became friends with television personalities, doctors, sports figures, and lots of beautiful black women. I became popular with a lot of women because I always knew the latest dances, some of which I had learned at the Old Plantation. I would flirt with women on the dance floor, but most times that was as far as I went. I was still hopeful I would meet a great guy at the Old Plantation.

I loved Rascals, with its polished bar, strobe lights, thumping R & B hits, and a deejay who would call out names of people he knew when they walked into the club or danced well. At Rascals, unlike the Old Plantation, I could always count on great music. Sometimes at the Old Plantation, fondly called O.P., I would have to wait for several records before the deejay would play something I wanted to dance to.

I had my routine down for Fridays: I would leave work a little early, get a haircut, and head to Rascals to secure a parking spot and a good seat before the well-dressed crowd would begin to arrive. It also gave me a chance to fill my body with liquid courage, which I needed so I wouldn't feel inferior to some of the people I might meet.

After a few drinks, I had no problem striking up conversations with people I considered famous. They didn't have to be a member of the Dallas Cowboys or on television; it could be someone who had a reputation for being a ladies' man or someone I perceived as attractive and confident.

With a good-paying job, I had become a member of the black brunch-eating bourgeoisie. Before I moved to Dallas, I didn't know what brunch was and how it gave you a reason to suck up some libations right after church. Armed with American Express and other credit cards, I was living beyond my means, but so was everyone else I knew. I created a middle-class background that would suit my newfound friends. I told people that my father, though deceased, had been a lawyer and later a family court judge and that I had attended prep school back east. The more I learned, the bigger the lies were about my background.

After Friday-evening happy hour wound down and patrons left for dinner and house parties, I would go to my apartment and change into tight jeans, a muscle shirt, and cowboy boots, and head to the Old Plantation.

Much to my surprise, I started seeing many of the same good-looking professional black men I would see at Rascals. I was beginning to realize that I was not the only black professional man who was seeking the same. I became friends with several of these men, and I began to develop my "sissy sense" or "gaydar," being able to detect gay men who were undercover about their sexuality. Without any type of initiation, I became a card-carrying member of another fraternity, black men who led dual lives. I would spend a great deal of time at the straight bars on Fridays trying to determine who I might see at the Old Plantation later. It never failed that some of the same womanizing men I admired on Friday would appear at the Old Plantation dancing with other men.

Despite my sudden social flurry, I wanted nothing more than to be with Mason. I was certain I still loved him, yet I didn't feel as though I was in the market for permanent companionship with either a woman or a man. When a woman would come on to me, I would cool the situation by telling her I was engaged to my college sweetheart.

Mason and I talked at least once a week, and occasionally I would receive a letter or card from him. At night I would wear one of the T-shirts he had given me, which made me feel close to him. When he had given me the shirts during my senior year, he had made me promise not to wear them on campus or anywhere in the state of Arkansas.

Sometimes when I talked with Mason, I could detect something was different. I got the feeling that he desperately wanted to be completely heterosexual, or he had discovered other black gay men in Fayetteville. He talked constantly about his girlfriend and other attractive black girls on campus, and he would occasionally ask me about certain members of my fraternity by quizzing, "So what do you think is up with him?"

When I journeyed back to Fayetteville for football games, I spent the majority of the time with my fraternity brothers and my ex-girlfriend Cherri and her sorority sisters. I tried to convince myself that life would be better if I could love Cherri the way I loved Mason. Then I began to hope she would marry me, especially since I had learned in Dallas that marriage didn't preclude one from having sex with men.

Mason and I would share stolen moments in Fayetteville and a few times in Dallas. Whenever we were alone in the same room, he would never mention his girlfriend or a desire to end our relationship. We had this private joke about the "same time next year," when we would get together for a weekend and would spend the entire time making love. Those moments were special, but so infrequent that I began to think about something more permanent. I wanted to be in love, and I convinced myself it didn't matter if it was a man or a woman.

THINGS WERE GETTING BETTER at IBM, and in the training program, I was making some treasured friendships with people I had nothing in common with. I was one of the few students whom some of the top students would help with assignments, maybe because they didn't see me as a threat for challenging them for the top spot when it came to class scores.

At times I secretly envied and despised them for their seemingly perfect lives. Everything seemed to come so easy for them, like understanding the right type of clothing and managing money. Once, one of the smartest ladies from my class, Suzanne Procter, a Harvard MBA, had a dinner party in her New York City East Side apartment, and she invited me because I was real tight with one of the best-looking white guys in the class, a former Princeton baseball player, Paul Pecka, whom I affectionately called Princeton Paul. Her apartment was like a page out of *Architectural Digest* and the dinner party was one of the most elegant I had ever attended at that point in my life.

IN MY FINAL IBM TRAINING CLASS, one based totally on sales calls and presentations, I finished near the top of my class. The applause I heard when I received one of five baseballs given to students who had received a superior rating on a sales call or presentation eased a great deal of the hurt and embarrassment I had felt at the beginning of my IBM career. I had proved that I could compete in this highly technical field. Yet I never considered if being a top salesman at IBM was something I really wanted to do.

After I completed the program, I got a promotion, a huge salary increase (almost doubling my entry-level salary), and my own sales territory. Since I was one of the few black salesmen not only in Dallas but in the country, I got a lot of attention. The regional personnel manager took me to several college campuses to help recruit minority students.

One of these trips took me back to Fayetteville, where I proudly walked around campus in my expensive navy blue suits, starched white shirts, and red power ties, visiting with professors and former classmates. I got to spend time with Mason and Hugh, with whom I had renewed my friendship. Hugh was a good friend, and my infatuation with him was over. I was able to convince the manager from Little Rock that Hugh would be a great employee. Hugh was on schedule to receive a degree in engineering and had a high grade point average. At first the manager from IBM resisted, saying Hugh appeared too shy and hadn't spent a lot of time with campus activities, with the exception of his fraternity, of which he was president. When Hugh took the aptitude test, he scored in the top quarter and was hired immediately for the Little Rock branch as a systems engineer trainee.

Back in Dallas, I immersed myself in work but still managed to have a social life. I also found a wonderful church located in the Hamilton Park section. I often traveled to Houston to visit Butch and the Cove, my first all-black gay bar. The Cove was a dive located behind a theater, but it was always packed with handsome black men and an assortment of colorful drag queens.

The Cove wasn't as big as the Old Plantation, but it had the most incredible energy. You didn't have to wait for the deejay to play a black song, and patrons didn't have to present multiple pieces of identification. I would dance with a freedom I had never known, not worrying about anybody whispering that I danced like a punk. Still, I refused to slow-dance with a man in public. I consider myself a private person and sometimes socially conservative, and I couldn't see myself doing something that looked like a sexual act rather than dancing in public.

In Houston, I hung out with friends that Butch had made at work, like Vanessa Gilmore, who would turn out to be one of my most treasured friends. Butch talked all the time about the stylish Vanessa, who had graduated from Hampton Institute and was also a good friend of Deborah Long. She could take twenty dollars and create a Sunday brunch in her apartment that would rival any four-star hotel's.

I also began having a string of weekend affairs that would start late Friday in the bar or in the adjacent parking lot and would last until Sunday afternoon when I drove back to Dallas. These men would come and exit my life in an instant, like a sweet, quick caress. Affairs as fleeting as lightning on a quiet lake.

None of those affairs had the traumatic effect that one in Dallas would have—a one-night stand that would remind me there was nothing gay about being gay when so many men wanted desperately to be straight.

One Sunday, while playing tennis at Southern Methodist University, I met an attractive black guy whom I knew to be one of the city's star athletes. He was smart, well built, and could turn on the boyish charm with great facility. It didn't matter that the name he gave me didn't match the name I associated with his handsome face. I knew he had to protect his image.

The night in my apartment was like a fantasy, a delectable romantic episode that made me think I was in love after one night. When he left my apartment early Monday morning, I began to make plans for a wonderful life with this already established sports hero that would make me forget Mason Walker ever existed.

I couldn't wait to get home from work to speak with him. I called him, hoping to make plans for the evening, but his warm voice from the weekend sounded distant and impersonal. He asked if he could call back. I agreed quickly. A couple of hours later, when I called to tell him I was going to bed, a female answered his phone, and when I asked for him she told me that my faggot ass had better stop calling this number.

When I called back a couple of days later, hoping there had been some terrible mistake, I got a recording informing me and other callers that the number had been changed and the new number was unlisted. I was humiliated. I didn't know how someone could be so cruel, even though lots of men showed me every chance I gave them.

THE INCIDENT BROUGHT ON another wave of depression. As a salesman I wasn't expected in the office every day since nobody there was buying computers, so many days I would drink rum and Cokes late into the evenings and sleep most of the day, waking up only to check with my secretary to see if anybody important was looking for me.

Although I was having some success with my accounts, Leon noticed the change and suggested that I join him and his wife Susan, a beautiful high-spirited Italian woman, for a meeting for an organization called EST that could change people's lives. Being from the South and the Church, I felt only God could rescue me from my pain. It didn't sound like something I wanted to be a part of, but Susan and Leon were relentless. I finally went to a couple of EST guest seminars and immediately came to the conclusion that I didn't think a bunch of white folks would understand the problems of a black man dealing with his sexuality. But Susan and Leon, along with the EST graduates/groupies, persuaded me that EST could solve all my problems. I was in pain, and God seemed too busy, and I was willing to give anything that would finally deliver the love of my life to my doorstep a chance.

When the time came for me to go to the EST seminar, I backed out, telling Leon that I couldn't afford the weekend sessions and didn't want to do the training in Dallas because I wouldn't be open if I might see people I knew. Leon offered to loan me the money and arrange an IBM advanced training class in another city where the EST training was being held.

Against my better judgment, I went to New York City to take the EST training at the New York Hilton hotel. I don't remember that much about the intensive program except the beautiful hotel and my sneaking out during the Saturday-afternoon sessions to watch parts of the Arkansas–Texas football game. I felt as though I was sneaking out of an all-important college class, knowing that if I got caught, I would have a heavy price to pay.

In a crowded ballroom, people I'd never met confessed deep, dark secrets about themselves. Some were in tears as they recalled horrible incidents from their childhood, many for the first time. I was expecting to uncover some type of sexual molestation from my childhood that would explain my attraction to men, but I knew nothing like that had occurred in my life.

At the end of the two-day session, everyone was hugging and saying that they had "got it." Forever the follower, I said, "I got it too." But in reality, what I had gotten was a weekend in New York City and further confusion about whether I was indeed gay and if change was possible.

When I returned to Dallas, I pretended to be more self-assured and confident when I was around Susan and Leon, especially when dealing with the evil curse of my sexuality. I didn't want them to feel as though they had wasted their money and I had squandered a weekend in New York, stuck in the hotel with a bunch of strangers in search of themselves. I was still in search of myself, and the trip convinced me that maybe if I couldn't find myself with EST, I could find a more bearable life in New York City.

CHAPTER 10

I t took me another two years, but in the fall of 1982, I did something I had long dreamed of but didn't think I would have the courage to do: I moved to New York City. I had visited Manhattan several times to check out Broadway shows and to party, but the fast pace and high cost of living always frightened me. The glow of Manhattan's skyscrapers that turned the sky a metallic blue, no matter what the season, had beckoned me only through movies and books. In my dreams I wanted to live there at least once.

Another catalyst for the big move was the dramatic ending of my first live-in relationship. For two years I had been involved with Andre, an SMU law student, but our relationship ended abruptly when Andre felt the need to sleep with one of my close friends. At least, I thought he was a friend.

The breakup was the talk of the closeted black gay community in Dallas. Everybody knew of Andre's secret affair but me. I was too busy working two jobs, one as a computer salesman, the other as a waiter on nights and weekends so I could pay the house note on a three-bedroom North Dallas condo.

It was a classic case of working too much to provide the material things in life, but not paying enough attention to the things that really mattered in relationships.

When the shit hit the proverbial fan, I got sympathy from our close friends. I actually caught Andre and "my friend" together at my alleged friend's house on a weekend when he was supposed to be in Austin, Texas, doing research. People I didn't know became involved in our Peyton Place gay drama.

I was heartbroken and felt once again that no one would love me totally. I told my Aunt Gee about the relationship, but I told her Andre was female, and she insisted that I visit Atlanta for a few weeks so that she could show me love and make me feel better. I knew my aunt's love was unconditional like my mother's, but I didn't feel ready to share who I really was. When I look back, I realize that I needed to share equal blame for the breakup. I think at the beginning of our relationship, Andre, who had pursued me, really loved me. I was too concerned with image and what other people thought; too busy trying to prove that I was the man in our relationship. Andre wasn't an athlete like Mason, but he was smart and handsome in a pretty-boy way.

I did some cruel things to my partner. On the weekend of my twenty-fifth birthday, I made him move all of his personal belongings from our condo because I had more than thirty-five friends I had made at IBM flying into Dallas to help me celebrate. I insensitively explained to Andre that my IBM friends, especially the women, wouldn't understand my having a much younger roommate who on the surface didn't have anything in common with me.

I had to protect my buppie-in-training image, but I didn't realize how much it would hurt him. He didn't protest my demands, and even came to the party as an invited guest. The strange thing is that it was on the weekend that I sent him away that I realized how much I loved him. I climbed into the bed, satisfied at the party's success, and reached to pull him close to my chest. He wasn't there, and I missed him. I realized later how insensitive I was.

When my relationship ended, the little self-esteem I had left over from college and a moderately successful sales career suddenly disappeared. In my own eyes, I wasn't good-looking enough, not smart enough, and not the lover I needed to be to have a successful gay relationship.

The first and only time I saw Andre and my former friend in a romantic embrace at the Old Plantation, the bar where we had met, I wanted to die. I wouldn't stay around to risk seeing them again. It hurt too badly. Since Andre had two years of law school left, I knew I had to be the one to leave.

While I was strongly considering moving to Houston, a bus ride from Atlantic City, New Jersey, became my first step toward making New York my home.

I was attending the Miss America pageant with Lencola Sullivan, the first black Miss Arkansas. Lencola and I had become friends after I wrote her a congratulations note when she won Miss Arkansas and finished in the top five in the 1980 Miss America pageant. At first we were pen pals of sorts, but later I invited her, and she accepted, to several of the parties I held in Dallas. We began to talk fairly regularly on the phone. During one of our conversations, she mentioned she was planning to return to Atlantic City because the pageant grapevine was buzzing that not one, but two, black young ladies had a shot at the title. When she suggested I join her, I jumped at the chance of witnessing an historic event, as a black woman winning the pageant would be.

Lencola, herself, I always felt was a year or two ahead of the times when it came to the pageant. She is a staggeringly beautiful woman, with skin the color of toasted almonds, thick long black hair, and the petite shape of a life-sized Barbie doll.

When I saw her in the Miss Arkansas pageant, dressed in a tight-fitting snow-white gown, looking like a young Diahann Carroll—well, it was one of those times when I wished women were the only thing my heart desired. I must admit to romantic fantasies about her, but as usual, we became close friends and nothing happened but a spectacular lifetime friendship. I couldn't believe someone so beautiful would be interested in me as a friend.

The Friday before Vanessa Williams's crowning, I left Atlantic City and took the bus to New York City. I walked into the offices of Wang Labs, located at 666 Fifth Avenue, and handed the receptionist a résumé. A few minutes later, I found myself being interviewed by a sales manager in her early thirties. I, of course, turned on the charm, and a few hours later, Cookie Morris told me if it was up to her, she would offer me a job on the spot, but since she couldn't she asked if I would consider coming back Monday and meeting her boss. I took this as a sign that now was the time to move to New York, and I could think of nothing else on the bus trip back to Atlantic City. By Thursday of the following week I had a job as a senior marketing representative with Wang Labs, one of IBM's main competitors in a new field called office automation.

I moved in with Richard Coleman, whom I had met while working at IBM in Dallas. We had instantly hit it off when he was promoted to the Dallas training center. He became my mentor and the big brother I'd always wanted. Richard was gay and seemed proud of the fact, although he sometimes dated women for IBM career movement and had a girlfriend, Stephanie, who lived in New York. He captivated me with his stories of growing up in New York City and what it was like to be gay in one of the world's most exciting cities. He was tall and extremely handsome, with sparkling green eyes, and was one of the kindest people I've ever known. Richard was the kind of man who, when he entered a room, both men and women, regardless of their sexuality, took note.

Richard had been promoted to IBM headquarters in White Plains, but we had kept in touch and I had visited him on several occasions. When he moved back east, he had purchased a huge older house on a corner lot in the town of Mount Vernon. The

house was so big, with its twelve rooms, that I was actually afraid
to stay there alone when Richard traveled on business, which
turned out to be quite often. I had never stayed in a house so big,
and it seemed to me that I heard every sound, and I would spend
half the night checking all the doors, windows, and the alarm.
My fear got so bad that whenever I found out Richard would be
traveling, I made arrangements to spend the night in New York
City with friends or stayed in a hotel.

Six months after moving to Mount Vernon, I got the opportunity to move to New York City, when Larry Stewart, one of the
best-looking guys from Little Rock, who was appearing in the
Broadway musical *Dreamgirls*, got a leading role in the national
touring company and offered me his apartment on the Upper
West Side at an affordable $450 a month. I grabbed the offer,
even though I knew Larry could return without much notice.

The benefits of living in New York were immediate. I was
able to walk to work, something that made me feel like a real
New Yorker. More important, my social life picked up dramatically, because now I could stay at the clubs as late as I wanted to
without worrying about having to rush to Grand Central to catch
the last train to Mount Vernon.

A couple of months later, I would get an unlikely roommate,
Lencola Sullivan. I convinced her that she belonged on the Broadway stage and not doing the weather in Austin, Texas. It wasn't
that we planned to become roommates, but when she said she
didn't have a place to stay, I offered her my apartment since I was
preparing to go to Boston for two weeks of training. Instead of her
staying at my place for two weeks, we ended up living together,
in a strictly platonic relationship, for more than two years.

DURING THE EARLY 1980S, New York City had several popular gay bars where attractive black men congregated until the

wee hours of the morning. Something called AIDS was only a rumor. The sounds of Stephanie Mills, Donna Summer, and Diana Ross were all a black gay man needed. I was amazed that on any given night, including Mondays, gay bars would be packed with attractive men in business suits, blue jeans, and preppy clothing.

On Wednesdays after work it was not unusual to see Broadway stars having a few cocktails between shows. The clubs included Better Days, The Garage, The Cotton Club, Ninety-six West, and the infamous Nickel Bar, a tiny hole-in-the-wall establishment located on Seventy-second between Broadway and Central Park West. The Nickel was more of a cruise bar because it was so small, but it did have a living-room-size dance floor in the back that jumped on Friday and Saturday nights.

Most people went to the Cotton Club in Harlem on Friday nights to dance, and to the Garage, located in the Village, on Saturday nights. Ninety-six West was like the Nickel with a slightly older crowd, and married men usually frequented it.

When the bars would close, the lines at the gay male bathhouse formed around the block. None of my young adult fantasies could ever imagine something as decadent as the bathhouse. I entered the bars looking for love, but the bathhouse was the place to go when you were looking for lust. Most times I was unsuccessful at both.

I went to the bathhouses only twice. No one ever spoke to me, and I had convinced myself that the competition in New York was too tough and I would never find love or lust. I couldn't even engage people with cocktail chitchat, and I felt invisible as I watched black gay men picking each other and going into tiny closetlike rooms that were rented by the hour.

Once I went to a bathhouse in the afternoon, thinking I would stand a better chance of getting chosen with less competition around, and I was right. Just as I was preparing to join a handsome stranger in his private room, I decided to check my office for messages. When I called the office, my sales unit secretary asked where I was and informed me that my boss wanted to see me and my sales forecast before the day's end. I looked at my watch and realized that I had less than an hour to get back to my office and turn in a sales forecast I hadn't even started. I quickly dressed and fled the four-story building on Forty-second Street without even saying good-bye or thanking the stranger for making me feel desirable.

Of all the places I frequented, the Nickel Bar became my favorite watering hole, and almost every Friday evening, I would leave my office around 5:30 and walk the twenty-plus blocks to the popular bar before it got too crowded. Armed with a vodka and grapefruit juice, I would take a seat at the corner of the bar, near the door, so I could get a view of all the men who would start to pack the place around 6:30.

Since the Nickel was so small, it seemed easier to meet people when they brushed against one another to order a drink or to get into the men's room. The Nickel had its regulars, and I knew a lot of people not by their names, but by smiles or what they usually drank, since I didn't budge once I got a bar seat.

Thanks to the Nickel, I would meet some of the best friends I'd ever had and another major love. The friendship happened first. They were a group of three, sometimes four, men and a woman who came to the Nickel every Friday. Sometimes they would arrive together, or when one came alone, the others were not far behind. They always seemed to be full of laughter, and I wanted to laugh with them, but I didn't have the courage to go over and introduce myself, fearful that instead of inviting me to join in their conversations, I might become a victim of their quick-witted reads I often overheard.

I learned from the bartender that the best-looking member of the group, with the soft and boyish face, was named Randy

Johnson. I did say hello to him once, and he returned my greeting with a warm smile. A few weeks later, I would learn the names and meet the other members of the group.

I first noticed the group not only because of the laughter but because they were all so loud. They seemed to know everybody who walked into the Nickel, and if they didn't, you'd never know it. Nothing stopped them from engaging in lively conversation. They were like the popular kids in high school you desperately wished would speak to you and get your name right.

One Friday evening the group came in and, after assembling in the corner, began giving Randy gifts. He squealed with delight as he held up a pair of aqua-colored bikini swimming trunks. Along with a couple of members of the group, Randy walked over to the bar. This time when he noticed me and gave me his usual pleasant smile, I finally got the courage to say something.

"Is it your birthday?" I asked.

"No, I'm going to Puerto Rico to celebrate finishing grad school," Randy said.

"Congratulations. Where did you go?"

"Columbia J School," Randy said. Just as I was getting ready to tell him that I had a degree in journalism, Randy's bespectacled and tall friend returned to the bar and noticed that Randy and I were engaged in conversation and said in a friendly voice, "Why are you sitting over there by yourself, darling? Come over here and join us. We don't bite unless you want us to."

I smiled shyly and moved from my barstool and went over to the corner and introduced myself to Randy and his friends. The group included William "Willa" Rhodes, the man who had invited me over; James, a handsome brown-skinned young man with wire-rimmed glasses and dark, short, curly hair, who when he had too much to drink loved to talk and sing in a high-pitched voice; and Denise Johnson, the lady in the group, a stout woman with skin the color of a cinnamon roll and a short Afro, who always seemed to be carrying a rolled-up copy of the *New York Post*. At first I assumed she was a lesbian, but I later discovered that she simply loved hanging out with gay men and reminded me of my friend Deborah Long from Dallas.

I told the group my name and immediately began to feel a little uncomfortable, like I was sitting at the cool kids' lunch table and I didn't quite belong.

"So where are you from, darling, with that cute old southern accent?" William asked.

"Texas. I just moved here from Dallas," I said, failing to mention that I'd grown up in Arkansas.

"Is it true what they say 'bout Texas?" he asked as his large eyes seemed to loom over his glasses and peer toward my crotch.

"What do you mean?" I asked stupidly. Even though I noticed his eyes, I really didn't know what he was talking about. I must have looked bama, like I was wearing a purple suit with matching tennis shoes.

"Now come on, darling. You know what I'm talking about." My face changed colors from embarrassment. Randy noticed, and he looked at William and said, "Stop it, Willa," then looked over at me, smiled, and said, "Forgive her. She doesn't mean any harm."

I smiled and said, "No offense taken."

We shared our first laugh. As the evening wore on, I learned more about the group. Willa was a graduate of Dartmouth College and Columbia University and was an elementary school teacher in Jersey City. Tall and regal-looking, he was my first male diva close friend. I remember one occasion when someone at the bar complimented him on his beautiful full-length mink coat and he replied as he draped the coat over the barstool, "You talking about this old thing?" One year for his annual birthday bash he sent out invitations with a photo of him lounging in the coat and leather pants and the question "What Becomes a Legend Most?" printed underneath in bold letters. One year the theme was "Dreamboys."

James had graduated with Randy from J School and had simultaneously completed a law degree. He was also a part-time preacher. He didn't have a church, but he was a preacher.

A Marymount graduate, Denise was an administrative assistant at one of the record companies. She was always full of good stories about famous people in the music industry and loved to twirl around on the barstools after a couple of drinks.

I discovered that no members in the group were lovers but simply good friends. Willa had some cute and usually sexual anecdote that he would share about almost every man who came over to speak to them. It was as though he was not only the leader of the group but the sexual historian of the Nickel Bar. If a couple met at the Nickel, Willa knew the details.

Over a long weekend, the group practically became my family in New York. They became my role models, because they seemed so self-assured, proud to be black and gay, while I was still unsure of who I was and if I would ever be comfortable with who I was, and the details of that identity. New York gay life was different from that in the South. Everything was out in the open and nobody seemed to care. I had a lot to learn, and they were willing to be the perfect teachers.

Members of the group cruised any man they were vaguely interested in with a staggering success rate that left me in awe. I would have been happy to simply take their rejects. The only time I had the courage to approach a man in a bar was after I had about four drinks, and even with the aid of liquid courage I was rarely successful in getting dates.

I have to admit that initially I found myself attracted to Randy. He was smart and his eyes were a smoky topaz color and his mouth seemed to form a perfect bow. But Randy made it clear in one of our early conversations, without being mean or bitchy, that I wasn't his type. He quickly added that even though he had several close friends, he was always looking for new ones.

With Randy as my friend, and with Willa's approval, I became a member of The Group, as I began to call them. It was like being a member of a small gay fraternity or gay gang. There were many nights when we would get drunk and terrorize gay establishments from Harlem to the Village. When I say terrorize, I mean making a spectacle of ourselves and anyone who crossed our paths. All, of course, in good fun.

On Saturday nights we would meet at one another's apartments for potluck dinners, drinking and watching *The Golden Girls* and *227*. We would be joined by two more of Willa's friends: Robert Mason, a banker and one of the nicest men I've ever met, and Stuart, Willa's schoolteacher cousin.

After the shows had gone off, we would gather in the living room and sit in a circle and talk about our hopes and dreams for the future. Randy wanted to be a famous writer and was already working on a novel, James wanted to become a world-renowned preacher like Reverend Ike, and Denise wanted to meet and marry a totally straight man. My only wish was to meet someone who would love me as much as I loved him. Willa talked about buying a huge house in either Harlem or Jersey City, where we could all live and grow old together, like the Golden Girls. After a few drinks we would head to Keller's, a bar in the village we liked because it was similar to the Nickel.

When we would become bored with New York, Willa would organize trips to Washington, D.C., Philadelphia, New Orleans and Chicago. He had a great travel agent and usually had close friends in these cities who would make sure we were welcomed properly, which usually meant some type of dinner party in our honor. Dinner guests would always include the best-looking gay black men the city had to offer.

Willa was born on the Fourth of July, and every year he threw a huge bash to celebrate his birth and the holiday, in that order. An invitation to Willa's party was coveted by many of the Nickel bar regulars, and Willa passed them out as though they were gold credit cards with no limit. One year he changed clothes every hour on the hour, producing a fashion show that would put any diva to shame. At the top of the hour Willa would saunter into the middle of the room, drink in hand, and twirl as the crowd roared its approval. Willa would smile, soak in the adulation, and say, "Well, darlings, it must be seven o'clock: Eight must be just around the corner." He ended the evening in a gold sequin bolero jacket and tight-fitting black slacks. The rest of the group could only smile and shake our heads as Randy whispered to me, "This bitch has lost his mind."

Life for me in New York was turning out to be wonderful, even though there were still remnants of my life in the South. I had three different groups of friends: gay, straight, and those who fell into a little crooked category, meaning they were not always straight when the lights went out.

Lencola was still my roommate and close friend, as was Tracey Nash, a successful New York model, a friend from my Dallas days whom I had met at Rascals and later at Southern Methodist University when I was taking some grad courses in the business school. Tracey was an engineering student. She is a lovely young lady whose kindness equaled her beauty. I never quite understood why she wanted to be my friend, because I knew her father was a big-time doctor in St. Louis, Missouri. Rumor had it that if you were born black in St. Louis, then Dr. Nash most likely was your pediatrician.

My lack of self-esteem was not limited to my involvement in the gay lifestyle. I basically thought that everybody I met during this period was better than I was. None of these friends, to the best of my knowledge, knew about my gay life or my new friends, who weren't going to pretend to be straight for anybody. Lencola knew only of my dates with women, not the men I brought home when I knew she wouldn't be there. At times I felt like I was living in my mother's house, with all of the sneaking and late-night creeping.

Tracey lived a couple of blocks from Lencola and me in a new high-rise on Ninety-sixth and Broadway and was always inviting me to great straight parties, usually attended by a lot of New York buppies from Ivy League universities with high-paying jobs on Wall Street. I was intimidated by a lot of these people, often envious of their education, occupations, and the air of confidence they seemed to possess. I would mask my insecurities by drinking and lying, creating more lies about my background and station in life. Even though I was making a decent salary at Wang, I was a terrible money manager and was definitely living above my means with the help of credit cards. On occasion I would meet young ladies who captured my attention and really made me feel like one day I could get married. I would send them flowers and escort them to Broadway shows and dinner at places like the Russian Tea Room and Sardi's. But once the evening or the weekend ended, it was off to the Nickel Bar and The Group, where I was slowly learning that maybe some of my truths could set me free.

ON THE FIRST WEDNESDAY in August 1983, a friend, Hank Lamar from Dallas, was visiting, so I took the day off, and along with Willa we went to a matinee of an off-Broadway play, *The Miss Firecracker Contest*, starring the future Oscar winner Holly Hunter. During the summers, Willa and I often went to plays, because being a teacher he was off for three months, and I rarely went into my office, scheduling sales calls and meetings from home around my social schedule.

After the play the three of us met Randy, James, and Denise at the Nickel for evening cocktails. Willa and I were sharing some of the play's best lines with the rest of the group when Willa noticed a tall, caramel-colored man with tender brown eyes and thick curly black hair sitting alone at the bar. He was wearing a white linen shirt, which was open enough to reveal think black chest hair, and he had on white walking shorts and black sandals. He was slim but not skinny, and there was a sense of athleticism about him. Willa was quickly smitten. He invited the young man over to join the group. The man agreed and introduced himself as Mario Robinson. He smiled and shook the hands of each member of The Group and gave Denise a hug like they were old friends. "Damn, you smell good," Denise said as she winked at Willa.

Good-looking men were a part of the regular fare at the Nickel Bar, but Mario had a sweet innocence that led me to believe that he had no idea how good-looking he was. Willa ordered another round of drinks for everyone and went into his witty routine of twenty questions.

I learned Mario lived in Harlem, was a software salesman like myself, and was the son of an African American father and Italian mother, which explained his smoldering looks. I could tell from Willa's questions that his forwardness was making Mario nervous. The poor man looked uncomfortable and cleared his throat several times. Trying to help out, I cut in and asked him how long he had a been a salesman. He gave me a smile of thanks as we talked about our mutual career interests.

When it came to men, Willa sometimes had the attention span of a fly, so when he noticed how well Mario and I were getting along, he shifted his attention to someone else. My eyes met Mario's in a swift, private smile as he turned toward the bar and ordered another beer. I started to offer to buy his drink, but before I could make a decision, a guy on Mario's left slammed money on the bar. Mario looked at him and gave him a polite smile and then turned back toward me.

About an hour later, Willa decided that it was time for us to move the party down to the Village, but before telling everyone he whispered in my ear, asking if I liked Mario. I smiled and said, "Yeah, I think he's real nice." I wanted to add that there was no way he would be interested in me, but I didn't because Willa was always getting on me about my lack of self-confidence.

"Okay, baby," he said. "Mother will close the deal for you." He moved over and positioned himself between Mario and the guy who had bought Mario's beer and quickly whipped out one of his cards. I heard him tell Mario he was having a dinner party on Tuesday of the following week and he wanted him to come. Willa could pull together an elegant party quicker than B. Smith and Martha Stewart working together. Mario looked at me with a tense look on his face, then asked Willa if he could bring his lover. I kept the smile on my face, but I felt my heart sink. Always quick on his feet, Willa leaned on Mario's shoulder and quizzed, "Do you really have to?"

"I think I better," Mario said.

As we were walking from the club and toward the subway station, Mario tapped me on the shoulder. When I turned around, he said, "I really enjoyed talking to you. Do you think your friend would mind if I put your home number on the back of his card? That is, if you can give me your number," he said, and smiled.

"Sure, I don't think he would mind," I said. I was wondering why Mario wanted my number, since he had a lover. I really wasn't looking for any new friends outside The Group. But I took the pen he held out and wrote my number on the back of Willa's card.

The rest of the evening, Willa and Randy kept teasing me about my fascination with Mario and his apparent interest in me.

When I protested, reminding them that he had a lover, they all agreed that didn't mean anything. Maybe they were hoping that my dream of finding a love of my own was about to come true.

MUCH TO MY SURPRISE and delight, Mario called me the next day and we talked for almost two hours. When we started to end our conversation, he said he was looking forward to seeing me again soon, and without a pause out came "How about Saturday?"

"Saturday. Sure, Saturday would be fine," I said. I knew I was wishing for something magical that day, but kept my wish hidden in my heart, which is almost always the safest place when it comes to romance.

When Saturday came, I was so nervous about seeing Mario again that I had to change my shirt four times because of perspiration. I had gotten tickets to the musical *Dreamgirls*, a show I had already seen more than fifty times and never tired of, especially when I got a chance to see it with someone who hadn't. After the musical, which Mario loved as much as I did, we waited at the stage door to say hello to a couple of the cast members whom I knew vaguely through my friend Larry. I had been backstage a couple of times, so I was a familiar fan.

I invited Mario for an early supper at JR's, one of my favorite restaurants. A lot of the cast members from *Dreamgirls* seemed to always be there, because it was conveniently located next to the Imperial Theater. Over steamed mussels and red wine, I learned that Mario was in his first live-in relationship—with an older man—and that it wasn't going the way he planned. He even hinted that his lover was physically abusive. I didn't understand why he would stay in such a relationship, but when I asked him if he was in love, he quickly said, "Yes." I made the decision then that even though I found myself attracted to Mario, I would be his friend, and I hoped The Group would like him as much as I did. I ended the evening by walking him to the subway stop and telling him if he ever needed to talk, he could call anytime. He smiled and looked at me like I was the first person to ever make him such an offer.

A few days later, my phone rang at about 2 A.M. It was Mario, and I could hear in his voice that he was upset. After I got him to calm down, he told me how his lover had gotten mad about our day out and had locked him out of the house. He asked if he could come over and talk, and I quickly said yes. An hour later, he showed up at my apartment visibly shaken. We talked for about an hour, and then we climbed into my bed, me in a bathrobe and underwear and Mario fully clothed. I could sense that he was uneasy, so I pulled him close to me and held him through the night like a protective friend.

For several months, my relationship with Mario remained platonic. The only physical contact was the occasional brotherly hug. It changed when I informed him I probably wouldn't see him on an upcoming weekend because I was expecting a guest from Washington, D.C. Right before I'd met Mario, The Group and I had made a trip to D.C. for a weekend of partying and club-hopping. During our stay, I had met Stan, a Howard University medical student, at a bar called Nob Hill. We had exchanged numbers when we met, I had invited him to New York, and he had accepted.

When Mario asked if my weekend guest was coming for a romantic visit, I told him I didn't know. He was quiet for a few moments, and when I asked him what was wrong, he said he wished I wouldn't do that. When I asked him what he meant, Mario said softly, "My feelings for you have changed, and I find myself wanting you in my life in every way." I didn't answer but simply kissed him for the first time on his beautiful lips. It was a long kiss.

The next day I called Stan and told him of my new situation, but left the door open for a visit since he had seemed so excited about coming to New York. When I told Willa what had happened with Mario, he asked for Stan's number, then called and offered Stan his apartment if he still wanted to come to New York. Stan came and stayed with Willa, but I didn't see him because I was too busy trying to spend every single moment with Mario.

A week later we made love for the first time, and Mario told me he would never return to his former lover, David. A few days later, when he was certain David would be working, Mario went to the Harlem apartment they shared to remove some of his possessions. For the first time since we'd met, he gave me the phone number at the apartment to use in case he didn't reach my place by a certain time.

I paced the floor of my apartment anxiously. I was both exhilarated and terrified—excited that Mario had chosen me, yet secretly afraid he might change his mind and never call me again. Finally, the doorman rang that Mario was downstairs and needed permission to use the service elevator to move in his things. I was so excited that I hung up the phone and rushed downstairs to help my new lover move in.

DURING THE NEXT TWO YEARS, I was under the impression that I was in the midst of the most wonderful love affair of my life. My dreams had finally come true. Mario hipped me to the music of Madonna, Sade, and singer/comedienne Sandra Bernhard. I introduced this native New Yorker to the joys of Broadway, a then-unknown diva-in-training named Jenifer Lewis, and establishments like Sweetwater's and Don't Tell Mama. He acquainted me with the tasty soul food dishes of Wilson's and Sylvia's, and I took him to restaurants like the Water Club and the Russian Tea Room. Every day seemed like the city and I were going through a magical transformation, like when a sudden snowfall turns the planet into an apparent crisis-free fantasyland.

Mario seemed as happy as I was, and I was so proud to have such a handsome lover to call my own. My self-esteem improved, and I hired a personal trainer to help trim the thirty pounds I had picked up during my first months in New York when my diet consisted of Popeye's Fried Chicken and lots of vodka and grape-fruit juice.

My relationship with Mario allowed me to be honest about who I was with a couple of important people in my life. Lencola had become a dear friend, and we were still roommates, even though we led separate lives. She had her own social life, and never questioned why Mario and I shared the same bedroom. When I finally told her about my relationship with Mario as we shared Chinese food in the small kitchen, Lencola took my announcement well. In many ways it made our friendship and relationship stronger. I also knew after years of living together that Lencola was not the type of woman who gossiped.

One of the things I loved about our friendship was that we always supported each other like loving brother and sister. As beautiful as Lencola is, she, like me, seemed to always pick men who couldn't love her like she could them. If there was a Mister Wrong in the room, that's where Lencola and I would usually end up. There were several New Years when Lencola and I would spend the evening at church and then come back to our apartment and pray that God would send each of us someone special. When we would meet someone and think our prayers were answered, Lencola and I would then find ourselves praying that they would treat us the way we treated them. We had many a good cry over the shape of our love lives and began to count on each other's friendship even more.

MARIO AND I ENJOYED an active sex and social life, and we made it a point to have a date alone at least once a week and spend one day a week talking at the dining room table about things that might be troubling us. This was my idea. I was trying everything in my power to make the perfection last forever. I was determined not to repeat any mistakes I might have made with previous relationships.

During some of our talks, I learned of the deep emotional pain Mario brought into the relationship. Some of these incidents were so painful, I often wondered how he had survived them. Many times he shared some of his family secrets with me, and would burst into tears, and I would hold him until the tears stopped. Listening to his childhood memories made me remember Ben but also helped me realize how blessed I was to have the mother and family I had. The pain Mario had experienced at such a young age made me realize why he accepted the emotional and physical abuse from David. The way he opened up to me made me love him even more, because I felt he needed me and his need gave me a tremendous feeling of self-worth.

I showered him with gifts, giving him full access to my ATM card and my American Express card. At first Mario was hesitant, because he didn't want me to think he was with me for my money. I convinced him that what was mine was his, and that we were a couple, a team. I really believed that everything I had belonged to Mario, and when he told me he couldn't give me the same, I told him all I wanted him to bring me was true love. He said that was easy.

We traveled often, taking romantic trips to San Francisco and Vail. I was making good money selling computers, and Mario was also doing well. He would ask for my advice on how to handle some of his customers when he was trying to close a big sale. Mario promised to take me to Italy when he closed his first six-figure sale. He wanted to introduce me to the Italian side of his family. I knew from some of our conversations that his family from Harlem and Italy didn't get along too well, but Mario took great pride in his biracial heritage.

But there were a few problems I chose to ignore. One was that with the exception of Lencola, none of my friends in The Group liked Mario. They tolerated him, and when I asked why, they told me they felt he was using me both financially and emotionally. My response was "Nobody gets to use me without my permission."

Mario didn't care for The Group either, so after we had our Saturday-night potluck suppers, he would retreat to Harlem and spend the weekend with his family. Despite their differences, the Robinson family seemed close-knit to an outside observer.

The funny thing was that Mario felt that I was much different from my friends and felt that they were using me, since it seemed to him that I was always paying for the drinks—and my friends could drink. I never saw my friends or lovers in a bad light. All I knew was that for the first time I had friends and a partner who loved me just for me.

But there were times when I began to doubt Mario's love. Sometimes I wanted and I needed him to be supportive of me. There were days when he became withdrawn, and when I asked him what was the matter he muttered, "Nothing you can solve." In my idea of a perfect relationship, I felt lovers should share everything. When his emotional swings started to interfere with our sexual relationship, and when holding Mario was not soothing enough, I convinced him to start seeing a therapist. He balked because of the cost, but eventually went to therapy when I told him he didn't have to pay any rent.

Initially, his therapy seemed like a good move. After a couple of visits, Mario no longer seemed depressed and our sexual relationship seemed to flourish once again. He started to spend more time with his family, trying to mend some of the rips and tears he felt they had caused.

But I would soon discover that therapy wasn't the only thing that was making Mario happy. One weekend, a close friend from Dallas was visiting New York and I invited him and his new lover to stay with Mario and me. This particular friend had a big mouth, and I knew I could count on him to spread the word back in Dallas about how fine my new lover was and how happy I was in my new relationship.

I asked Mario to forgo his normal weekend trip to Harlem and help me host my friends. At first he resisted, but later agreed to stay home Friday and spend Saturday night at his parents' home. Although it wasn't what I wanted, I figured one night was better than nothing.

The weekend came, and Mario and I took my friends to a couple of shows, including a popular off-Broadway show called *Mama I Want to Sing*. We stopped at the Nickel Bar for drinks afterward. My friends were impressed with Mario and my life in New York— so much that they tried to convince him to stay home Saturday night so that they would have a chance to spend more time with him. He was polite but said he couldn't change his plans.

Early Sunday morning, while my friends were sound asleep in my living room, something very strange happened. I woke from a deep sleep at around 3:00 A.M., with a strong sense that something was wrong. I got up from my bed and went and looked out of my bedroom window onto Eighth Avenue, and then I picked up the phone. I was going to call Mario's parents, but instead I dialed the number of Mario's former lover as if I dialed it every day. When a deep male voice answered the phone, I very casually asked to speak to Mario. I was praying he would say I had the wrong number or shout that Mario didn't live there anymore. Instead he said, "Hold on." A chill swept over my body. Moments later I heard the voice of my lover, in a groggy voice, say, "Hello." I was stunned and quickly hung up the phone.

Tears started to stream down my face, and I turned to the

window and watched the cars pass and a few people walk down the street. I was so devastated and wanted to leap from my ninth-floor window. I was thinking, *How could this happen again? How could someone I love, who said he loves me too, be spending the night with somebody else?*

THE NEXT AFTERNOON, Mario returned home. He had a huge smile on his face as he hugged and kissed me while saying how much he had missed me. I returned his kiss, because at the moment I desperately wanted to forget about hearing his voice over the telephone earlier that morning. I was seriously trying to convince myself that the previous night hadn't occurred. My lover was back in my arms, and that was all I needed.

Mario asked me if my friends had gotten off all right and if I had gone to church. When Mario started showing signs of depression, I had encouraged him to turn to God, and so we went to church together often. I answered, "Yes" and "No"—I hadn't gone to church because I was too tired from the weekend.

Mario went into the bedroom, and a few minutes later I heard the shower running. Minutes later, he came out with a towel wrapped around his waist and asked me to dry his hair. He sat on the floor between my legs as I dried his curly hair in silence. When he asked if everything was okay, I told him everything was fine.

Mario then turned around and looked up at me directly in the eyes and asked, "Do you know how much I love you?"

Something went through me like an electrical charge, and I could no longer contain my anger.

"So is that why you had your ass over at David's house last night? Is that what loves means to you?" I screamed. I wanted to call him all kinds of bad names, but I didn't because I wanted him to tell me something that would make me forgive him instantly.

"What are you talking about?" he asked. "I haven't seen David since the day I moved in with you," he lied.

"Who in the fuck do you think called you last night, Mario? Who do you think it was?"

His face dropped, and suddenly tears filled his eyes. "I'm sorry. I'm sorry. Please don't leave me. I love you," he cried.

His tears and pleading made my anger rise. I wanted to tell him to get his shit and move out, to go back to his former lover, but I knew I was in love with Mario and I wanted him in my life forever. I asked him if he wanted to move back in with David and he said no, that David still hadn't changed. I asked him if he really loved me and wanted to live with me and me alone. Mario said he truly loved me and wanted to make our relationship work. My anger subsided, and I told him I felt we could work things out, but only if he was going to be totally honest with me. He promised he would, and on that dull Sunday I chose to believe him.

I had to.

THE WEEKS THAT FOLLOWED Mario's betrayal, I barely touched him. I didn't want him to leave, but it hurt my heart deeply that I again had a lover who chose to be unfaithful. I became depressed and unsure of myself once again. I confided in Randy and asked him not to tell the rest of The Group, because I didn't want them to dislike Mario even more. Randy suggested I get out of the relationship immediately, but I told him I still loved Mario.

Mario was doing everything he could to show me that he loved me. He was cooking dinner for me almost every day, and he was initiating romance, even though I still couldn't bring myself to finish the lovemaking. Since I felt no one could truly understand what I was feeling, I started to see a therapist myself.

In therapy, I began taking responsibility for Mario's infidelity. I told my doctor that if I had been a better lover with a perfect body, he wouldn't have had the desire to be with someone else, and that in some way I had failed Mario. My doctor didn't agree with my assessment, and tried to have me focus on building my self-esteem.

With both of us seeing therapists, my relationship with Mario seemed to have a chance, and for a couple of months things returned to normal. Mario was attentive to my needs, and there were no more overnight trips to his "family." I had convinced myself the relationship had survived the first major storm.

When he started therapy, Mario had started to keep a journal. I suppose the doctor suggested it. He kept the red book in the closet right above the rack where we kept our underwear. I saw it every day but was never tempted to read its contents.

But one day, when I was feeling a little down about our relationship, I couldn't resist. Maybe I thought the journal would give me hope about our future. I reached for the journal and anxiously flipped it open to a page that included a type of plus-minus chart, with my name at the top of one column and David's name on the other. Under my name he had written things like: *loves me an awful lot; a good provider; honest; really, really loves me.*

Under David's name he had: *says he loves me. Great lover, great sex.* Again I began to feel the devastation I had felt on the night of the phone call. I flipped back a few pages and read an entry where he recounted his recent birthday. He wrote about a surprise party I had given him at Memphis, a popular Upper West Side restaurant.

Mario wrote how it was the first time anyone had given him a party but he couldn't help but notice that most of the people there were my friends, like Tracey and Lencola. He went on to write how he had enjoyed the Broadway musical *Cats*, but how he hated spending the night at the Harley Hotel and making love. He said he felt obligated because of my generosity. As I read his handwritten words, my tears started to flow onto the pages of the journal. I slammed it shut and threw it against the bedroom wall. What a fool I had been. It was clear to me that no amount of therapy was going to save this relationship.

Still, for some reason, I couldn't leave Mario. I felt like he needed me and this was my last chance to have a successful relationship with a man, one where we could grow old together. I was thinking of my relationships the way most of my straight friends viewed theirs—long-term. I wanted to be loved, and I thought I could make Mario feel the same way. The only thing I wanted from Mario was honesty—something he couldn't give me for reasons still unknown.

THERE COMES A TIME in every hopeless relationship when you have to give up on it. For me, the final straw in my tortured alliance with Mario came with yet another surprise. One afternoon, the secretary from Mario's office called. She said she had beeped Mario several times but he hadn't called back. When I told her he wasn't home, she told me that one of the company's service technicians was locked out of his apartment, to which Mario had a set of keys, and the technician was tired of waiting out in the cold. When I asked the technician's name, she said the one name I knew I would hear—David Taylor.

After promising me that he had broken it off with David, I found out that Mario and David had worked for the same company for more than a year and that Mario had helped David secure the job.

For me that was it. I confronted Mario, and again there were tears. This time, though, he suggested maybe it was time for us to take a break. When I asked him if he was moving back in with David, he said no. Over the next two weeks, I helped him find a studio apartment in Harlem near his family.

I was hoping that maybe Mario's being away from me would bring him to some startling realization that he couldn't live without me. During this time, I continued to see my therapist. The Group picked up the social slack by planning more and more out-of-town trips, introducing me to anybody they thought I might be remotely interested in.

I met a few guys that I found interesting, but I was still in love with Mario, even though I was convinced he was using sex as a bargaining tool when he wanted something from me like a nice dinner or a sympathetic ear. Mario and I would see each other sometimes twice a week. There were some painful moments, like when he would show up at my apartment dressed nicely in a sweater or jacket that I had given him as a gift.

Sometimes when we had dinner, I would inquire about his plans for the weekend and he would look at me and say, "I don't think you want to know." I took this to mean he would be spending the weekend with David.

Everywhere I went in New York reminded me of Mario and the time we had spent together. I stopped therapy because the doctor couldn't provide me with a way to save my relationship. I became depressed again, and the only solace I found was with my friends and vodka.

At night when I went home alone, with the knowledge that Mario was probably enjoying himself with David, I would drink alone and cry. The tears flowed plentifully though silently. Those days would be among the worst of my life.

CHAPTER 11

When the American Airlines jet landed and the flight attendant announced, "Welcome to Chicago," warm tears slid down my face. It was the third day of the New Year, 1986, and hopefully another new beginning for me. But when the passengers started to move toward the door, I wanted to scream, "Turn this muther around and take me back to New York City!" My emotions were all over the place: from gratitude to fear. Would Chicago really be different for me? I wanted to be back in my apartment, in my bed with Mario beside me, gently stroking his hair and listening to him say how much he loved me. I knew that wasn't going to happen ever again, but it didn't stop me from wanting it.

That fall I was seeing less of Mario, and he was seeing more of David. I couldn't stand it anymore, so I decided I needed to leave before I embarrassed myself. I chose Chicago, because I had had a great time when The Group and I visited the city on one of our weekend excursions. As a big city, Chicago offered many of the things I loved about New York. In Chicago you could walk along busy streets and think about life, and maybe find true love on Michigan Avenue.

The day I arrived was a cold, drizzling day, with the sky low and gloomy and no sign of the sun. Fully aware that it was January, I longed for warmth and wondered if I was making another mistake.

When I had started to think about leaving New York, I contacted an executive recruiter who arranged for me to interview with several Chicago computer companies. I decided that if I got an offer, then it meant that Chicago was where I needed to be. When a small computer company offered me a job after a four-hour interview, I figured it was a sign.

I knew that I was wearing out my welcome at AT&T because of my constant absences. I had only worked there less than a year. I left Wang because I thought AT&T sounded more impressive. AT&T had just started a new computer division located at 2 World Trade Center and hoped to compete with IBM. I was hired after only two interviews, possibly because of my IBM background and because I was black. If I had learned anything since I had left the University of Arkansas, it was how to interview. Almost every honorary society I was a member of required an interview.

I was still dealing with a dormant kind of depression by partying into the wee hours of the morning and often showing up at work without sleep. Things came to a halt one day when I fell asleep, snoring while morning drool crept from my mouth, during an important meeting with a Smith Barney customer. My boss was present, and I'm still amazed I wasn't fired on the spot.

But I knew that if I stayed in New York I would remain in the emotionally abusive relationship with Mario. In one of our last conversations before I left New York, he had told me that I was the kind of guy you married, and he wasn't ready to get married.

The months before I left New York I had become more severely depressed, wearing my friends' nerves down with my constant moping and crying about the love I had lost. When I moved to Chicago, I thought about finding a therapist, but didn't. I was meeting new people, but I couldn't bring myself to become involved with anyone. I still held out hope that Mario would come to his senses and beg me to come back to New York.

In Chicago I quickly fell into another damaging pattern. I tried to mask my pain and lack of love in my life with material things. I moved into a new apartment on Chicago's Magnificent Mile and paid cash for a brand-new navy blue BMW. I quickly made friends with several high-profile personalities whom I had met in straight clubs, as well as with several gay men who lived their lives in the closet. I became a regular at the lowest-of-the-low black gay bar in town, another hole-in-the-wall called the Rialto, located under the el tracks in downtown Chicago.

The Rialto could be tough and was often filled with trade, masculine men (some ex-cons) who would make you feel good for a couple of beers and a couple of dollars, even though they didn't consider themselves gay or bisexual. I was constantly reminded how harsh and mean black gay men could be. Once, after accepting a couple of drinks, a man I had my eye on told me that he had no interest in going home with me. He added insult to injury when he told me I could be attractive if I lost some weight. I was so drunk that I told him to kiss my fat ass and I moved to the other end of the bar.

For a while, I pretended things were fine. Even as I actively pursued a new life, I still thought about Mario every day. He even made a few trips to Chicago—at my expense, of course—and we had decent times. The trips stopped when I realized after each visit that he had made phone calls to David's number.

I decided to go back to therapy to deal with my self-esteem issues and sexuality, but I stopped seeing my black female doctor when she told me there was nothing she could do to change my sexuality, that there was no magic pill. Despite my constant trips to the Rialto, I still prayed that being heterosexual was possible. At least that's what I prayed for when the depression returned. I blamed my depression on my homosexuality. I thought if I could change my sexual attraction to men, happiness would be waiting.

About a year after I had moved to Chicago, things began to

come apart during my most severe bout of depression. The kind that paralyzes you. I woke up one day and simply didn't think that I could live another second. I found more comfort in darkness than sunlight. My drinking had increased to the point where I was now mixing my alcohol, starting with wine before dinner, vodka afterward, and ending the evening with cognac or something similar.

One cold, especially gray Chicago morning, I was consumed with the fear that I wouldn't see the end of the day. Somehow I felt that this particular day would be my last on earth. I knew I needed help, so I called a medical hot line and told them how I was feeling. When I told them I was afraid to drive my car because my father had been killed in a car wreck and that I felt I was doomed to the same fate, they quickly recommended a doctor who was close to my apartment.

They asked for my phone number, and about ten minutes later a doctor called. We talked for about thirty minutes, and with a cool, soothing voice he convinced me that I owed it to myself to at least wait until the following day to meet him and see if he could help me. I don't know why, but I believed that this man whom I had never seen could help me.

The next day I walked to an office building on Michigan Avenue, about eight blocks from my apartment, and entered the small office of Dr. Gary Willer. He was a fragile white man with ocean-blue eyes and light blond hair. He wore wire-rimmed glasses and walked with a slight limp. He had a kind smile to match the voice that had gotten me through the previous night, and I immediately felt safe with him.

Our first session, scheduled to last one hour, went on for more than three hours, with me tearfully telling Dr. Willer about my stepfather, Ben, my life as a black gay man, and my recent relationship with Mario. I talked about the friends I had left in New York, how they had been among the best friends I had ever had in my life, but that I didn't understand why they wanted me as a friend. I told him I feared I would die before I ever experienced the one thing I wanted most in my life: true love.

Dr. Willer prescribed a medication he said would help me sleep and reduce my anxiety. When he warned me it would be dangerous to mix the medication with alcohol, I promised him that I would stop drinking. I lied. The pills didn't help me sleep, I thought, but alcohol did. So what if I never remembered taking off my clothes and climbing into bed?

Over the next four months, I saw Dr. Willer five times a week, every morning at 10 A.M. A week after I started therapy, he filled out a form that qualified me for permanent disability, since during this time I felt safe only in his office. The bookshelves lining the walls and the floral-covered furniture made me feel like I was at home. I would lie on the sofa and share my innermost thoughts with him.

During those dark days, I felt I could trust nobody but Dr. Willer. I confessed feelings to him that I had never admitted to myself: I felt bad about being born out of wedlock and felt like it had been a curse on my life; that men were not interested in me sexually or romantically unless there were financial rewards; that I felt I could only have sex with men if I had been drinking. Even though I knew my family loved me, I didn't think they would understand what I was going through. Maybe I required more love than my family or the world was willing to give. Every now and again, when I had moments where I felt I could sound happy, I would call my mother and Aunt Gee and tell them I was doing fine. I didn't want them to worry about me. It seemed that ever since I moved to New York I had distanced myself from the very people who had loved me unconditionally—my family.

Slowly Dr. Willer convinced me to rejoin the world, to start doing things I once enjoyed, like going to the movies, the theater, and to sporting events. I didn't tell him that I was still occasionally drinking, but I was convinced he could tell, because on the days I drank I would invariably be overly dramatic and far more depressed. When I was away from the safe confines of Dr. Willer's office, I needed alcohol to fall asleep faster. When I slept, I didn't feel pain and I wasn't afraid.

There were times during my therapy when I felt I was making progress, when I saw a glimmer of hope, usually when I talked to Dr. Willer about my dreams of finally loving myself. In fact, it was to him that I first voiced my desire to be a writer. I dreamed that if I could find the words to describe the pain that I felt being black and gay, maybe it would help someone else. When Dr. Willer encouraged me to write some of my feelings down and pursue a career as a writer, I would retreat, telling him that Randy was the writer of The Group and that I could never compete against him, since he was one of the few people I felt loved me despite knowing everything there was to know about me.

In his always dimly lit office, I began to deal with the anger I felt toward Mario and Andre. I spent entire sessions screaming and yelling at my invisible former lovers, telling them how badly they had hurt me and how all I wanted to do was to show them love. The exercises helped, but whenever I got a call from Mario, who now was trying to be my friend, my anger would return.

I don't think Mario really meant to hurt me, but he didn't seem to understand that I didn't want to hear about his trip to Paris with David for the Christmas holidays or how happy he was. During this period of inner struggles and healing, I confided only in Randy and sometimes Richard, who didn't believe in depression. Richard thought I should just say "fuck it" and get on with life, while Randy, as hard as he tried, could take only so much of my doom and gloom.

THERE WERE A FEW BRIGHT SPOTS in Chicago. I met friends like Chris Martin, a talented photographer with a wicked sense of humor who always made me laugh, sometimes even at myself.

I had met Chris on a visit to Chicago with The Group, and we had kept in contact. He was the first person I called when I moved to Chicago.

I also met another hopelessly heterosexual man who would be the object of my attraction for a time. I met Troy Donato at a sales conference in California. He is a handsome man with a smoldering sensuality. Troy has milk-coffee-colored eyes that are lively and flirtatious, and a smile that is so contagious it makes him look like he is beaming. We hit it off immediately, and I thought, once again, I had met the love of my life. I invited Troy to Chicago, and he made the trip a couple of weeks after we met.

I had never considered dating someone I worked with, but I was willing to make an exception. Troy had a lot of the qualities I'd admired in Hugh, but this time I was going to try and be honest about my feelings right away. On the Sunday Troy was going to leave after a wonderful weekend, I sat on the sofa next to him and told him I was gay and interested in him. Troy smiled and his face softened, and a tenderness came into his eyes as he said, "I'm not, but I would still like to be your friend." Thank God I said, "Sure, I'd like that." Even though romantic love had escaped my grasp once again, the chance to have someone willing to love and treat me the way I treated them had not. This was the first time I had met a man so comfortable in his skin that he didn't consider my sexuality a problem, but rather an opportunity to expand his view of the world.

IN THE MIDST OF MY THERAPY in the late 1980s, AIDS became a part of my life for the first time. Around the last week in March, I got a call from Randy telling me that Willa needed to see me. When I asked him why, he said Willa wanted to tell me in person and would pay my way to New York if I didn't have the funds. I had spoken with Willa a couple of weeks prior and he had sounded like he always did, busy and in perpetual party-planning mode.

Two days later, as I was leaving my apartment headed for New York, I got another call from Randy.

"Bill passed," he said softly.

"Passed where?" I asked.

"Child, didn't you hear me? Willa's dead."

When I asked what had happened, he simply said, "You know."

I didn't go to New York that day, but two days later—for the Saturday funeral. It was the first time I had attended a funeral of a close friend. The service was early, and the spring day was beautiful as we entered William Rhodes's church in Jersey City. The Group all sat together holding one another's hands for support. We all had these strange looks on our faces like we couldn't believe Willa was dead. There were no tears until a youth choir from the school where he taught sang the gospel song "I'm Going Up Yonder." Denise started crying first, then James, then me, and soon the church was filled with loud sobs.

After the service, we followed the casket outside and were greeted by a driving thunderstorm. Later we would joke that Willa was already in heaven creating havoc and had ordered the storm to get even with the people (namely, regulars from the Nickel Bar) who had shown up for curiosity's sake.

Later that afternoon, we had a potluck supper similar to our Saturday evenings in the past, and then we went on a tour of all the bars in New York that we had frequented when Willa was alive. Of course, we all got drunk, and by nightfall every single song we heard provoked tears—anything by Phyllis Hyman and especially "That's What Friends Are For," the popular AIDS anthem, which Willa had sent to us right before the holidays. I learned that Randy had known about Willa's illness for a couple of years but had been sworn to secrecy.

Following Willa's death, I knew I had to come back to the real world. I felt I had to get over my depression so that I could be a better friend to Randy, who had just lost his best friend and was also now dealing with the illness of his lover, Deric, a handsome married man Randy had been seeing for almost five years. Deric's illness shocked me, because during that time there was a feeling that the only people getting AIDS were bottoms (passive men), and from outward appearances and what I had picked up from conversations with Randy, there was nothing passive about Deric.

I would soon learn that Willa's death was just the beginning; two weeks later I lost another friend, Larry Stewart. I had always loved and admired Larry because he was from Little Rock and had been so nice to me when I moved to New York. Larry was in the hotel business, but when he moved to New York had decided to pursue his childhood dreams of becoming a performer. When I ran into him in New York, he was starring in one of the hottest shows on Broadway, *Dreamgirls*, and had appeared on the soap opera *All My Children*. He was a few years older than I, and I remembered thinking how handsome he was when he'd dated my baby-sitter, Jean.

After I moved to New York, during one of my trips to see *Dreamgirls*, I stood at the stage door of the Imperial Theater to get Larry's autograph. When I told him I was from Little Rock and reminded him of Jean, he took an immediate, protective-big-brother stance toward me.

One summer, Larry's then eleven-year-old son, Sean, came up from Little Rock to spend the summer with his father. Sometimes when Sean didn't want to sit backstage, Larry would drop him off at my apartment, and since Sean wasn't a baby, I would Sean-sit, instead of baby-sit.

The last time I saw Larry, he seemed in great health and spirits. He was in the national touring company of *Dreamgirls* and it was playing in Milwaukee. I drove the ninety miles from Chicago to see the show, and then Larry decided to come back to Chicago and spend the night because he could get an easier flight to Little Rock from there. Larry's father had taken ill and he wanted to get home to see him. The next day, while driving to the airport, Larry told me not to give up on my standards and hopes of finding someone who would love me for me. He told me I was too nice to not have love in my life. That was our last conversation.

I didn't return to Little Rock for his homegoing service, because when I called to get the time of his funeral, the receptionist at the funeral home told me she had gone to high school with Larry and that he looked so bad she didn't recognize him. I didn't think I could handle seeing Larry that way. I wanted to remember the smiling face I saw when he waved good-bye as he walked into the American terminal at O'Hare Airport the last time I saw him.

I was beginning to face the fact that it was going to become harder to ignore death and AIDS. When the disease first appeared, many in the black gay community thought it was affecting only white gay men and black men who dated white men. I knew that couldn't be totally true, because I never knew Willa to date white men. It also dawned on me that for as much as Willa flirted, I rarely remembered him being involved in a relationship or even a one-night stand. He seemed like more of a voyeur than anything when I met him.

ANOTHER STEP TOWARD HEALING some of the wounds of my childhood was a return to my faith. One Sunday morning, as I thumbed through the *Chicago Tribune* trying to decide where I would go to brunch or what movie I would see, my phone rang. When I picked it up, I heard the voice of a good friend, Deborah Crable. She was the host of the nationally syndicated *Ebony/Jet Showcase*, an African American entertainment program. I had met Deborah during my first months in Chicago at a party to which one of the few blacks living in my building had invited me. Deborah and I became fast friends, but since she traveled a lot she hadn't noticed that I had dropped off the social map. The only time I went out was when Troy returned to Chicago to visit.

"When I woke up this morning, you were on my mind," Deborah said.

"I was?" I quizzed. I didn't understand why someone as popular as Deborah would be thinking about me.

"Yes, you were, and I got someplace I want you to go with me," Deborah declared.

"Where?" I asked, thinking she had discovered some new restaurant with a great brunch.

"Church," she said.

"Oh, I would love to, but I already made plans," I lied.

"Well, change them. I'm not going to take no for an answer. I'll pick you up in front of your building in about fifteen minutes." The next thing I heard was a dial tone.

I looked for my phone book and found Deborah's number. I had to call her back and tell her I wasn't going to nobody's church. After several rings, her answering machine picked up.

I jumped out of my bed and started to put on some jeans and go downstairs and tell her that I couldn't go, but instead, for reasons unknown, I showered, then picked out a suit I could still fit into since I had picked up the thirty pounds I had lost plus an additional twenty.

A half hour later, I found myself on a crowded pew in the packed Apostolic Temple of Faith Church on the edge of Hyde Park. The church was rocking, with its large choir and friendly members. The dynamic Bishop Brazier preached and moved like a human tornado. I found myself mesmerized, weak in the knees, and my body felt warm.

I had always identified myself as a Christian. When I was twelve, I had joined and been baptized at the Metropolitan Baptist

Church in Little Rock. I later joined the North Little Rock Church of Christ, which my Aunt Gee and her family attended, mainly because I wanted to please my aunt and not because I believed the teaching of the non-music-playing Church of Christ. In college and in Dallas, I had returned to my Baptist roots.

But on this Sunday, something happened to me that had never occurred in church. I don't know if it was something the bishop said, but I felt as though he was talking only to me. I found myself standing up, my hands stretched in the air with tears rolling down my face, repeating, "Thank you, Jesus. Thank you." Then I felt my knees go limp, no longer able to hold my body, and I collapsed in the pew alongside Deborah. On that day I felt the Holy Ghost and knew that Jesus was real. I realized that He didn't expect me to be perfect and He might even understand the gay thing. I knew if anybody could save me from the pain and loneliness, He could. I was ready to give Him a chance.

WITH THE REDISCOVERY of my faith and thrice-a-week therapy, I thought I was on the road to recovery. I returned to work after being on sick leave for six months. My boss was surprisingly sympathetic. He shared with me that he had a close friend who had suffered from depression and was supportive of my recovery. Since I had been receiving my full salary and spending little money on food and entertainment, I had a nice little savings account, so to celebrate my return to the world I traded my BMW for a new Mercedes.

I joined a health club and hired a handsome, former pro football player to help me get my body back in shape. Three months later, I was planning a weeklong trip to Jamaica to celebrate my new body and attitude. Then I made the mistake of inviting Mario. I felt like a new person, and I thought this would give Mario one last chance to realize what he was passing up. Sadly, I failed to realize that I could always use things like trips and gifts to get his attention. When I first invited him, he was hesitant, but I convinced him the trip would do us both some good.

The first three days of our trip were pleasant. Mario seemed happy to see me and my new body, even though he barely touched me. He chose to sleep in the spare bedroom. When we reached the resort, the one-bedroom suite I had reserved had been given to someone else, and a nice Jamaican lady thought she was doing us a favor by upgrading my reservation to a two-bedroom suite.

We were like two friends on a trip, spending the day eating and swimming and then retiring to separate quarters. I guess I could have lived with that until the fourth night, when I was in Mario's bedroom and I noticed a postcard on the desk addressed to David. Again, reading something not addressed to me was going to cause me pain. There it was in Mario's handwriting: *David, Having a great time in the sun. Wish you were here. We'll have to do this sometime soon, Love Mario.*

I WENT BALLISTIC, smashing my hands into the wall. Suddenly I saw blood splash from my fist as I started pulling pictures from the wall. Tears rolled down my face as I screamed at the top of my lungs, "How long am I going to let you fuck over me?" For about five minutes I shouted obscenities like "You faggot mutherfucker. I hate you." I called him names I had only thought of when he'd made me angry before.

Mario had a look of shock on his face, and I, too, was startled by my fury and resentment. It was one of the few times in my life when I wanted to hit another human being, to make him hurt the way I was hurting inside. It was the first time I used the term *faggot* to hurt another gay person.

The next morning, I left about one hundred dollars on the kitchen counter and headed to the airport without saying good-bye, giving up the three days of hotel time I had previously paid for. I headed back to the cold wind of Chicago with my hand covered in a bandage.

When I arrived back in Chicago, powerful hail the size of ice cubes was pelting the city. I arrived at my apartment, dropped my luggage at the door, put on a Whitney Houston CD, and began to cry again. Just as I was preparing to pull off my clothes and open a bottle of wine, I heard a knock at my door. I lived in a doorman building, so I figured it must be one of my neighbors, and I was not in the mood for neighbors. When I looked out the peephole, I saw my trainer Brad at my door. The health club where he trained a lot of his clients was located in my building, which meant the doorman didn't have to announce him. I opened the door, my eyes red from crying, and just looked at him with a *What are you doing here?* look.

"How was your trip?" Brad asked.

"Don't ask," I said. I wondered why Brad had stopped by, since I had told him I'd be gone for a week. I had assumed Brad was straight from the way he was always talking about women and from the attention women paid him at the club. I had put on my tired old straight act by telling him that I was going to Jamaica with an old girlfriend. All I had to do was remember to change Mario to Maria, and I could share with Brad what a rotten bitch *Maria* was and get sympathy from my handsome trainer.

Brad had the body of life. He was 6'3" and about 215 pounds, with the legs of an Olympic track and field runner. He had played college football and run track, participated in the Olympic trials as a hurdler, and even played one year as a wide receiver for the Los Angeles Rams.

Brad informed me he didn't know when I was returning, but since it was raining so hard he decided to see if I was home, so that he could hang out until the rain subsided. We drank wine, listened to Whitney's mellow voice, and talked about sports.

Before I knew it we had finished a liter of some cheap wine I had found in the back of my refrigerator.

The rain didn't stop; in fact, it seem to pick up force. So when I became tired from the long trip and the wine, I informed Brad I was going to bed.

"Hey, man, do you think it would be okay if I crashed here?"

"No problem," I said. "I'll get you a pillow and blanket and you can sleep down here on the sofa."

"Where do you sleep?" Brad asked.

"In my room," I said as I pointed toward the stairs that led to my bedroom.

"If it's cool with you, then that's where I will sleep," he said.

I didn't try to dissuade him, and the body-by-God trainer slept in the bed with me. Nothing happened during the night, and the next morning there was the bumping of knees and the touching of toes, but no sex. I figured he had simply had too much to drink.

Three days later, Brad showed up at my apartment after the gym had closed. Again we drank wine and listened to music. But this time when I announced it was my bedtime, Brad followed me like a puppy dog, and when I reached the top of the stairs I could feel the heat of his body behind me. When I turned around to face him, he stuck his tongue down my surprised mouth.

The next morning, Brad assured me that he was not gay. He told me that I was the first man that he had ever kissed besides his father, and that he loved pussy more than anything in the world. I had heard this story before, so I knew how to respond— by assuring him that our night of passion was a secret that was safe with me, and I, too, was into women and fucked around with men only on occasion. I couldn't wait to get to therapy and share this escapade with Dr. Willer.

Dr. Willer had advised me against taking the trip with Mario. Nevertheless, he was quite shocked when I told him with faint

emotion what had happened and that I had little interest in discussing it. He also thought it was good that I was thinking about
someone other than Mario, but he warned me that someone so
unsure of his sexuality might not be good for me either. I assured
him that I would never fall in love with someone like Brad, but
at least I had wonderful sex with someone who seemed to enjoy
sex with me.

I'd met guys like Brad before and knew the drill. You enjoyed
the sex and never let love and romance enter the picture. Besides,
beautiful Brad was a tremendous boost for my damaged ego, and
before I knew it, Brad had moved in with me.

He did it slowly, by leaving a pair of jeans at my place, and then
maybe a T-shirt or warm-ups. When his underwear started showing up regularly in my laundry, I realized he was more than just my
trainer. Brad still had a girlfriend. I learned he was staying with her
when we met, and he still spent the majority of his free time with
her. In the beginning, this arrangement didn't bother me.

Brad took my mind off Mario. It excited me that a handsome
jock who didn't associate with the black gay world found me
interesting and attractive. Depression was still a part of my life,
but now it seemed to come in soft waves—waves I hoped to erase
with my newfound faith, romance, and Dr. Willer.

I reentered the social scene with my handsome roommate. At
his suggestion, many of my friends and his girlfriend believed he
was my cousin. I started to entertain at home and went to church
at least twice a week. I was feeling so much better that I even
reduced my therapy to one day a week. On the surface, it looked
as though I had made a full recovery. The tears in my sessions
with Dr. Willer disappeared and were replaced with laughter.

ONE FRIDAY EVENING at happy hour, I ran into a tall and
striking young lady who remembered me from my IBM days. We

struck up a conversation and she told me about the exciting new job she had gotten as a regional manager for a large software company. Right before she left, Vickie slipped me a card and said, "Give me a call and let's have lunch and talk about you joining my team."

Even though I was happy with my sales position, I was intrigued. Of course, I was familiar with the software giant Vickie was going to head in Chicago. She said what I wanted to hear: Working for a black boss, I wouldn't have to put up with the endless skinning and grinning necessary to have a good relationship with white male superiors.

My boss at the time, Myron Weintraub, was white and Jewish, and he was probably one of the fairest men I had ever worked for. Myron didn't make me feel guilty about the time I spent on sick leave with my depression, and he seemed to think that I could do no wrong when I was operating with all jets going. Even though I was not open with him regarding my sexuality, I think he would have handled it with class. He seemed interested only in results and sales. Myron was right: When I was feeling a hundred percent, I could sell the devil fire.

Vickie was not going to take no for an answer, and she wore me down with expensive lunches and tours of her company's new downtown office, telling me if I was first on board I could have my choice of office and territory. When she asked me how much my base salary was, she promised to make an offer that would include a twenty-thousand-dollar increase. The job would require travel, which would include New York City, where I felt I was ready to return. I missed Randy and The Group, even though they'd already made three trips to Chicago once I started to feel better.

So against the advice of my big-brother mentor, Richard, I took the job. Richard felt that I owed my current boss and company some loyalty since they had stood by me during my illness.

He also warned me that my black female boss might be a night-mare if she found out I was gay. When I told him she was married and wasn't like that, he again warned me that black women, married or otherwise, didn't take kindly to gay black men who looked and acted like me. Troy encouraged me to consider the position, since it was a big jump in pay. I didn't tell him what Richard had said. In the end it was my decision to make, and as difficult as it was to tell my boss, I resigned. I wasn't quite honest in my resignation. I told Myron and the company president that I felt my depression was returning and I didn't think it was fair for me to request sick leave again. I almost changed my mind when Myron told me he would rather have me at fifty percent than a lot of salespeople he had interviewed at a hundred percent.

The first weeks at my new job went smoothly enough. I had a beautiful office, an expense account, and I was working for a black woman who thought I hung the moon. During those early days, Vickie was always inviting me out to lunch or for drinks to discuss sales strategies. I thought this was odd, because one of the things we had discussed in early conversations was our disdain for after-hours meetings over drinks and dinner. I was interested in getting to the health club and home, in the hope that Brad might be there. He was dating and seemed to be smitten with a beautiful young actress/model in Chicago who would later become nationally known. I told myself that was cool with me, because I wasn't interested in falling in love but I also wasn't willing to give up the passionate sex life we shared.

I was working hard on my new job. I was the only black salesman out of six whom Vickie had hired, so I wanted to be better than the rest. I was at work every morning before 7:30 and often worked on weekends. Some evenings I would call Randy and talk for hours, or Richard, and tell him how well it was going. When I brought up my life at home with Brad, Richard cautioned me to be careful what I said on the office phone. He reasoned that as a manager he sometimes monitored the calls of his salesmen to see where they were spending their time. I told him I wasn't worried, that Vickie was cool.

When I had been two months on the job, things changed. I was preparing to close my first big sale with a public utilities company in Minnesota. I had made several trips and appeared poised to bring in the first significant sale for the new regional office. I was so focused on closing the sale that I turned down an invitation from Vickie to join her and some of the other sales force for dinner after work. In the coming days I found Vickie's attitude toward me chilly. At first I assumed she didn't want the other salesmen to know how close we had become during the interview process. That was cool with me. But the week I was to return to Minnesota to close the deal, Vickie called me into her office and said, "This situation is not working for me. I will pay you two months' salary if you have your desk cleared out before the end of business today."

At first I thought maybe she was playing some cruel joke, but I soon realized from Vickie's stoic face that she was not playing. When I asked her what I had done, she repeated her opinion that the situation was not working out. I was shocked and devastated. I started to plead with her not to do this, but Vickie's face and cold attitude didn't change one bit.

I returned to my office near tears and threw my few personal belongings into my briefcase and went home. I immediately called Richard, seeking his advice on whether or not I should take her offer of severance or get a lawyer. At first he took an I-told-you-so tone, but when I broke down in tears, he became more sympathetic, advising me to take the money and run back to my former employer.

The experience was so demoralizing, and I knew I couldn't go back to Myron and admit I had lied about my mental stability. If he took me back and my depression returned for real, then I would be in a boy-who-cried-wolf situation. My pride was getting in the way, and I wasn't so certain Myron and the president of the company would take me back. I couldn't take the additional rejection.

During the weeks that followed, I found my solace once again in vodka. I started seeing Dr. Willer twice a week again, using his office as a place to scream obscenities at my former boss for destroying my life when things were suddenly looking up. I cussed Mario and my stepfather again for good measure and came to the conclusion that Brad was with me only because I let him drive my new Mercedes and kept him supplied with tennis shoes, workout clothes, and sexy underwear. I had to get rid of him before he realized I was a loser with a shrinking bank account.

I felt failure and helplessness seeping into my being. I called Deborah and turned back to church, something I had slacked off on when my affair with Brad was in full swing. I did get him out of my life. In a crowded restaurant, I told Brad that the relationship was no longer working for me—the same words Vickie had used with me. His reaction surprised me.

The big muscle-bound jock and ladies' man started crying in the restaurant, demanding to know why I would do this to him after I had roped him into this illicit relationship. He said he thought he could depend on me. When I pointed out all the ladies that constantly called for him on my phone, he said that made our relationship special because I knew about them but they didn't know about me.

I tried to ease the blow by saying that I felt if I spent another night with him I would fall in love, and after being hurt, I couldn't bear that again. Looking back, that was true. I loved having someone like Brad in my life. I enjoyed the look of envy I saw in the eyes of the few gay friends who knew the real deal about our relationship. I loved the fact that Brad totally dispelled the stereotypes I had about gay or bisexual men, and in a strange way he fulfilled some of my youthful fantasies.

Still, I saw how Brad treated women. I heard him cursing them out on the phone, calling them names. I was the one who consoled them when they came to the apartment looking for him after he had stood them up or when he owed them money. I told myself that if he treated these beautiful women like that, eventually he would treat me the same or worse. Deep down I knew he didn't love me, as he had said when I broke off the relationship, but loved what I had to offer him materially.

Unable to find suitable employment, and not having the benefits of a salary and health insurance, I returned to some of my old destructive habits: partying every night of the week, drinking in excess, and not taking my medication or seeing Dr. Willer because I felt as though I had let him down, since I'd returned to my old routine.

One night, I went to the Rialto and spent the evening buying drinks for potential one-night-stand suitors. When the bar was about to close, I went to my car ready to head home for another night alone. Before leaving, I pulled my silver Mercedes in front of the club as men started to pile out. Many were paired together as couples. I noticed an attractive brown-skinned guy standing alone, smoking a cigarette. I blew my horn, and when he looked up, I lowered the passenger-side window and motioned him over to my car. When he walked over and asked "Whatsup?" I responded, "You. Come ride with me." He smiled and jumped into the car, and that's where my memory lapses.

I vaguely remember driving home and bringing the stranger with me through the lobby of my building and speaking to the late-night doorman. What happened after that will forever remain a mystery to me. All I know is that the next morning I woke up with a hangover from hell, and most of the expensive clothes from my wardrobe were gone along with my Louis Vuitton luggage. My first thoughts were to call the police and look for my keys. When I didn't find them immediately, a fear swept through me that the stranger had also stolen my car. I found a pair of jeans and a sweater and raced to the parking lot. I was relieved to find my car still there.

Back in my apartment, I located my keys in the freezer, which told me I at least had enough sense to hide them, but my wallet was missing. Again I thought of calling the police, but didn't because I didn't know what I would tell them. So I did what I usually did when I got in trouble: I called Richard.

Richard was sympathetic for about a minute. Then he tore into me, telling me that I needed to get myself together and stop all the dumb shit. He told me that instead of worrying over clothes, money, and luggage, things I could replace, I should be on my knees thanking God that the stranger hadn't taken my life. I told Richard that I knew he was right, but that I just wanted someone special in my life. He calmly replied that I was not going about it the right way.

For the next three days, I stayed locked in my apartment, not eating or drinking. My thoughts about what would happen next swirled in my head like damp autumn leaves. I was feeling so lost, so inconsequential. I didn't even have a career. Even though I wasn't that crazy about some of my previous jobs, I did get a feeling of satisfaction when I closed a big deal. I wasn't answering my phone, and on day four, Richard contacted a friend of mine and asked him to come to my apartment and check to see if I was all right and for me to call him immediately.

That evening I called Richard, who had been promoted to a job in the Washington, D.C., area. I tried to put up a brave front but later broke down in tears again. Richard said, "Pack your shit up, bitch. Put it in your car and bring your ass to D.C." At first I protested, saying how much I loved Chicago and that my doctor was here. Richard responded that D.C. had doctors, and he could help me find employment in the computer industry. He added that I could help him out for a change with some of the finishing touches on the new home he had built right outside Washington, D.C.

After hanging up, I thought maybe Richard's suggestion made sense. Washington was close to New York and was the mecca for black gay men. Maybe the love of my life was waiting there. Maybe with Richard's wisdom and big-brotherly love, I could pull it together.

At different points in my life I'd tell myself that if I found someone who truly loved me, and it didn't matter if they were male or female, I could get myself together. I could live up to the promise so many people said they saw in me. It never really dawned on me in my search for love to look in the mirror. On those rare occasions when I was brave enough to look at myself, I saw sadness in my eyes and I understood how lonely my future might be. I needed more than my faith; I required more than my family and my friends with their wonderful lives, who just didn't understand the pain the loneliness in my life was causing.

After giving friends most of the furniture I had bought while living in Chicago, I was on the road again, searching for peace of mind and looking for love.

CHAPTER 12

At times Washington, D.C., can be heaven for an African American gay man. Yet in many ways it can be hell. I liken it to heaven because of the large number of attractive and successful black men living in the city and the thousands who visit the nation's capital regularly. But when solitary nights blend seamlessly, one into another, it becomes an abyss of loneliness.

During the next three years of my life, I would experience a little bit of heaven and a whole lot of hell that only depression can bring. And without even knowing it, I would learn valuable life lessons and begin to grow up mentally and spiritually.

I had been to D.C. countless times with The Group on our annual, unofficial black gay celebrations over Memorial Day weekends.

On late Sunday afternoons when the music was playing and I immersed myself in the packed and popular club Tracks, D.C. was heaven. I mean, never in my life had I seen so many beautiful black gay men. But hours later, after the music had stopped and dusk arrived, I watched so many of my friends leave the club with the loves of their lives or love of the night, while I went home alone. There were times when I was desperate enough to settle for a one-night stand, when my standards were nonexistent. I still couldn't meet someone with whom to share at least a couple of good nights, much less my whole life.

I began to feel that I needed to be perfect. The reason I wasn't attracting someone was that people could see my weakness, they smelled my fear. I had always felt a certain amount of anxiety when I walked into a gay bar. There was a fear that if I spoke with someone or asked him to dance, he would base his decision on whether I looked like a suitable bed partner. This didn't happen with me in straight clubs. I was never afraid that a woman would say no, but when one did, she was always polite. In D.C., on the surface there seemed to be so many more choices, yet rejection was still a possibility and I was once again reminded of how cruel men could be.

My home life was good. Living with Richard brought a certain degree of stability for me. He had rules I had to abide by, like keeping my room clean and making sure I put things back in their proper place. I hadn't done that since I had left my mama's house.

I found a new job the first week I arrived. It was a sales position with a medium-size computer firm. The white sales managers were still quite impressed with a black man who had been successful as an IBM salesman.

Whenever I felt depressed, which was at least five times a week, I just went upstairs to Richard's (whom family and close friends called Richie) huge master bedroom and talked with him. With his quick wit and wonderful sense of humor about life, I wouldn't stay depressed for long. I felt safe in his four-bedroom ranch-style house, located in an integrated neighborhood in Mitchellville, Maryland.

On many weekends, his wonderful father and mother would make the trip from upstate New York, and I felt like I was a part of a big, happy family. The first couple of times when they came I would get a hotel in D.C. because I didn't want to get in the way, but after spending just one weekend with the Coleman clan, I looked forward to their visits almost as much as Richie.

Richie's mother would cook big meals, while his father seemed to always be tinkering on the large mobile home he drove. After dinner, there would be card games and drinking while the Coleman family talked about the good ole days as we watched family movies on a projector flashing images on the den wall.

Some weekends Randy would make the trip from New York. I would get a hotel room and we would enjoy all the gay clubs D.C. had to offer. I made a few new friends, and renewed friendships with black gay men I had known in Texas and New York. It seemed everybody was moving to D.C., and though I didn't think it possible, 1987 ended on a good note.

THE FINAL TWO YEARS of the eighties would have a lasting effect on the direction of the rest of my life. The year began festively enough. Randy came to D.C. to celebrate his birthday and the New Year. I rented a two-bedroom suite at the Grand Hyatt and had a small birthday party. On New Year's Eve, I decided I didn't want to start the year in a gay bar, and even thought about finding a church holding midnight service.

Randy wanted to go to Nob Hill, one of his favorite D.C. spots, but I talked him into staying at the hotel until midnight. He did, and at the stroke of midnight, we hugged and drank a champagne salute to Willa and Deric, Randy's lover, who we knew were up in heaven partying. The champagne made me sleepy, so I decided to go to bed, while Randy caught a taxi to the club for an early morning of partying.

The day after New Year's, as Randy was preparing to catch the train back to New York, I rushed to look for my jeans and car keys so I could give him a ride to Union Station, but for some odd reason Randy said he wanted to say our good-byes in the suite, pointing out that every time we had parted lately there were always tears. The hotel suite didn't prevent the tears as

Randy whispered he loved me and said he would see me in a couple of weeks when I visited New York.

Richard's parents came the weekend I was going to New York, and I tried to convince Randy to come back to D.C. He told me he had a hot date with a Vietnam vet he had met on a job. Randy and I talked with each other almost every day, and I told him I would see him soon.

On the first Wednesday of February I spoke with Randy, and he said this might be the last time we talked for a while since New York Telephone was going to cut off his phone at day's end for nonpayment. When I offered to help pay his bill, he declined, saying I had already done enough. I told Randy my offering to help was selfish in many ways because I looked forward to talking with him every day. He told me I could make it a couple of days without chatting and that he had a few freelance writing assignments coming up and after he got paid he would get his phone turned back on.

I missed talking to Randy, and a few days before Valentine's Day I sent him a card with a fifty-dollar bill and signed it "From a secret pal." I knew Randy could make some great but cheap meals for a couple of weeks on fifty dollars.

Around the end of February, the void of not talking to Randy became too much and I realized I had to take matters into my own hands. I called New York Telephone and arranged to send a check Federal Express so Randy's phone could be turned back on. I was feeling pretty good about my plan and couldn't wait to tell him what had been going on since the first of February.

I knew Randy talked to his mother frequently even when his phone was off, by calling her collect from the pay phones that lined his block, around 106th and Broadway. Randy and his mother, Pinky, were very close. He had given me her number to use in case of emergency, so as I sat in my office, I picked up my phone and dialed her. When a lady answered the phone, I asked to speak to Pinky and she told me Pinky wasn't in.

"Do you know when she will be back?" I asked.

"I don't know. She's gone to New York," the female voice said.

"Oh, she's gone to visit Randy?" I asked.

"No, her son is dead, and she went up there to identify his body," she said.

"Oh, who?" I asked, not thinking for one moment that she was talking about Randy. He had two other brothers, and I thought one of them lived in one of the other boroughs of New York.

"Randy," the lady said.

"No, not Randy," I said as I closed my office door and felt a chill ripple through my body so fast that it felt warm.

"Who is this?" the caller asked.

"This is Lynn. I'm one of Randy's best friends. Are you sure it's Randy?"

"Yes, baby, I'm sorry, but it was Randy."

"What happened?" I shouted.

"I don't know," she said. Just as I was getting ready to ask another question, one of the secretaries from my sales unit knocked on my door. When I said: "Come in," she peeked in and said she had an emergency call waiting for me. I hung up the phone without even saying good-bye. When my phone rang I recognized James's voice, and he said, "Lynn, baby, I've got some bad news for you."

"James, is it true? Is Randy dead?"

"Yes, baby, it's true."

"What happened?"

James told me that right then nobody knew. He told me that Randy's super had called the police to open Randy's apartment when his neighbors began to complain about a stench coming from his place. Once inside, they had found Randy's badly decomposed body between his bedroom and bathroom, wearing only a pajama top. They had estimated that Randy had been dead for almost three weeks, and it was going to take some time to determine the cause of death. I thanked James and told him I would be in New York the following day.

After telling my boss what had happened I headed home, but before I reached Richard's house, I stopped at the liquor store and bought a liter of Randy's favorite vodka. I got to the empty house and quickly poured a naked glass of the vodka and drank it like it was water. Standing in the kitchen, I suddenly fell to the floor in tears, calling out Randy's name. I prayed that this was some tragic joke. I finally composed myself enough to call Richard at work, and when I told him what had happened he told me he was on his way home.

My body ached with pain and misery so intense that I felt I couldn't stand it for another second. Never had the death of a friend or anyone I loved felt like someone had hit me in the stomach with a boulder.

Richard and Randy were not friends. In fact, they didn't like each other at all. Richard had always thought Randy and the group were a bad influence on me, while Randy thought Richard was too pretentious. Still, both respected my friendship with the other. Before Richard got home, I'd finished half of the liter of vodka and had crawled into my bed, fully clothed, and passed out. Later that night I heard a knock on my bedroom door, and Richard came in with a cup of hot herbal tea. We talked about Randy and speculated about what had happened. Richard asked me if I thought Randy had AIDS, since his former lover had died from the disease. I told him I didn't know. Then I remembered that Randy had often said AIDS would never be a part of his reality. Whenever he said it, I believed him.

There was no funeral for Randolph Leland Johnson and no conclusive information on the cause of his death. By the time

I arrived in New York, Randy had already been cremated, but the coroner had kept some tissue samples and the police were treating his death as a possible homicide.

That weekend, several of Randy's friends, including what was left of The Group, gathered at Robert's Jersey City condo for our Saturday potluck dinner and to pay respects to our lost friend.

We promised to keep the evening upbeat, recalling the happier times with Randy. We each went around the room and shared our stories of how we had met Randy and a funny or special time we'd spent with him.

I talked about the time Randy and I had gone to Barbados for a weeklong vacation. I had planned the trip shortly after Willa and Deric had died to help Randy deal with his quiet grief. Five days into our trip, we grew bored with the island because it wasn't like either Puerto Rico or the Dominican Republic and seemed homophobic.

Randy and I had spent the majority of our time at the hotel's beach bar and restaurant, enjoying elaborate meals and drinking ourselves sick. When we got ready to check out, I went down to the front desk to get a copy of our charges. I was shocked. It was more than twelve hundred dollars, and I knew my credit card couldn't stand that kind of bill.

I went back to the room and told Randy. We pooled our cash but came up about five hundred dollars short. I told Randy I had a plan. He would leave the hotel and take a taxi to the airport. I would leave from the terrace of our room and walk on the beach to the hotel next door and catch a cab from there and meet him at the airport.

"Have you lost your mind, bitch?" Randy asked.

"What? You don't think it will work?" I asked.

"What do you think people are going to think with you walking across the beach fully clothed and carrying a full set of designer luggage?" he said, laughing.

"Then what are we going to do?" I asked, realizing how stupid my plan was.

"Visualize the clerk punching in your credit card number and the approval coming across the machine," Randy said.

I was thinking, *Yeah right*. We would probably end up in a Barbados jail for theft of services, and I didn't know a single soul I could have called to send me the money. But Randy had been right, I told his friends. My credit card was approved. In fact, Randy and I had used our visualization technique to buy Baccarat crystal and upgrade our coach tickets to first class for the flight to New York with the same credit card that I knew was past due everywhere except, apparently, in Barbados. I ended my story by telling everyone how we got drunk on champagne during the flight. Once we arrived at the airport, we were so proud of our tans that we rushed to Randy's apartment, dropped off our luggage, and headed straight to the club. As we entered the subway station, Randy looked at me and said, "We look so good with our tans, men are going to be lining up to buy us drinks. We'll be the most hated bitches in the club tonight."

Everybody laughed and said almost in unison, "That was Randy."

Our trip to Barbados was not the first time I had encountered Randy's visualization theory. Randy shared a few of his beauty secrets with me and told me the most important one was visualizing meeting the finest man available that night. So whenever Randy was going to the club, he would look into the mirror after getting dressed, and tell himself, "You're smart, you're handsome, and tonight you're going to meet your king." Randy always had his choice of good-looking men, and I dreamed of being as confident as he was.

There were whispers that maybe he had committed suicide, but those of us who knew Randy didn't believe it. At the time of his death Randy had completed his first novel and had shot a television pilot with good friend Lajoyce Hunter Warlick, who also spoke at the party. It was a black version of *Entertainment Tonight* and was the big break for which Randy had been waiting.

Months after Randy's death I was still walking around in a daze, trying to figure out what had happened to my friend. I found it difficult going to some of the bars Randy and I had frequented in the district. I tried desperately to piece together information about his last days. The card I had sent him had been found with the money still inside. The only person I knew who had seen Randy was Mario.

He called about a month after Randy had died to offer his condolences. "Even though I didn't like him, I know how important he was to you," he said. He told me how he had seen Randy at Keller's on Valentine's Day night. When I asked how Randy looked and what he was doing, he said, "I didn't speak to him, but he looked fine to me. He was just being Randy, flirting with some man and drinking." No one else, including his building superintendent, recalled seeing Randy after Valentine's Day.

I TRIED TO GET ON WITH MY LIFE, which continued to change daily. Much to my surprise, Richard had decided to marry his longtime girlfriend, Stephanie, which meant I had to find an apartment of my own.

When I asked Richie why he was getting married, he told me simply that he was tired of being alone. With his family and good friends, I had never thought of Richie as being lonely. I was happy for him and Stephanie, and nervous and excited about having my own apartment once again. I wanted to get a place in the heart of D.C. near the clubs, but Richie talked me out it, reminding me of the danger in the city and his concern that I would revert to my old Chicago ways. He pointed out that Randy's recent death should be reason enough for me to stay in the suburbs. Richie was convinced that Randy had been killed by some rough trade. I didn't believe this, because Randy dated only good-looking and usually responsible men. Still, I took Richard's advice and found a two-bedroom apartment about five minutes from Richie's house.

Even though I lived near Richie, I didn't see him that often and just assumed that he was settling into married life. But one evening I decided to pay him a visit, and I was shocked when I saw that he was losing weight and walked like he was in a great deal of pain. Naturally, I got worried. When I asked Richard about his health, he told me his car had been rear-ended in an accident—thus the pain he was experiencing in his back. I believed him.

About a week later, Robin Walters, a very good friend of mine from my college cheerleading days and IBM, called to express her sympathy about Richard. When I asked Robin what she was talking about, she paused. I told her that Richard had been in a car wreck but was okay.

"I don't think so, Harris," Robin said softly. "I have a friend who works in IBM benefits who told me Richard is out on disability because he has cancer."

When I told her she was wrong, she told me she was certain. Robin was not the kind of woman who gossiped just for the sake of it. I knew she was calling me out of concern because she knew I thought of Richard as a big brother. I hung up the phone and went to my car and headed to Richard's house. When I arrived I used my key, and I was on my way upstairs to Richard's and Stephanie's bedroom when I heard Stephanie ask, "Where are you going?"

"Upstairs to see Richie," I said.

"He's not here," Stephanie said.

"But I saw his car in the garage," I protested.

"He's not here. I'll tell him to call you when he gets home,"

Stephanie assured me. There was a strange look on her face like she wanted to tell me something but couldn't. I'd always gotten along great with Stephanie and couldn't understand why she was lying to me. Richard never went anywhere without his prized gold Mercedes, which he didn't allow anybody to drive.

Later that evening I called Richard's house, and for the first time in several weeks, he answered the phone. He sounded like Richie, with his strong and forceful voice. We talked a few minutes about my jobs, and he joked about how many I had had since leaving IBM, which when I thought about it had been numerous.

"When are you going to find out what you're really supposed to being doing down here?" Richard asked.

I laughed, and then I asked Richard if he was really all right, and he very firmly said, "Yes, I'm fine."

I said good night, and when I hung up the phone I wanted to believe Richie, I needed to believe him, but I sat on the floor and cried. I became numb with fear that I couldn't bear to lose another close friend, one who had become a part of my family.

The following weekend, I returned to Richie's house determined to see my big brother. I came under the guise of needing to wash my car. Again I saw Richie's car in the garage, but there was no sign of him. It took me about two hours to wash my car, and afterward I went into the house to talk to Stephanie. She was in her usual perky mood, talking about her new job and how Scotty, her pre-teenage son, was adjusting to his new school and neighborhood.

When I asked about Richie, she told me he was upstairs sleeping. In all the years I'd known Richard, I couldn't recall his ever taking naps. Now I was convinced something was wrong.

I was trying to figure out how I could go upstairs to Richie's bedroom, when suddenly I heard his cheerful voice almost singing, "Is that Lynn Harris I hear? Come on up here and talk to me."

Stephanie and I exchanged a quizzical glance and I moved slowly toward the stairs.

When I entered Richie's sanctuary, the master suite complete with wet bar and fireplace, I saw him sitting in his maple canopy bed propped up by several pillows. I was shocked by what I saw. He looked like he had lost fifty pounds since the last time I had seen him, which had been just the month before. Only his smile and killer green eyes made me certain it was Richie. I walked over to his bed to give him a hug and felt tears forming. As I pulled back, Richard saw my tears and quickly said, "If you're going to cry, then you can't stay up here."

"So what are you telling me? That I'm going to have to grow up?"

"Yep, you've got to grow up, 'cause it doesn't look like Richie is going to be here to keep you from doing dumb shit."

I tried to stop the tears, but when I realized I couldn't, I raced out of Richie's room and into the bedroom I'd called my own for more than a year. I tried to pull myself together, but every time I thought of the way Richie looked, the tears would return. Only a short time before, in that same room, I had drunk myself to sleep when I found out that Randy had died. I thought about how much I missed Randy and how badly I would miss Richie.

About a half hour later, I walked back into his room and asked Richard if there was anything I could do. He said he was fine and asked how I was doing.

"I'm fine," I said. Then I asked, "Does it hurt?"

"I have a little discomfort, but I'm a Coleman, and we come from tough stock," Richie said with a smile.

I smiled back, but I was heartbroken.

IT WAS JULY WHEN I LEARNED of Richie's illness. He told me the doctors had given him a couple of months to live but he wanted to make it until October and his fortieth birthday. I decided I didn't want to miss any of Richie's last days, so I quit my job so I could spend as much time with him as possible. It wasn't like he needed me. Stephanie and his family made sure Richie didn't want for anything, but I would just sit on the edge of his bed and watch television with him and talk whenever he felt like it.

Every time he coughed or had difficulty breathing, I would jump. At that point I was very squeamish and had never really been around anyone so seriously ill.

Surprisingly in a place where death loomed, the Coleman household was like a Fourth of July celebration most times. Many of Richie's friends, nieces, and nephews would come and spend the weekends. There was a lot of cooking, card playing, and laughter during those days. That's the way Richie wanted it.

Richard's illness taught me how short life can be and the importance of friendship. I wanted him to know how much his friendship meant to me, so almost every day I would leave him a card or a letter. The letters were always written on expensive paper, and I would remind Richie of some of the good times we had shared and what I had learned from him. Sometimes I would see tears trickle down Richie's face, and he would ask me to finish reading the letter aloud.

One day after reading one of my letters, Richie looked at me and said, "You know, you write great notes and letters. You should give up this sales bullshit and write a book."

"What kind of book?" I asked.

"You could write about us. Not just me and you, but all the children. You should tell our story," Richard said firmly.

"You think I can do that?"

"Why not?"

"I don't know."

Richard placed his hand on top of mine and looked at me and said, "Promise me you'll think about it."

"I will."

OVER THE NEXT FEW WEEKS, Richie and I replayed the many wonderful moments of our friendships. He thanked me for introducing him to college football and many of my southern ways, and I thanked him for being the big brother I always wanted.

One afternoon when the house was quiet and the two of us were talking and laughing about something in our past, he looked at me and said, "You know, I feel okay about leaving now, because I know you'll be okay. I've seen you grow up so much these last two months, and it makes me proud. I know you're worried about how you're going to make it without me, but you'll be just fine."

I didn't know if I believed Richie, but I did feel as if I had grown through his illness. I realized the world didn't revolve around me and my search for love and self-esteem. I learned that I could face the tough obstacles of seeing someone I loved dying and still maintain my faith in God. I was reminded of the power of family, and the lie that black families were homophobic was dispelled by the love and support every member of Richie's family showed him every day, not because he was dying but because he was their son, husband, brother, uncle, cousin, and friend.

THE FRIDAY BEFORE Richie's birthday, we watched *Dark Victory* with Bette Davis. It was a sad movie I had never seen, but Richie said he had watched it many times. Afterward we watched the pilot of *In Living Color*. Donald Gasden, one of Richie's best friends, was a lawyer for Fox television and had left the tape after one of his visits from the West Coast. We laughed so hard, we would rewind the tape after every sketch. Richie especially liked the "Go On Girl" sketch and the gay film critics.

One Saturday something amazing happened. When I went into Richie's room he wasn't there. His car was gone, and nobody seemed to know where he was. We were all worried, but about an hour later in walked Richie with a smile on his face. Everyone wanted to know where he had been, and his mother fussed at him about getting everybody worried.

Richie told us he had gone to McDonald's because he wanted a hamburger and a Filet-O-Fish sandwich, and he had had his car washed. Then he walked upstairs and back to his bedroom. He told me he wanted to get some rest so that maybe he could dance at the fortieth birthday party Stephanie and his family had planned for him on Sunday evening.

I WENT TO CHURCH Sunday morning and prayed for God to perform a miracle on Richie. Afterward I went to Richie's house, where everybody was either cooking or putting up decorations for Richie's birthday celebration. There were three generations of Colemans there, and many of Richie's close friends. Many, like Donald, had flown into town for the celebration. It was a happy day, almost a combination of Thanksgiving and Christmas in terms of the amount of food prepared.

When the evening ended, I went up to say good-bye to Richie, who had been excited most of the day but now looked exhausted. I sat on the edge of his bed and rubbed the blankets. Richie's once-powerful runner's legs now felt like bones. But I didn't care; I just wanted to be close to him.

"So we made it," Richie said, smiling.

"Yeah, we did. Now let's see about staying around until Christmas. Maybe I'll start that story for you," I said.

"You promise?"

"Yeah, what else do I have to do?"

I kissed Richie on his smooth face and whispered that I loved him. I heard him tell me that he loved me too. When I got to the door of his bedroom, I looked back at him. He smiled and gave me the okay sign, and I returned the gesture.

It was the last time I would see Richard "Richie" Coleman and his wonderful smile. He died the next day, early that Monday morning—peacefully, I am told, in his sleep.

CHAPTER 13

After Richard died, things got worse for me. He had warned me against moving into D.C. because he knew I would continue to allow people to take advantage of my low self-esteem. But a couple of months after his death, and after his family had sold his house and returned to upstate New York, that's exactly what I did.

I leased an apartment in the Northwest section of D.C., within walking distance of the White House. It was a neighborhood of splendor and squalor, a perfect setting for a novel. The three-story walk-up where I lived was brand-new. I was the first resident. The apartment had marble fireplaces in the living and bedroom areas, parquet floors, and a washer and dryer in each unit.

A few doors away was a four-story tenement that had to be among the worst in the District. Some of the windows had screens covering them, some didn't, and many were cracked. People went in and out of the building constantly, and I soon found out one of my neighbors was selling crack. I was told by the leasing agent that the area was "slowly changing," but most of my suspect neighbors didn't seem aware of the change.

Right outside my apartment was a gas station where several homeless men and addicts would offer to put gas in your car or wash windows for a price. I became friendly with a couple of them, and they always made sure my Mercedes was protected when I was in a hurry and parked it on the street.

Later two men, a Harvard-educated lawyer and a Georgetown law student from the West Coast, moved into the building. Both were nice enough, but I didn't spend a lot of time getting to know them, especially after the Georgetown law student wanted to know why I wanted to watch a bunch of fairies when I bumped into him on my way to see the Dance Theater of Harlem at the Kennedy Center. I didn't respond, but I made a mental memo to never get into any deep conversations about sexuality with him.

I became a frequent patron of the Brass Rail, a bar-diner located on Sixth and K. The Brass Rail had strip shows on Friday nights and drag shows on Sundays. The bar attracted all types, from drag queens to professional working men to rough trade, selling their sex for drugs and dollars. The bar was always packed on the weekends, and was the site of a few stabbings and barroom brawls.

I was drinking more than ever. By now my craving was more than a simple thirst for a glass of wine to relax me. It was a penetrating, irrational need to get me from moment to moment. It was amazing that I even got home several nights and wasn't stopped for DWI. Sometimes when I felt the depression returning like a ghost from a Toni Morrison novel, I would take a taxi so I wouldn't have to worry about driving.

There was something different about my drinking in D.C. For the first time I was experiencing blackouts. I didn't consider the Chicago incident when the guy stole my clothes a true blackout, because I remembered some of what happened. I told myself that I had just fallen asleep on a date. Now there were some mornings when I didn't remember the night before. The few friends I had would call me the next day and mention something that had occurred, and I would have no recollection of the event. Once I got upset with a friend because I hadn't heard from him, only to find out that he had broken his leg and I had been there when it happened.

While I lived on N Street there were periods when I would forget vital information. Once, while filling out an application for a check-cashing card, I couldn't remember my Social Security number. I left in embarrassment without completing the application.

The only time I even thought about pulling myself together was the spring of 1990, when my fraternity invited me to be the guest speaker at the annual Founders' Day Program. Butch was the only member of my fraternity whom I kept in contact with, and he had shared with me that he was HIV positive, and encouraged me to accept the invitation, even though he knew I was having a hard time dealing with Richard's and Randy's deaths. He told me there was no way of knowing if this would be our last chance to spend a weekend in Fayetteville. Emotionally I hadn't dealt with the death of my friends, because deep down I expected them to give me some sign to let me know they were safe. There were many nights I sat up in my bedroom in darkness, waiting for Randy or Richie to return and let me know they were okay and offer me some direction.

I began to think that a trip to a place where I had some fond memories would help. Then I felt I might be a big disappointment to my fraternity brothers who expected so much from their former president. What would they think if they knew of my alcohol-induced zombielike existence?

A month before the event, I cut down my drinking substantially to only a couple of glasses of wine a day and started working out at a gym at least two hours each day. When I arrived in Fayetteville, I felt confident. I had updated my résumé; it now stated that I had my own consulting company, which wasn't a total untruth. Several small computer companies had contacted me about representing them in Washington, D.C., but I really hadn't pursued the leads with much vigor.

The weekend of Founders' Day coincided with the first Annual Black Student Reunion at the University of Arkansas, an event designed to bring back black alumni who had never returned to the Fayetteville campus.

It turned out to be a nice weekend. I was able to put on a good front. I embellished my dating life with women, even telling fraternity brothers how I had been close to getting married a couple of times. I envied my fraternity brothers who were married with children, because they seemed to have it all together. Many times during the weekend I would have given anything in the world to change places with them. All I thought about was that they had someone to wake up with each morning and someone to talk with late at night. It was during times like this when I prayed for a magic pill that would render me straight so that I could get married, have children, and never feel lonely.

I was of little support to Butch, who was dealing with his HIV status. Butch, always cheerful like he was leading songs with an Up With People group, told me he was determined to beat the disease and was pursuing his lifelong dream of becoming a lawyer. He had been accepted to the University of Oklahoma Law School and suggested that since my HIV/AIDS tests had come back negative it was a signal from God for me to pursue my dreams as well. I just didn't know what I was supposed to be doing besides drinking and looking for love.

I left Fayetteville that weekend determined to get my act together and make some of my lies become truths. I thought if I didn't owe it to myself, I at least owed it to my family and friends.

My resolve was short-lived. I returned to D.C., and within a week I was drinking even more because I realized there would never be a magic pill to cure my loneliness. I was drinking alone most times, and I never waited until sunset to have my first drink.

I STRUGGLED THROUGH several more months of uncertainty when the shadows of deathlike depression loomed heavy, like a slab of concrete. I locked myself in my apartment and took up permanent residence on my black leather sofa in front of my television, which was usually on mute. I would get up from time to time for another drink, and sometimes brought the bottle near the sofa.

I left my apartment only to get more liquor, and all that I seemed to relate to was the closing time of the local liquor store. I didn't want to have to think about going through the night without a drink.

One Sunday I was gazing at the television, not really paying attention to what was on. I could tell that it was some kind of awards show, from the parade of people going to the podium to accept tiny statues. There wasn't anything unusual about this, because I had loved awards shows since I was a kid. Halfway through the program, a bespectacled, frail-looking white man caught my attention. I think I noticed him because he reminded me of Dr. Willer. I was thinking about the time when he warned me about discontinuing my therapy too soon and how I missed our sessions. He had been one person who I felt could help me, who had helped me.

When they displayed the name of this funny-looking man, I sat up from my prone position and turned up the volume. The name that scrolled across the screen was Michael Jeter. His last name was spelled the same way as my father's. Even though he was white, I felt strangely connected to this man.

Michael Jeter had just won a Tony Award for best featured actor for his role in the musical *The Grand Hotel*. In his acceptance speech I felt as though he were talking directly to me. I don't recall word for word what he said, but the gist of it was about kicking drugs and alcohol. He looked right into the camera and said something like, "I know that there is someone out there tonight battling these demons, and I want to tell you tonight that you can beat them. I'm living proof of that." Tears started to stream down my face. For the first time I realized that alcohol had truly taken control of my life and that I needed help.

I DIDN'T STOP DRINKING, but the actor's face and words never left me. I attempted to call Dr. Willer to see if he could prescribe some type of sleeping pills. I felt that if I had something to help me sleep, then I could stop using alcohol. Since I was blacking out even more during this period, I doubt I would have known if Dr. Willer ever returned my calls.

I was able to get a prescription for sleeping pills from a gay doctor friend I had met at the club Tracks. He warned me that the pills could be dangerous with alcohol. I picked up the pills from the pharmacy, but for days they sat on my bathroom counter. I was still using liquor to put me to sleep.

When I had been in therapy, one of the things Dr. Willer used to tell me all the time was that when depression became too much, try and think of the things that made me happy. I couldn't think of anything. My beloved Razorbacks had one of the top basketball teams in the country, but I wouldn't realize that until much later.

I felt my family and friends could survive without me. I didn't want to share this part of my life when I was so miserable, because I wanted them to remember me in happier times, or when I at least appeared happy.

I knew that being gay and not accepting it was going to destroy me. I was still driving around the dangerous streets of Washington, D.C., looking for companionship, if only for a few hours. Most nights I would come home alone. The couple of times I found takers, they became the new owners of some of my personal items like my leather jacket or part of my CD collection. Looking back, I'm still astounded that I wasn't harmed.

I've heard that people who take pills in suicide attempts really don't want to die, but just want attention. All I know is that taking pills was the only way I knew how to kill myself, since I had never held a real gun in my hands. I wanted to die. I was curious about what was on the other side, and I felt that being there was the only thing that could ease my pain. No matter what I tried to do, I just couldn't bring myself out of my ocean-deep depression.

Nothing mattered. My bank account had dwindled to almost nothing. It didn't matter that my landlord was threatening me with eviction or that the Illinois bank that had financed my Mercedes was looking for the car. In her messages, the bank loan officer reminded me that if I was sick or not working, I had insurance that would cover the monthly payment if I would fill out some forms. I had forgotten about the insurance, and when she sent me the forms via FedEx, I couldn't even fill them out, partly because I still couldn't remember my Social Security number. So my car ended up being repossessed. One day when I went to the parking lot and didn't see the car, I assumed it had been stolen. The police informed me that was not the case, that the bank had taken it back. I really didn't care, and in many ways I was relieved.

I wouldn't need a car in heaven.

I HAD SEEN THIS LOOK BEFORE; it basically said that if you don't start no shit, there won't be none.

I was in a session with a new doctor, whom I had been referred to by another doctor friend after the night of my suicide attempt.

Dr. Dove was a big black man with a stern face that at times looked gentle. During our first session, I told him I didn't think a black straight male doctor could understand why I no longer wanted to live. Briefly, I told him about Ben, Mason, Andre, and Mario, and that being black and gay had become too much for me to bear.

He responded with a deep-voiced presence, speaking in carefully chosen words, using pauses and peering over his glasses to emphasize his seriousness. Dr. Dove told me what doctors had told me before, that there really wasn't a cure for homosexuality. But he also told me something that no other doctor had ever said. Dr. Dove said my depression could be related to a chemical imbalance that could be cured with drugs. I had always assumed that my depression was related to my childhood, failed relationships, and wanting romantic love so desperately.

I started to see Dr. Dove every day, just as I'd done with Dr. Willer, but he refused to give me any drugs until he had completed his evaluation and was certain that I wasn't going to drink again. He threatened to check me into the hospital if I wasn't willing to get my life in order.

I told him how I needed the liquor to sleep. He suggested Alcoholics Anonymous or a possible drug-treatment stay. I told him I had never taken drugs and I couldn't afford rehab. Plus, I didn't want a whole bunch of strangers in my business. I couldn't admit to myself that I might be an alcoholic. I understood that alcoholism was linked to heredity. My mother and grandmother never drank, and since Ben wasn't my biological father his drinking didn't count. I didn't really know about my father. The few times I saw him I couldn't recall him drinking. I was willing to admit that I used alcohol to make myself feel better, knowing full well that when I stopped I would feel dangerously depressed.

My sessions with Dr. Dove were proving to be helpful. He was tough, and that's what I needed. He wasn't willing to let me go on with my drama of the tragic gay man. He made it clear that my life was totally up to me. He was just there to get me started on the journey.

I started looking forward to my daily visits at Howard University Hospital with Dr. Dove. In my mind I was still living in a let-me-make-it-through-the-next-minute-hour-day mode.

I was gaining confidence in Dr. Dove, and he in me. After a physical, it was determined that I was suffering from a chemical imbalance. The news gave me hope. I had cut my drinking down drastically and I had no desire for sex of any kind. Still, I was having trouble sleeping. I left my apartment only for my sessions with Dr. Dove. The ringer on my phone remained off.

Dr. Dove was still not going to give me medication until I stopped drinking. I know I could have told him I had stopped, but I felt this was my last chance and I wanted to start being truthful with myself. One night I got on my knees and prayed like I had never prayed before. It was like I was challenging God. I told Him since He wasn't ready for me but hadn't answered my prayers to change my sexuality, I was going to give Him one more chance. If He was God and so powerful, I wanted Him to take my desire for vodka away because I couldn't do it alone. That was August 27, 1990, and I have not had a drink of hard alcohol since. That experience alone has convinced me of the power of prayer. When I finally looked Dr. Dove in the eyes and told him I wasn't drinking, he gave me the prescription for the drug Trazodone.

I was starting to feel better, even though my surroundings were crumbling. Days away from being evicted, I was depending on public transportation, which made finding a suitable job almost impossible. Still, I felt that I couldn't let anything get in the way of my recovery.

For the first time in my adult life I became aware that I had choices. I always felt that I didn't have a choice in my attraction to men, but I did have a choice when it came to living a life I felt uncomfortable with. There was a huge difference between being gay and living a gay lifestyle. I realized that maybe it was the way I was living my life that was causing me the pain, not my sexuality.

I was also learning to respect the power and pain of depression. In Chicago and New York I had convinced myself that my depression had more to do with Mario than a chemical imbalance. There were times when I had wished for some type of physical ailment that would justify the pain I was feeling in my heart. It seemed impossible to remove the thoughts of hopelessness.

A DAY BEFORE THE SHERIFF showed up to evict me, some of my new friends, Tim Douglas and Bruce Fuller, who had remained my friends despite my depression, helped me pack up my belongings and put them in a storage bin. I had met them at the Rail and later at church. They offered me their pullout sofa. I didn't know Bruce and Tim that well or why they would offer me a place to stay, but I was in no position to question their kindness. During this period it wasn't that I had no friends; I simply kept them at a distance as I did with my family and longtime friends, like Lencola, Robin, Vanessa, and even Troy.

I knew I couldn't spend every moment with Dr. Dove, even though he had mentioned that a hospital stay might not be such a bad idea. I didn't know how to explain depression to Bruce and Tim, or if they would understand my prolonged silences. All I know is that they were doing everything in their power to make me feel at home. I thought briefly about going back to Arkansas or Atlanta, but I felt that with Dr. Dove I was on my way to recovery and I couldn't give that up.

I slowly began to manage my affairs, or what was left of them. The medication seemed to help, and I started to plan for the future. I checked out my insurance policy and learned I still had disability insurance. I was broke except for some money from my mother, Aunt Gee, and a good friend from Chicago, Regina Brown. I didn't realize that I could be getting paid since depression was one of the illnesses covered in my insurance policy.

When I contacted my insurance agent, he assured me everything would be fine and I would get the forms right away. I completed the forms, but a couple of weeks later my agent called me and said my policy had lapsed but he thought there was some type of clause that would cover the period when the automatic transfer I had set up didn't pay. A couple of days later, he called and said they were still trying to deny payment. He told me he thought it was because of the amount of money they would be required to pay and because my doctor could not give them a date as to when I would be able to return to work full-time.

Normally this information would have made my depression grow deeper. I kept Dr. Dove informed as to what was happening, and he assured me he wouldn't stop my treatment. I was worried about how I would pay him, even though he never mentioned costs.

During this time I started to talk with my family on a regular basis and realized how much I had missed them, how much I loved them. It was wonderful to reconnect. I'd had to cut them off during the height of my illness. When I did talk to them on birthdays and holidays, I assured them I was fine but I kept the calls short.

One night while talking with my Uncle Charles, an Atlanta attorney, I mentioned the problems I was having with my insurance policy and how the agent had said the company was trying to get out of paying me. He told me that if my agent had actually said that, it would constitute bad faith on their part and could be grounds for a lawsuit. He asked me if there was any way I could prove he had in fact said that. I told him my new roommates had been there when I had the conversation, but he said that might not be good enough. He suggested I try to get the agent to repeat his statement, and this time have a witness present.

Well, let's just say my uncle is a brilliant lawyer. The next day, I called my agent and brought up our previous conversation. Again, he stated that the company he represented was trying to avoid payment, but this time I recorded the conversation on the answering machine. When I got a rejection letter on my appeal for benefits, I took the letter and tape to the insurance commission.

Two weeks later, a representative of the company flew to Washington, D.C., met me at the Howard Hospital cafeteria, and offered me $25,000 to give up my battle. While I'm certain I could have gotten more, I was concerned about maintaining the progress I was making with Dr. Dove and I didn't want to be tied up in litigation. Besides, I was broke and tired of depending on the kindness of family and friends.

I was feeling a bit better and started to think about returning to work, even though I had burned several of the computer contacts I'd built early in my career.

Still, there were days when it seemed I was powerless over my depression and that no amount of money or therapy would make me feel better. I felt a strong desire to be around family, but I didn't want to go to Little Rock and have my mother worry about me.

Again, that old faith thing happened. I guess God was trying to show me that He *was* hanging around. During my depression I dreamed a lot, but I never remembered them. One night I had a dream about Randy and it was as if he were still alive. There were still several questions concerning his death, questions I one day hoped to pursue.

In the dream, Randy told me to call Carlton, a friend of ours who lived in Lithonia, Georgia. He kept saying Carlton needed me. Randy and I had met Carlton and his identical twin, Calvin, on one of our trips to Atlanta. I'd fallen hard for Carlton. I even asked him to be my date for a birthday party I gave myself at New York's Plaza Hotel. Nothing happened sexually or romantically, but Carlton was so special that we became good friends.

We were friendly, but we didn't talk to each other regularly. I didn't understand why Randy wanted me to call Carlton, but the dream was clear. Call Carlton.

I told Dr. Dove about my dream, and he didn't offer any strong advice either way. A couple of days later, I ran across Carlton's card and called him at work. He was excited to hear from me, and we talked about the new home he'd just built, his job, and new love. It sounded like everything was going great for him. I told him I was great as well. I had this habit of never letting anyone who had rejected me know when things were a little tough.

Just as I was getting ready to hang up, I mentioned my dream and that his twin Calvin was also in it. My impression was that despite the fact that they were identical twins, they had very different personalities. Carlton is one of these organized individuals, always planning, whereas I got the impression that Calvin was sort of a free spirit. Calvin had acknowledged he was gay at a very young age, whereas Carlton's first experience with a man happened in his late twenties.

"How is Calvin?" I asked. For a moment there was silence on the other end of the line, and then Carlton said softly, "Oh, Calvin isn't doing so well."

I had heard the "he's not doing well" comment more times than I wanted to recall. It had become code language for saying someone was sick with AIDS.

"Oh, what's the matter? Is he not working?" It was not only a question, but a secret prayer that Calvin was actually fine.

As I suspected, Carlton told me that Calvin had been ill for a while and had recently moved in with him. I didn't ask what was wrong; I just assumed it was AIDS. I ended my conversation with Carlton by telling him that if there was anything I could do to please call. He thanked me, and we agreed to do a better job of staying in touch.

ARMED WITH MY INSURANCE settlement money, I continued my daily therapy. Dr. Dove still hadn't mentioned money, even though he knew of my settlement. I had now added the gym to my daily schedule but didn't realize I was losing weight until one day Dr. Dove mentioned it. During my depression I had ballooned to 232 pounds, the most I had ever weighed in my life. I knew it had to be the alcohol, since I was never really a big eater. I was currently weighing around 190 pounds. Randy used to tease me about worrying about my weight, especially whenever I would race to the gym and work out for hours after I had felt I had eaten too much. He once joked, "If you were a white lady, they would call you anorexic."

Recalling Randy's wonderful wit made me realize how much I missed him, Willa, and Richard. On days when my depression tried to overwhelm me, one of them would always say something that would cause me to laugh out loud. Now, even though they'd passed away, I got the feeling that maybe they were still with me in a spiritual sense, helping me fight my battles.

DR. DOVE AND I STARTED to discuss the next step in my treatment. I told him that I was afraid that if I went back into sales I might revert to my old ways, which would include drinking. I also knew that going back into sales might mean creating new lies about my background and romantic life and I was getting tired of the lying Lynn.

I'd already passed my first big test of being able to say no to drinking. Dr. Dove had suggested I start hanging out with friends who I was certain were true friends, people who really had my back.

One day my friend Regina from Chicago called and I just opened up and shared what I had been through. Regina had a wonderful ability to put things in perspective. When I told her my doctor had given me some pills and I was certain they were going to make things all right, Regina responded, "What kind of magic pills are they? Are they gonna pay your rent when they put your shit out on the street?"

I laughed so hard that it hurt. When I told Regina they had already put my ass out, she responded by joining in my laughter.

Sensing I needed a trip, Regina, who was working for singer Whitney Houston, invited me to Fort Lee, New Jersey, to spend the weekend at one of Whitney's residences. She told me she was going to be there working on some business and Whitney was going to be out of town. Regina told me not to worry about any money, that she would take care of everything. So with Dr. Dove's blessing, I caught a train to New York.

It was great seeing Regina, and she kept me laughing. We went to a couple of wonderful restaurants where we received the star treatment because the owner knew Regina worked for Whitney. We spent one evening with Whitney's mom, Cissy Houston, and on Sunday we watched football with her father, John.

That's when I was tested. While watching the game, Mr. Houston offered me a glass of wine, which he said cost $500 a bottle. I'd never had a glass from a $500 bottle of wine, but I resisted. Mr. Houston, ever the perfect gentleman, didn't appear offended as he and Regina enjoyed a glass. I had never felt so proud of myself and couldn't wait to get back to D.C. to tell Dr. Dove.

A couple of weeks later, I passed another big test. Mario tried to reenter my life. He was on a serious mission to win me back and even drove to D.C. from New York and paid half the money for a hotel room for us to share.

I didn't tell him what I had been going through, and it was nice to have him chasing me for a change. We had a decent time, although he spent the majority of the weekend begging me for sex, which was a first. I had made a promise to myself to remain sober and celibate until I got myself together. I was under the misguided impression that maybe if I stopped drinking I would lose interest in men, too. I found myself still attracted to Mario, possibly still in love with him, but I'd made a commitment to myself that I planned to honor. I knew that if I allowed him to hurt me again, I'd be left devastated.

I realized that he always sought me out when things were not going well for him and David. So, as with the offer of wine, I said, "No" to Mario. That alone seemed to erase some of the pain my relationship with him had caused.

Around Thanksgiving 1990, I was still making progress but felt I needed to keep looking over my shoulder for the ghost of serious depression. Holidays had always been tough for me. I was thinking of going to Atlanta, having dinner with my family, and deciding on my next step. Deep down I knew it was time to leave D.C. and start a new life someplace else.

I HAD ALWAYS FELT ATLANTA would be the perfect city to settle down in. But since I didn't have any prospects, I didn't know if Atlanta was where I needed to be. Atlanta did have something Washington, D.C., or New York didn't have: family members who I knew loved me and would help me with my recovery.

My Aunt Gee was there, and she had always been the one person I could talk to. I tried not to bother her with a lot of petty things, because she had a husband and four sons. Her kind and gentle spirit always made her the one person I knew would understand me. Aunt Gee had always made me feel special, like I was her son. The great thing about this was that my mom understood and was not threatened by our relationship. As it was during their childhood, Mama and Aunt Gee remain more like best friends than sisters.

In 1990, Atlanta was the new boomtown, and I felt that finding a job wouldn't be hard. Dr. Dove was supportive and told me to check things out and decide after the holidays. If I stayed in

D.C., I would eventually have to find my own apartment, and that would be difficult with the eviction and credit rating.

I spent Christmas in Atlanta with my family, and it turned out to be the medicine I needed. I had a wonderful time. I went out and spent the day with Carlton at his beautiful home. Calvin had died recently, and Carlton seemed to enjoy my company. I shared with him what was really happening with my life. He reminded me of my dream and asked me to be his roommate for a while so we could help each other out during our difficult time.

That night over cheesecake and coffee I talked things out with Aunt Gee. She told me how much she would love having me close by so that she could give me a hug whenever I needed one. I knew that if the depression returned full force, I'd need something I hadn't tried with my previous bouts: one of Aunt Gee's powerful, restorative, and loving hugs every day.

CHAPTER 14

A t the beginning of 1991, I made the Atlanta area my new home. I moved into Carlton's three-bedroom house in Lithonia, about twenty miles from downtown Atlanta. Emotionally, I still felt as fragile as ice on a river in late spring, but for the first time, I was feeling hopeful about summer. I had my faith, family, friends, and medication. I was beginning to feel stronger, and had finally realized I didn't have to fight the battle against self-doubt and depression alone.

I started to send out résumés to several computer sales organizations. I had a few interviews, but now companies were telling me I had too much experience. I guess it was a nice way of saying I'd had too many jobs. During the final interview for a position I was certain I was going to be offered, I started to daydream. I was beginning to realize that cushy sales jobs were a part of my imitation-of-life image—trying to create an image I thought the world would accept. I would always tell prospective employers how I dreamed of being the top salesman in the organization. If it was a dream, it was one filled with rain and occasional thunder. I also knew I could never totally be myself working for such companies.

I had always stayed in sales because of the money I could

earn and because it allowed me to mask my emotional problems and drinking. I thought of the countless times I had woken up with a hangover and simply called my office and said I was at a customer location or preparing to leave for an out-of-town meeting. Many times I could get my customers to cover for me, bribing them with expensive lunches and dinners when I finally got around to visiting their sites.

"So are you going to accept our offer? I know it's less than you're used to making, but the cost of living is lower in Atlanta," the rail-thin sales manager said. His question brought me out of my trance.

"I don't think so," I said boldly, surprising even myself.

"Excuse me? I thought you said you dreamed of being the top salesman here."

"I think it's time for something different," I said. It was time for some new dreams. I needed to listen to my heart more, and then dreams of my own would come.

While in therapy with Dr. Dove, I had once again brought up the idea of writing. When he asked why I didn't pursue it, I told him maybe nobody wanted to read what I wanted to write about. He told me I'd never know unless I tried.

I still had a little money, and Carlton wasn't asking that much for rent. If I managed my money right, I could live for maybe six months without working. I decided that writing was what I wanted to do, but I had to be sure.

I also thought about going back to school. I felt an academic environment would be a safe place for a new start. I looked at Columbia University but didn't think I was ready to go back to New York. Besides, I didn't know how somebody could teach me how to put what I was feeling on paper without the final product being their thoughts and not my own.

Even though I was no longer in therapy, I kept my mind clear by doing things like going to the gym, taking long walks, and having long conversations with Carlton, my Aunt Gee, and my fraternity brother Butch Carroll, who was on a cloud attending law school. He was finally living his dreams. All three were a source of inspiration for me, especially Butch, who was studying for exams with the shadow of AIDS hanging over his head.

I started to go to church regularly with Carlton and his partner, Jerry. One Sunday I ended up sitting next to a cute little boy, whom I imagined to be around eight or nine years old. He was sitting with his very attractive mother, who appeared to be in her late twenties. Every time I would make eye contact with the little boy, he would smile. It was obvious from his constant squirming and animated behavior that church was the last place he wanted to be, and for a moment he reminded me of myself when I was his age.

It must have been the first Sunday of the month, because it seemed like every fifteen minutes an offering or something was being taken, and my funds were getting exhausted. When it came time for the mission offering, which I remembered from my childhood as being a token of silver, I realized that I didn't have any change. The little boy noticed me searching my pockets and coming up empty-handed, and in a gesture that touched me deeply, he took one nickel and one dime from his tiny hand and placed them in mine and gave me a magical smile.

His mother noticed our exchange, and after the service she came up to me and introduced me to her son, Daniel. She then asked me if I was a part of the mentoring program the church had, and I told her I was only visiting. She went on to say that she had never seen Daniel so taken with someone and wondered if I was interested in spending some time with her son. I squatted so that I was eye level with Daniel and asked him if he would like to spend the following Saturday with me, and he very shyly said, "Yes." I exchanged numbers with his mother, who told me her name was Dellaresse Jones. I noticed she was smiling at me just as much as Daniel. It was a smile that warmed me more than the minister's sermon. I wanted to ask where her husband and/or Daniel's father was, or whether it would matter that I was gay, but I didn't.

The next Saturday I rented a car and went to meet Daniel. He lived in the southwest section of Atlanta with his mother, grandmother, and several cousins. When I walked into the medium-size, wood-framed house, it was like walking back in time. The house looked and smelled like my grandmother's. I met Daniel's grandmother and promised to have him back before evening, and the two of us took off.

It was a marvelous day with a special little boy. We played basketball, went to an arcade, and then had lunch at a downtown restaurant. Daniel won my heart with two very innocent actions. When the day started, I gave him twenty dollars to pay for his portion of lunch and some of the games, but I usually ended up putting the quarter in the slot before he had the opportunity.

After lunch we passed a store, and Daniel asked if we could go inside. When I asked him what he wanted, he said he wanted to get a gift for his mother. That touched me deeply, because I remembered how much I loved buying gifts for my mother when I was a little boy. No matter what it was, Mama always loved my gifts. Daniel made his purchase of a piece of costume jewelry, and as we were returning to the car, Daniel grabbed my hands and looked up toward me with his lively brown eyes and asked, "You know what, Lynn?"

"No, what?" I responded.

"I wish I had a daddy like you," he said. I didn't respond, because I was too busy trying to hold back tears.

FROM THAT FIRST SATURDAY, Daniel and his mother became a part of my life and recovery. Daniel and I spent almost every Saturday together, and we sometimes did things during the week. He was a humbling influence in my life, and I considered resuming my job search so that I could do more for Daniel than give him the occasional five dollars, which was a lot of money for me at the time. I realized that I had spent so much time looking for love from all the wrong people, and here was a little boy who saw something good in me. I wanted him to be as proud of me as I was of him.

I was still thinking about school, so I began filling out the extensive application for Columbia University Journalism School. I didn't think I wanted to leave Atlanta, my family, or Daniel, but realized I had to keep all my options available. If I got in, I would consider my acceptance a sign from God. While completing the application I came to a portion where I had to write about myself. I started to think about the fascinating, though sometimes pitiful, life I had led.

I couldn't help but notice how I enjoyed putting it on paper. I started to think about what Richard had said about my writing, and I thought maybe he had a point. Just as quickly as I decided I might write about my life, I started to question who would be interested in reading a story about a sexually confused black man who had basically wasted every opportunity given to him. There was no reason for me to believe that I could write a novel. I had never written a short story or even a poem.

About a week after I had finished the application and a make-believe version of my life, I was watching *Oprah Winfrey*. The show was about closeted bisexual men. Everyone on the panel was white with the exception of one black guy who was the stereotypical fierce, finger-snapping queen. After the show, several of my closest gay friends called to talk about it and how women didn't have a clue when it came to spotting closeted gay men. They had a point. When I looked through my old phone books over the last decade, I came up with more than fifty men I knew who didn't look or act gay. The same evening, I read an article in *Jet* magazine stating that minority women were the fastest-growing segment of the population infected with HIV.

I thought about all my close female friends, like Vanessa, Regina, Deborah, Lencola, Cindy, and Robin, and wondered if any of them had dated bisexual men or ever found out about their secret lives. I began to think about how I would feel if I started to lose my female friends like I had lost my male ones. These women had stuck by me through all my depression drama and the deaths of Willa, Randy, Larry, and Richard. Even when I had tried to shut these female friends out of my life, I knew they were there if I needed to talk.

Since I had always gotten along with women, I was beginning to realize that I had taken these important relationships for granted. So many times when I was in one of my love hangovers, I would separate myself from them as I did with my family, even though they had never given me any indication that my sexuality mattered. As Robin once told me, "Harris, you're the only one who makes it an issue."

A few days later, watching *Oprah* once again, I was finally motivated to take a chance and follow my dream. I had spent so much of my life following what I have come to know as my rain dreams: the ones that I could hear, those I thought the world wanted for me, like being married and successful in my career. I remembered how I wasn't all that impressed with taking a job with IBM until I heard the sound of awe from my classmates. I finally realized that up until this point in my life everything I'd pursued was in order to impress others so they might love me more.

But this dream of writing was becoming powerful and silent, like snow. It was one of the few times that I listened to myself without worrying about what others would think. I saw that just like snow, writing could provide me comfort, but I felt if I shared my dream with a lot of people they might bring on the rain, washing away this wonderful new vision of my life. I had to be careful who I shared my dream with.

That evening I asked Carlton to drive me to the store and I bought a desktop computer. When I came home, Carlton allowed me to set it up in his office and then I went upstairs to my bedroom, got on my knees, and prayed. I asked God to guide and direct me on what to do. I prayed that if it was His will, He would give me the words and courage to write, to tell the story of people like Richard, Randy, Willa, Larry, and myself and make people realize that being gay wasn't about just sex, but about love. I went back downstairs and turned on my computer and began to write the words I was hearing inside my heart and head.

I ORIGINALLY SET OUT TO WRITE a story for me, because I realized I might be the only one who would read it. I wanted to write a story that would capture the pain and joy of being black and gay. I wanted it to be a love story, because the one problem I had with admitting that I was gay was that I had to give up having true love like in the movies.

Every author, I think, takes a little bit from his or her life in their first novel. I started my book with something from my own life, at a time when I thought I was happy. This took me back to Fayetteville with Mason, but in my novel, it became a college town in Alabama. I didn't want anyone confusing this as my life story, and I figured the University of Alabama at Tuscaloosa and the U of A had a lot in common.

Since my dream of being a writer was coming in the form of images of snow, my first scene was a beautiful winter night when the main character, Raymond, and his lover, Kelvin, meet and frolic in the snow after Christmas break. In real life, a situation like this had happened with Mason and me after the fall semester.

We had both returned to Fayetteville early so we could spend some time alone. There was a snowstorm, and when I had to pick him up, my car got stuck. We were so anxious to see each other that we both agreed to walk and ended up embracing and kissing on a snow-covered Fayetteville street. I had to be in love to take such chances in Fayetteville. If anybody had seen us, we would have spent our college days somewhere else. We ended the romantic night eating popcorn, drinking beer, and watching the movie *Sparkle* on cable. We spent the night sleeping in each other's arms, listening over and over to LTD's "Love Ballad." For years I couldn't hear that song without my thoughts going back to that night, recalling Mason's scent and touch like it was yesterday.

I wanted my story to be one where women, if they decided to read it, would think about the choices they made when it came to men. I wanted my heroine to be a beautiful black woman with a beauty pageant background and southern naïveté, and thus Nicole was created. I wanted the lead male character to be so handsome that whenever he walked into a room, both men (even hopelessly heterosexual ones) and women would take note. I named him Courtney but soon changed it because I thought Courtney sounded feminine, and I wanted a more powerful, black-sounding name, so Courtney became Raymond.

After my first night at the computer, I found myself looking forward to the next day when I could return to my new friends. I was amazed at how these characters, which now included Sela, were coming to life in my head.

When I had about thirty pages, I started to share them with Carlton, Lencola, and Tim, whom I kept in touch with and who had become like a little brother to me. They all loved what I read them, but they were close friends and were just happy to see me happy. I needed a second opinion.

I had become friendly with Dellanor Young, a lady who owned a travel agency near Carlton's house, when I had walked into her agency to buy a ticket to Washington, D.C., for a visit and update with Dr. Dove.

I learned that Dellanor loved to read, and when I told her I was writing a love story with a twist, she offered to give me an honest opinion of my work. I told her all my friends loved it and she responded, "They're your friends—what else are they going to tell you? You need to get somebody to be honest with you." So even though I was nervous, I gave Dellanor the first two chapters of my novel and she promised me she would read my work that evening.

The next day, I rushed over to see what Dellanor thought. She looked at me and shook her head, saying, "This needs some work." I was disappointed and asked her what she meant. She had all these questions about Raymond and his motivations. Every question she asked me I knew the answer to, and she told me that was great but it wasn't showing up on the page. When I asked her what I should do, Dellanor looked at me and said, "You have to become Raymond." When I asked how, she said, "Just become him and tell his story."

I destroyed all the pages I had written in the third person and began my novel over. I became Raymond Winston Tyler Jr., and the words came like water from a river. It was easy to just flip the switch and give Raymond the life I had often dreamed for myself. I had heard that Mason had gotten married, and I wondered what would happen if I ever bumped into him and his new wife. I had heard countless stories of gay and bisexual men marrying and actually having former lovers in their wedding parties. I thought of some of these women and created Candance, who was smart and beautiful, but clueless when it came to men and the secrets they protected with their life.

Over the next few months, I became obsessed with writing. I stopped looking for work, even though I was pretty close to being broke again. I was getting support from Carlton, Aunt

Gee, and my mom. Dellanor was now serving as my unofficial editor, and I knew I was onto something, because she would call me early in the morning and ask for new pages to find out what was happening.

The only thing I was doing besides writing was spending time with Daniel and praying. When I had access to a car, I found myself spending hours in bookstores looking at novels and reading books about publishing. I finally saved enough money for a book that listed all of the New York publishers and agents and what was needed to get a novel published. I was almost finished with the first draft of my novel, and I was letting women whom I didn't know read it, and their responses were encouraging. During these days my depression was a storm that now seemed far away.

June came and as I edited my novel, Deborah Crable from Chicago asked me to help out with a program she had started called the Ovation Arts Council. The two-week program held at Georgia Tech University was Deborah's brainchild. She took disadvantaged minority students with C averages and encouraged them to reach a little higher. Deborah asked me to come in as head counselor for the forty teenagers from hell, as she and I affectionately called them.

I was glad Deborah asked me to help out, because I learned that when you spend time worrying about the well-being of others, you are left with very little time to fret about your own problems. During the camp, Deborah had a chance to appear in a movie back in Chicago, and the day-to-day operation of the enrichment camp fell to me. Suddenly my major concern was keeping sex-starved teenagers separated at night, but as I sat guarding the dorm floors I would think and edit my characters in the early hours of the morning. I was burning the candle at both ends, but had never felt so energized. After the camp was over, I returned to my novel feeling better about myself and my future.

At the end of July, I had completed the second draft about a young black man from the South who during the course of the novel falls in love with two women and two men. I was now spending my days and nights at Kinko's, making copies and sending my novel, *Invisible Life*, to New York publishers. I also sent a copy to Janis Lunon, a friend from college who owned the only black newspaper in Arkansas, *The State Press*.

Weeks later, I got the manuscript back from Janis with an encouraging cover letter, but when I opened the manuscript I saw red everywhere. Janis had circled the errors and scrawled down questions she had. I became angry when I realized that I had sent this error-filled novel to so many New York publishers. But the errors and Janis's questions were important.

I spent the next week correcting the errors and answering the questions, and sent the manuscript back to Janis and to my good friend from my New York days, Tracey Nash-Huntley, who was now married and living in Dallas. She had called to see what I was up to, and when I told her about the novel she offered to read it. I had forgotten when I sent the novel to Tracey that I had never been honest with her regarding my life; I assumed she still thought I was straight.

When she called me back a week later, I could hear the shock in her voice. Tracey kept repeating, "Lynn, I didn't know. I didn't know." I told Tracey this wasn't my life story, but the manuscript did give me the chance to tell Tracey the truth. I realized she was one of those people in my life whom I really loved, but I had told her nothing but lies about my life. Tracey assumed not only that I was straight but that I had come from a middle-class family; thus, it was very easy for her to believe that I was Raymond. My main character's background was another decision I had made early on. I didn't think anyone wanted to read about someone who was poor, black, and gay.

During my conversation with Tracey about my book, I

shared some things I hadn't even admitted to myself. I still wanted to be straight. I told her that at her wedding in 1988, I had been in tears for reasons other than her happiness.

Tracey and her husband, David, had one of the most beautiful weddings I had ever attended. It was in the middle of the summer at a stately old church in St. Louis, Missouri. I was fine when I arrived for the wedding weekend, because I had the chance to see a lot of people I'd known in New York. When I saw Tracey walking down the aisle as a beautiful bride, I started crying dime-sized tears. At that moment I realized that I would never experience what David and Tracey were sharing, and it made me terribly sad. I also admitted to Tracey how I never understood why she wanted me as a friend.

I confessed that I envied her for being the daughter of well-respected parents in St. Louis. I felt that if she really knew who I was, she and David would not have wanted me at their wedding, let alone counted me among their close friends. Tracey was very sympathetic about my feelings and told me she wished I had shared them with her sooner. She told me she and David loved me for me, because I was a kind and gentle person, not because of my sexuality and family background. Conversations like this helped me on my road to accepting myself and gave me encouragement to write with honesty. It eased the letting go of my rain dreams, like getting married and being totally straight, and allowed me to see that if I wanted love in my life I had better listen more carefully to what I called my silent, more truthful snow dreams.

WRITING AND GETTING MY NOVEL published became my new therapy. My characters became my new friends. I was taking my medication and praying daily, and I remained sober and celibate. The few times I went to gay bars in Atlanta, it was okay for me to come home alone, because I had my novel. When people asked me what I did for a living, I said I was a writer. When they asked me what I had written, I told them I was finishing up my first novel and very soon they would hear more about me. I had never felt so self-confident about my future.

The confidence didn't disappear by late September, when I had a stack of rejection letters almost as big as my novel. I had been rejected by a slew of literary agents, and a lawyer friend who had agreed to help me find a publisher was no longer returning my calls.

Amid all the rejections, there was some encouragement. I sent my manuscript to an agent at the William Morris Agency. I got the agent's name after reading the acknowledgments in Tina McElroy Ansa's first novel, *Baby of the Family*. I figured any agent who received mention in an author's acknowledgment had to be good. About a month after sending my novel to the agent, I received another rejection letter stating that she wasn't taking on any additional clients but she had been impressed with my novel. I picked up my phone and called the agent to see if she really thought my story had potential. Of course, she wasn't taking calls, but when her secretary asked me what I wanted, I told her about the letter I had received. She asked my name, and when I told her, the secretary said, "Oh, I remember you. I read your manuscript, and I think it's really good."

"You do?" I asked eagerly.

"Yes. Don't give up. You'll find someone to represent you soon."

I hung up the phone excited about what the secretary had said. I was getting emotional and financial support from family and friends. The mere fact that they didn't look at me like I was crazy when I said I was writing a book about gay and bisexual men was support enough. My mother came to my rescue again, by adding me to her Visa account so I could rent cars when I needed to. My Aunt Gee started putting checks and money in my hand when I would hug her good-bye after my weekly visits, just like my grandmother used to do when I was a little boy. Carlton told me not to worry about rent or helping with the food. He hadn't read any of the novel since those first destroyed pages. He simply said that if writing was making me happy, then he wanted to do anything he could to help. So many family and friends protected my snow dream.

One day, while waiting in line at Kinko's after printing copies of the third revised draft of my manuscript, I noticed a book titled *How to Self-Publish*. I picked up the book and began reading it. When it came time for me to pay for my copies, a young black lady with whom I had become friendly was working the cash register and asked if I was purchasing the book. I looked at the price and realized I didn't have enough. She looked at me, winked, and smiled as she slid the book in with my copies. There it was—another dream protector, another sign.

I spent the following days reading up on how to publish your own book. After finishing the book, I decided that if the New York publishers, who were still rejecting the revised drafts, didn't think my book was good enough to publish, then I would do it myself. From my marketing background I knew that sales got people's attention and remembered something a manager had once told me: "Nothing happens until something is sold."

I was still getting positive feedback from regular, everyday people who loved to read, and I felt I had to get my novel to the public and let them decide. In the back of my head I knew that if I took the multitudes of nos as a final answer, the shadows of my depression might appear. For the first time in a long while, I wasn't feeling sorry for myself about not having love in my life, and I had something to look forward to every day. I was working harder than I had ever worked in my life. I knew I had to keep moving and stay focused on my dream.

CHAPTER 15

With my novel revised and completed, I became a one-man publishing company at the end of October 1991. I didn't like rejection as a salesman, and I didn't like it as a writer. I was warned that the publishing industry didn't look kindly upon self-published authors, but I couldn't wait until some editor in New York discovered my novel. I would have to take a chance.

I was beginning to believe that the novel would have an impact not only on my life but on my family and other families like mine. One night while talking to my Aunt Gee, I mentioned that I was becoming comfortable with spending my life alone since I was gay. As I have said before, my aunt has always been supportive of me, no matter what. But during this talk, she said something that hurt me deeply.

"Baby, if I had raised you, I don't think you would have been gay."

A chill went through my body, and after a few moments of silence I said, "No, Aunt Gee, you're wrong. I might have learned to love myself sooner, but I still would have been gay."

I knew she didn't mean any harm, nor did she understand that she was implying that my being gay was a product of my environment. This is a very common misconception, even today.

My mother didn't raise me to be gay. Nothing she ever did, including divorcing Ben and never remarrying, had anything to do with my sexuality. In fact, my mother went out of her way to make sure I had positive male role models like my uncles, and even though she would have loved for me to be home over the holidays, she always let me spend Christmas with Aunt Gee and Uncle Charles and my male cousins. I was lucky to live in a family where I was never molested by uncles or male cousins who were older and bigger. I told my aunt that she didn't understand what being gay was about and that I couldn't wait until my novel was published so it could help people understand that being gay was as much about being attracted to the same sex as it was about my spirit and soul.

"Maybe I should read your novel now," my aunt said as we prepared to say good night.

It was the first time since I had begun writing the novel that it dawned on me what the book might mean to my family. Would they be humiliated, or would they be embarrassed? Aunt Gee was really the only one who knew what the novel was about. I suddenly considered the advice of a closeted media friend who had advised that I write under a pen name. Initially I laughed at his recommendation, but suddenly make-believe names floated through my head. When I got into bed, and despite my medication, I endured a restless night. I had visions of faceless people laughing and pointing at me while they chanted, "Silly, nigger faggot." A thin film of sweat formed around my neck, and I felt both angry and afraid.

The next day, I delivered a copy of my novel to my aunt. A couple of days later, just before midnight, I got a call from her. This was very strange, because for as long as I could remember my aunt was always in bed by ten, unless you count the holidays when she was up late preparing meals.

When I made sure everything was all right with Uncle

Charles and my cousins, I asked why she was calling me so late, and she said something that warmed my heart.

"Baby, I just finished your novel, and it's beautiful. Will you please forgive me for what I said the other day? Now I finally understand what you were trying to tell me," Aunt Gee said. Through my tears I told her that of course I could forgive her and thanked her for calling. That night when I went to bed, I knew nothing was going to stop me from publishing my book.

The following week, I started contacting printing companies and getting price quotes on what it would cost to produce my book. It didn't matter that I didn't have the money to even print a book proposal.

Greg, one of the local salesmen from a printing company I had contacted in Nashville, called me to make sure I had gotten his price quote. We talked about what I was trying to do, and he suggested we talk over lunch.

In a heartbeat I went back into IBM mode. I put on my best blue suit, white shirt, and red power tie and met the young white salesman at the Colony Square Sheraton. I was as confident as a seasoned politician as I laid out my plans for my novel. I explained to Greg how my novel, though controversial, would be a big seller, basically because one like it had never been written. Greg was impressed, and even though he made it clear that he had little interest in my novel's content, he thought we could do business. He suggested I form a company, submit a credit application, and see what happened.

Since my credit was as bad as milk left out in the sun, I felt my neck stiffen and began to think about how I was going to raise the money to get my novel printed. I got more encouragement from Carlton and Dellanor and came up with the name Consortium Press. A couple of days later, I rented a closet-size office on Peachtree with a loan from my aunt and cousin Kennie and submitted my application to Nicolstone Printers.

A few days later, another prayer was answered when one of the first calls I received in my new office was from Debbye, an employee at Nicolstone. She told me she was going to approve my application despite the fact that she couldn't find any credit references for Consortium Press. Another dream maker, another sign.

THE EMPLOYEES AT Nicolstone Printers in Nashville, Tennessee, treated me like I was their biggest customer on my trips to review the page proofs and the color separations for my beautiful cover, which was designed free of charge by Deborah Roberts of Austin, Texas, a wonderful artist who had assisted me with the Ovation Arts Council program.

Nicolstone rushed production so that I could get my 5,500 books before December 10. I originally wanted to print only 1,000 books, but the salesman convinced me it made more business sense to go with the larger press run. I hoped to get the books into local bookstores before the holiday shopping season, and thought it would be the perfect way to celebrate my first year in Atlanta. It didn't matter that I had zero commitments from bookstores. A couple of the stores I had talked to explained what an important commodity shelf space was during the holidays and couldn't offer much hope that they could stock my book.

Yet it seemed that every time an obstacle would appear, a dream angel would magically move it away. I wanted to kick off my career as a writer in my hometown of Little Rock in front of my family. After reading the corrected proofs of *Invisible Life*, my friend Janis offered to have her newspaper host a reception in my honor. She also got a local minority AIDS organization to cosponsor the event.

In my excitement about the publication I hadn't given much thought to how my family in Little Rock would feel about my

first work, especially when even I felt a little uncomfortable reading some of the content aloud as I practiced in front of a mirror.
I still hadn't had a conversation about my sexuality with my
mother, although like most mothers of gay children I was sure
she knew not to expect a lot of grandkids from me. I called my
aunt and asked for her advice, and she said I should at least tell
my mother what the book was about. When I expressed my
apprehension, my aunt agreed to help. I didn't think I could take
being rejected by my family or my hometown. I was prepared to
point out that the novel was not a picture of my life but just my
imagination in overdrive.

I don't know what my aunt said to my mother, but whatever
it was it worked, because when I called my mother, she seemed
excited about my coming home and my book. Her being happy
that I was coming home wasn't something new, but she actually
mentioned the book. She told me that my grandmother, sisters,
uncles, and cousins were excited also.

Two days before the Little Rock reception I received a call
informing me that the books wouldn't be ready in time. When I
told the customer service rep about the reception and how it was
too late to cancel, she promised to have ten copies waiting at my
hotel. At least I would be able to read and show the book.

I was really nervous when I entered the reception area of the
Legacy Hotel. A few minutes before I came downstairs, my
cousin Jackie came up and wished me luck, and she, Dellanor,
who had flown in from Atlanta, and I formed a circle and prayed.

When I walked into the room, I noticed that the crowd was
smaller than I had hoped for, but about fifty people were there,
including more than twenty-five of my relatives and a few childhood friends. I had told Dellanor before we left Atlanta that I
hoped more than a hundred people would show up since Janis
had sent out more than two hundred invitations. But there was a
proclamation and a personal note of congratulations from then

Governor Bill Clinton, presented by one of his top black aides. Lencola had flown in from New York to introduce me and offer moral support. Though it had been more than ten years since Lencola had been Miss Arkansas, she was still as popular as ever in the state.

The reception was great. I started off by saying that if nothing else, writing the book afforded me the opportunity to publicly thank my mother and grandmother for all their love and support. Being able to express my love and thanks was something I had dreamed of doing since I was a little boy. The only way I had been able to tell them how much I loved them in years past was in cards or letters. I thought about what my mother and grandmother had done for me, and I felt tears forming in my eyes, but I blinked them back.

It was smooth from that point on. I read the first chapter of the book, and no one booed or threw anything. In fact, the applause at the end was warm and supportive. My mother and grandmother were the first people in line to congratulate me and tell me once again how proud they were of me and how much they loved me. There was no mention of the book's content or what I had said in my talk about how writing the book was forcing me to deal with my own truths.

In many ways, it was in that hotel reception room, in front of my family, that I took a huge step in dealing with my reality, even though I didn't say, "I'm a black, gay man." I was just beginning to say it to myself and be okay with that.

Looking into my mother's eyes, I recalled what she had once told me when I had called her, drunk out of my mind, crying about how sorry I was about not being married and making her proud. She told me I was her baby and she loved me no matter what. My mother's love was unconditional, but it had taken me most of my life to understand what that meant.

Before I left Little Rock, I had my first taped radio interview and got about thirty people to pay $12.95 for a book I promised to send once the finished product arrived in Atlanta. I left Little Rock feeling like home was always a place where love and support could be found in ample supply.

I was now ready to face the rest of the world.

I BEGAN PLANNING for my Atlanta debut, where I was assured that my books would be available. One of my fraternity brothers and Carlton's partner, Jerry Jackson, along with Carlton, had agreed to sponsor my Atlanta party, and they sent more than two hundred invitations for a Sunday-afternoon signing the week before Christmas.

Late Friday evening, I was sitting in my empty office awaiting the arrival of my books. When a gruffy-looking trucker knocked on my office door, he told me he had to collect twelve hundred dollars for shipping freight before he could start to unload the books. I didn't have twelve hundred dollars, and I didn't know what to do, so I went down to Dellanor's office, which was in the same building, and once again sought advice. She thought about writing a check from her business, but she knew I wouldn't be able to pay her back and that her business partner might get upset. We spent about fifteen minutes thinking of people I could borrow the money from. Every time we thought of someone, I would realize they had already done something for me and I didn't want to seem greedy. It was almost six o'clock, and everything was getting ready to close, when Dellanor pointed out that Nashville was an hour behind Atlanta time. She suggested I call the printer to see if I could get someone there to help me.

I called Nicolstone and located someone in accounts payable who didn't know me from the man in the moon. I explained my problem and how important this was, my voice cracking and almost pleading that she help me out. There was silence on the phone for what seemed like a minute, and then she asked to speak with the driver. I went outside and got him. When he got on the phone, I couldn't tell from his expression what was going on. All I know is that he hung up the phone and started moving the books into my office.

I was ready for my close-up in my literary birthplace.

SUNDAY CAME, AND I WAS full of nervous anticipation. Several friends chipped in so that I could have a suite at the hotel where the book signing was being held. I got there about noon to dress and make sure everything was in place. Tim Douglass, my "little brother," had come down for moral support, and another close friend, Ken Hatten, flew in from Dallas with several beautiful sports jackets for me to choose from. I ended up wearing a beautiful cobalt-blue wool jacket that Tim had brought to wear himself. It looked nice with my black slacks and beige pullover. It seemed like it had been years since I had money to purchase anything new.

Paul Dedman, a tall and extremely handsome ex–pro basketball player I had met coming out of a Federal Express office, also came early to see if he could do anything to help. Paul was straight and ended up being the hit of the party. There were so many people, men and women, who wanted to know who Paul was. He didn't seem interested in meeting his new admirers, telling me he was there only to support me.

The one-bedroom suite was full of hope and love. I had another circle of prayer and I went into the reception and was greeted by more than one hundred people. Some were familiar faces, some not.

My reading and talk about why I wrote the book went smoothly. There was one very touching moment when I acknowledged little Daniel, who had been understanding when I cut down on our visits to write and learn about publishing. We still saw each other often, and I called him almost every day to see how school was going. When I thanked Daniel for bringing a new type of love into my life, this tough little man-child broke into tears and buried his face in my chest. It took everything I had to hold it together as his mother and I gently massaged his close-cut head.

After the party, Dellanor and I learned that we had sold forty-three books. I had hoped to sell at least one hundred, but I felt the party had been a success. Back in the suite, several well-wishers came up for wine and snacks, and many of them had already started reading the novel and were telling me how good it was. I was focused on staying sober and celibate and really felt happy and proud—something I hadn't experienced in a long time.

The next week, armed with my letter from a future president of the United States and copies of my book, I returned to several local bookstores. Christmas was approaching, but I found very few bookstore managers in a holiday mood and I was still facing rejection. One store, Oxford, which at the time was the largest independent bookstore in the South, did agree to take ten books on consignment. This meant they wouldn't pay me until they had sold the books.

I was starting to feel the pressure as I thought of the 5,000-plus books in an office space I could barely pay for even though the rent was under three hundred dollars. Still, even in my worried state, some good things were happening. Many of the forty-three people who had purchased the book were calling trying to get additional copies. I was driving all over the metropolitan Atlanta area, delivering books from the trunk of Dellanor's maroon Toyota.

One of the guests, an Atlanta hairstylist, K-Lavell Grayson, who actually crashed the party, called and asked if I could bring ten books to his midtown salon. He was convinced he could sell them. K-Lavell's call and kindness would play an important role in the future marketing of my novel.

As the year was coming to an end, I had sold only 117 books, including the ten at Oxford, which had placed an order for fifteen more. There were no calls from any of the magazines and radio shows to whom I had sent complimentary copies, and I was beginning to feel I had made a terrible mistake by self-publishing. A few days before the New Year, I walked around the grounds of Carlton's home, gazing at the golf course that was right behind his house. There was a hammock that I had swung in many times during the summer months, and it still looked inviting on this cold and gray December day.

I climbed into the hammock, and after a few minutes I started talking to God in a voice barely above a whisper. I told Him that I felt writing was what He wanted me to do but that I needed a sign. I basically wanted to make a deal with Him. I said to God and myself that if I sold more than two hundred books before the beginning of the year, I would pursue my new career with such vigor and passion it would make Him proud.

After I prayed and made my deal with God, I was still nervous about ways to get rid of the books, even if it meant passing them out on street corners. All the calls I received from people whom I had met at the Atlanta book party were positive, and I told myself that by publishing a book I had accomplished what I had set out to do. I had accomplished a big goal, and now I knew I could do anything if I put my heart and mind to it.

On December 29, 1991, I got an answer to my prayer in the form of a phone call. I was downstairs in the kitchen, drinking coffee, when Carlton yelled that I had a long-distance call. For some strange reason, I raced upstairs to Carlton's room rather than take the call on the wall phone in the kitchen. I was hoping maybe it was a magazine or radio station wanting to do an interview, something that might provide me a reason to renegotiate my deal with God. When I answered the phone, the caller told me his name was Dr. Henry Masters and he had met me briefly at my signing in Little Rock. I recalled the olive-brown man who had come in late as we were packing up. I had a couple copies of the novel left over from my ration of ten, and I gave him one since there was no one around. Dr. Masters apologized again for being late but went on to say how much he had enjoyed my novel.

Then my life changed. Dr. Masters explained that he was responsible for AIDS education at a clinic in Pine Bluff, Arkansas, and he thought my book could be a powerful tool in educating the African American community about AIDS. He went on to say that he had discovered he had some extra money in his budget that he would lose if he didn't spend it before the year's end. Then he asked me if there was any possible way for me to ship and bill him for one hundred copies of *Invisible Life* before noon the following day.

A chill came over my body that had nothing to do with the winter cold. For a few seconds, I was speechless. A huge smile broke out on my face, and I started jumping up and down. Carlton started smiling without even knowing why I was so excited.

I told Dr. Masters that I would get him the books quicker than he could finish an Arkansas hog call. I hung up the phone and shared my news with Carlton and breathed a huge sigh. I went into my bedroom and got on my knees and gave a prayer of thanks to God for His sign. I pulled out my little black book where I was keeping track of sales and determined that with Dr. Masters's order my grand total was now 233 books sold.

I borrowed Carlton's car and quickly drove to my office and picked up the books and shipped them via Federal Express that evening. I went back to my office to prepare an invoice to fax to Dr. Masters.

As I was leaving my silent office, I noticed that the soothing winter dusk was draping the city. It felt like snow was coming. I thought of all the people who had made my dream possible and I thought of my "angels"—Richard, Randy, Larry, and Willa— and how proud they would be. How proud they were. Then I looked at the boxes of books lining the walls. As I closed my office for the last time in 1991, I had a vision, or as Randy would say, "I visualized." For the first time since the books had been stored there, I imagined my office the way it had looked when I first signed the lease. I pictured it empty. Before July of 1992, it was.

EPILOGUE

Weeks before Richie died, he gave me some important advice: "Spend some time alone, Lynn," he said. "You might be surprised by how much you'll learn to like yourself."

Richie's suggestion at the time seemed impossible. My entire life I'd always wanted to lead any life other than my own. Why would I want to spend time with me? Yet when I became a writer, I joined one of the most solitary occupations in the world. As it turned out, I'd picked a profession that would allow me no other choice than to spend many days and evenings alone.

IT'S EARLY SPRING 2003, and I've spent the bulk of the winter in New York City writing the final chapters of this book, which has been a part of the last seven years of my life. And since snow and what it represents has always been so important to me, it's fascinating to note that many of those days were marked by record snowfall.

It was difficult at times to write my memoir, as I was forced to relive the tragic parts of my life. There were moments in my youth that I didn't include here because I didn't want this to be a "woe is me" memoir. At other times, I was afraid this book might jolt me back into a depression or that maybe some of my family members and friends would not want their lives shared with the world. Late at night I would worry that my fans, who always seem to be waiting for my next novel, would be disappointed to read about *my* life instead of the lives of Raymond Tyler and Basil Henderson.

So I decided to take a break and clear my head before I tackled the epilogue. I took a trip to Houston, Texas, to visit one of my best friends, Vanessa Gilmore, and her son, Sean, who happens to be my godson. Vanessa is now a federal judge and a single mom, and I was honored and thrilled when she asked me to be Sean's godfather. I take my godfather duties very seriously, so I visit Sean and Vanessa as often as possible.

The evening I arrived, Vanessa told me that she'd run into my good friend Tracey Nash-Huntley at church the previous day. Tracey and I have been out of contact for a couple of years because of my writing and touring schedules and her busy life as a wife and mother. We've kept in contact through mutual friends, though, and whenever I show up in her hometown of St. Louis, a member of her family, one of her sisters, or her mother shows up to get a book signed and give me an update on Tracey, her husband, David, and their boys, Porter and Calhoun.

On a lovely Monday evening, Vanessa, Sean, and my assistant, Anthony Bell, arrive at the Huntleys' for dinner. I'm anxious to catch up with my friends and show them the cover of the memoir, something I am quite proud of.

Their house, a sprawling brick home with a well-manicured yard, looks like the perfect fortress for the TV Huxtables if they lived in Houston, and I mean that in a good way. When Tracey greets us she looks even more beautiful than when she was a New York model many years before; motherhood and married life obviously agree with her. I can't believe that she and David have been married for more than sixteen years, and when I walked into their foyer I could immediately feel that the house is filled with love. Porter and Calhoun have grown into handsome and courteous young men, and I was very moved when they invited Sean, who is still a toddler, upstairs to their room to play.

Over a dinner we talk and laugh about old times. It seems like only yesterday when we'd done the same thing in their Dallas home. Just as we are finishing the first course, David, Tracey's husband, comes home. David and I had met when he was an intern at IBM and while he was serving as President of the Student Body at SMU. I knew when I met him he would be successful at whatever he pursued, and David has not disappointed. We hug and talk about our tennis game, and then David suddenly spots the cover of the memoir. He reads the title of my memoir and says, "This sounds so sad."

I know David is concerned because he has been privy to the hard times in my life, but I look at him and say proudly and truthfully, "Oh, David, but it's not. This story has a happy ending."

And it does.

When I wrote *Invisible Life*, I thought I'd written it for me, but several days earlier as I talked to my editor, Janet Hill, she suggested that maybe my dream of writing was connected to someone else's; that maybe someone was waiting for me to write my book so that their life could be changed. Janet had learned about this idea in a Bible study group, and even though it sounded a little unusual at first, maybe there was some truth in it. I started to think that nearly ten years after writing *Invisible Life*, maybe what Janet said was true. I'd followed my dream and had the courage to write *Invisible Life*, a story that no one had yet dared write in the early 1990s. Maybe lives had been enriched and hearts transformed. At the time, I didn't view writing *Invisible Life* as an act of courage, but rather as a way to escape a place of deep, deep pain.

But in the aftermath of *Invisible Life* and my seven other novels, nothing has changed more than my own life. By truly embracing the three F's I've never been ashamed of—my faith, my family, and my friends—today I'm thriving in a world that over a decade ago I didn't want to be a part of.

I have remained prayerful and thankful throughout my journey. I pray before I start each book, before I get on a plane to go to an engagement, and before I stand at the podium. During the early years of my career as a writer, I gave up things I once thought I needed like liquor and sex, so that I could follow my dream and one day look myself in the mirror and smile like that little boy on the front of this book.

When I started writing, I never imagined that I'd eventually sell over three million copies of my books. Or that my name would repeatedly appear among the nation's top authors as I took my place on *The New York Times* and *Publishers Weekly* bestseller lists as well as on a host of other national and regional bestseller lists. I would never have thought that thousands of people would wait in line to have their book signed by me, a reformed high-school prankster, a deeply lonely child who would do anything to be loved. Even a dreamer like me couldn't imagine having photographers yell, "Hey! E. Lynn, will you stop for us!" as I walk the red carpet at premieres and other extraordinary events. I can't act or sing, so why would I ever think that I would get to appear on Broadway in my favorite musical of all times, *Dreamgirls*. (I didn't sing, but as the emcee I still had a speaking part.)

On countless occasions my faith has pulled me through, and I've learned to "keep the faith and keep on stepping," because as the Bible says, "Faith without acts is dead." Faith has gotten me through many tough experiences: the deaths of my beloved grandmother, my close friends Butch and Tim, and my ex-lover Mario. Sure I was sad and heartbroken—I mourned for a time, but as the scripture says, "Joy cometh in the morning." As I've grown older I've come to understand that death is a natural progression, a part of the circle of life, and that I will always hold my loved ones in my heart.

Before I started writing this book, I got on my knees and prayed, as I do with each of my novels. First I thank God again for giving me this wonderful gift of allowing characters and stories to reside in my head. I humbly ask for direction and that somebody will be touched by something in my novels. I ask God to never let me forget that the life I have now is a blessing and that the way I show my appreciation for my gift is to share it and the benefits of this talent with others. I thank God for allowing me to experience dreams more magnificent than even I could ever have imagined. I thank Him for helping me realize that He placed a dream inside my heart and gave me innate gifts to combat life's obstacles. Now I understand that life may never be perfect, but it can be rich and rewarding nonetheless.

In 1997, after I wrote *If This World Were Mine* and while I was starting to write *Abide With Me*, my depression returned as simply as opening the door/window to get some air. But my despair resurfaced like a chilly unwelcome wind. "The black dog," as many call depression, had returned.

But this time I took control. I was living in Chicago, and I immediately found a doctor and resumed therapy. For a short period, I took medication and I didn't block out my family and friends. Instead I made them a part of my healing process. I continued to pray fervently, and I got great results: The depression disappeared almost as quickly as it had come. In a quiet moment, I realized that this bout of depression was different from the others—this time I had my writing to rely on. So I never stopped writing, and my characters provided a welcome and healthy solace.

Writing has allowed me to craft and sculpt a magnificent life and touch the lives of others in ways that still awe and humble me. Every day I receive e-mails from fans who let me know how much my books mean to them, and how their lives have been enriched and changed. Writing is my lifeline.

Writing saved my life.

I've also learned how to accept love in my life. I now know how important the love of my family is. Recently my mother turned seventy and we had a surprise party for her. Even though it was Mama's special day, I felt warm and near tears the entire evening as I looked around the room at my sisters, cousins, uncles, aunts, and other family and friends who'd come to join in the celebration. I thought how all these wonderful and amazing people had been there for me my entire life. Fans often ask if my family treats me like a star when I return home, and I reply, "My family has always treated me like a star." Not because I have gained notoriety as an author but because I am their son, brother, nephew, cousin, uncle, and friend.

Although I have made many new wonderful friends since I became "E. Lynn, bestselling author," the thing that brings me the most joy is that many of my friends from *back in the day* are still the people I depend on the most. They've all celebrated my success like it was their own, and they should, because I couldn't write novels about the importance of friendship without thinking about the love and kindness that they've shown me.

For years I felt that being gay meant that I'd have to give up on having true love in my life. But I've discovered how amazing it can be when you are finally willing to look at yourself honestly and live your life in truth. For almost a decade now, I've shared my life with a wonderful man who is good and kind to me. I have love in my life, and that's all you need to know. . . .

But please don't think that my life is wonderful now just because I've achieved a level of success as a bestselling author. My life's journey has shown me that material possessions and notoriety can't compare to learning to love yourself and appreci- ating and loving your family and friends. Money doesn't measure up to the feelings I get when I dream up a new storyline or cre- ate a sizzling new character or when I give a fan a warm embrace at a book signing. All the fame in the world is meaningless without the love of God, family, and friends.

When I look at my life now, my longtime love, my family and friends, and my precious little godson, Sean, I realize that because I had the courage to dream a dream and follow it, I've been able to write myself into the very life that I always wanted.

Now I know that I never have to be brokenhearted again. And neither do you.

Go ahead. No, I dare you. I double-dog dare you.

Live.

Dream.

M O R E   T H A N   Y O U   K N O W
(Featuring the Stars of My Life)

When you write your life story, a lot of people come into your head. Some of these visions make you smile and others make you sad or sometimes mad. When I told my mother that I was writing my memoir, she advised me not to waste a lot of time on people who'd tried to hurt me. For the most part I agreed, but of course there were people and situations that, in many ways, still affect the way I live my life today. Although my stepfather Ben died in 1989, the shadows of his abuse lingered over my life until I started writing. Writing allowed me to finally erase the pain he'd caused me. I'm also proud to say that for the last five years I have managed to maintain a happy life without the use of therapy or medication. I depend on the power of prayer, family, friends, and my life's work. So let's end on a happy note. I wish I could have mentioned and shared stories of all the amazing people who have come into my life, but space would only allow so much room. I couldn't imagine writing my life story without mentioning certain people in my life. So consider these "Acknowledgments, Part Two," as I include the names of people who've passed through my life and warmed my spirit with their kindness, people I love more than words can ever convey. Still,

I know I will forget someone, but charge it to my head and not my heart.

I'll start by mentioning the members of my family. I have included several of them in my previous books' acknowledgments, but this time I'm bringing the whole crew. My sisters, whom I love and don't see enough: Anita, Zettoria, and Jan. My nieces and nephews: Corey, Roshanunda, Tony, Whitney, Jasmine, Makel, Raven, and Ray Lynn and Eric Jr.

My Aunt Gee's family, starting with my Uncle Charles, who has been more like a father to me than any man I know and is a man whom I love, admire, and respect deeply. The sons of the Phillips clan and their families: Kennie and Larecia, Chuck and Karen plus Chaz, Tony and Delecia, Carlos and Denise, plus Morgan and Malcolm. Thanks Kennie, Chuck, Tony, and Carlos for always making me feel like your brother.

Uncle James and Aunt Hattie and my cousins (The Williams Clan), whom I always looked forward to spending weekends with as a child and still look forward to seeing today. First, my wonderful cousin Jacquelyn Johnson, whom I mentioned before, and her husband, Charles Wayne, and her son Michael and three lovely daughters, Corshaunda, Courtney, and Jennifer.

My cousins Robbie, Gary and his wife Joann, Sidney, Michelle, Pam, Virginia, and Amy.

My Uncle Arthur Lee, who always seemed like an older brother, and his wife.

In Michigan, my cousins (The Allen Clan), whom I mention in the memoir and made me always look forward to the summers. Cousins Lenora, Clarence, Roy, Juanita, Carolyn, Clarence Jr., Rickey, Wayne, Ervin, Lawrence Jr., and Jeanette.

My adoptive family in Tulsa, Oklahoma, who have loved and accepted me with open arms and have reveled in my success: the Smith family, starting with the lovely Mrs. Rose Smith, and her children Robin, Rhonda, Roy, and the adorable Reggie and Sherrie. I can't forget Desiree and Stephanie Smith, who have become an important part of my life.

I have five very close female friends who have always been there for me for over twenty years. They sometimes jokingly called themselves "Lynn's Angels." The funny thing is these talented, beautiful, and amazing women are all very close friends, and they all met through me. So don't ever let anybody tell you that beautiful women can't get along. My angels here on earth are Lencola Sullivan, Vanessa Gilmore, Robin Walters, Cindy Barnes, and Pam Frazier. Thanks for all the love and support, ladies.

I also have several other female friends who aren't a part of that group but who have been there for me as well. Some have been my friends for twenty-plus years, while a few have swept in and made me feel like they were loving me for at least that long. Much love and thanks to; Regina Daniels, Debra Martin Chase, Dyanna Williams, Linda Johnson Rice, Deborah Crable, Garbo Hearne, Sybil Wilkes, Yolanda Starks, Brenda Braxton Van Putten, Janet Hill, Rose Crater, Blanche Richardson, Sanya Whittaker Gragg, Sonya Jackson, Juanita Jordan, Sandy Matthews, and Dellanor Young.

Sean Harrison Gilmore is my heart.

Rodrick L. Smith is my heart and soul.

My real-life dreamboys are not boys at all, but men who are very important in my life and who've shown me a love I would never have imagined: Troy Donato, Sean James, Hugh Watson, and Brent Zachery. Thanks, fellows. Who said handsome men could only love themselves?

Two friends who feel more like the younger brothers I always dreamed of? Lloyd Boston and Anthony Bell. I couldn't imagine my life without either of you.

Carlton A. Brown has been a brother and a friend, and without him *Invisible Life* might not have ever happened.

Derrick Gragg is a person whose friendship I depend on and don't know how I survived so many years without. Thanks for reminding me of the important things in life.

Kevin Edwards, Reggie Van Lee, Derrick Thompson, Gordon Chambers, Andy Phillips, and Lee Daniels for their friendship always being only a phone call away.

There were some good times during my childhood in Little Rock. I liked all my teachers and classmates, but a few stuck out. (You know they had to stick out for me to remember them today.) It's funny but I can happily say that I went through school without ever having a fight with one of my classmates. (I did, however, narrowly escape a scrape with my elementary school friend Albert Cutts when I carelessly said something about his mama, but today, Albert and I still keep in contact via e-mail and class reunions.) Studies have shown that children who grow up in abusive households sometimes either become abusers or very gentle people. I'm glad I'm in the latter group.

There were other children I grew up with whom I'd like to mention besides Albert. Gary Nunn who is now Gary Nunn, M.D., Collette Finley, Robert Elmore, Robert Vault, Carl Vault, Beverly Stewart, Michael Stewart, Ronnie Hill, and Jarvis Anderson. There were some older young adults whom I also admired and were always kind to me, like Joseph Nunn Jr. and his sister, Rita.

The entire Morris clan were like cousins instead of friends. I spent many hours in their home enjoying the company of Marilyn Jean, Gail, Richard, Terrie, Rose, and Winston.

My favorite elementary school teacher was Mrs. Janet Gant, whom I had in the third grade. In junior high, my favorite teachers were Susan Adams, who taught journalism; Ann Young, who taught math; and Mr. Miller, who taught civics. Many of my other teachers were great, but these three make me smile even today.

In junior high I did make some friends whom I enjoyed hanging out with at school and at their homes. Besides the lovely Rose Crater, I must mention Valerie Rice, Wanda Nelson, Gertrude Stubbfield, Jocelyn Hester, Rodney Brooks, Kennie Gee, Beverly Rice, Mavis Dunn, Tony Rainey, Doris Palmer, William Sparks, James Jennings, Lanky Wells, Dexter Reed, Brenda Richardson, Sandra Myers, and Dwight Scott.

In high school, I loved my senior English teacher, Ms. Carol Martin. She had the greatest laugh and would read us Shakespeare aloud and chuckle to herself at some points that I didn't really understand back then. She made reading the classics fun. On my last book tour, Ms. Martin came to one of my signings and it almost brought me to tears. She still looked the same and still had her infectious smile. I consider Mr. Weldon Faulk, the principal at Hall High, and Luscious Powell, the then vice principal, as positives images who went out of their way to make sure I stayed focused and out of trouble.

I also had much love for two teachers who were also coaches, even though I despised gym as much as I hated taking showers in a room full of much bigger boys. Coach Oliver Elders and Pat Jones always believed my excuses for missing gym, even though I know they knew I was lying. Coach Jones would look at me with a smirk and a smile when he would say, "What's your excuse today, Lynn?"

After Becka and Karen, I formed several more friendships with women while in high school. These people were always very kind to me, even though I was at a point in my life where I wasn't willing to really reveal who I was. I mention the following people not because we were close friends but because they tried to offer me something I was desperately seeking but didn't know how to receive. They were Leslie Hankins, Cynthia Greer, Betsy Bracey, Connie Blass, Debi Thomas, Sherri Kaufman, Karen Moore, Carolyn Pledger, Shawn Shannon, Carla Hill, Harry McDermott, John Garr, and Eric Heizman.

In college, of course, I made close friends with my fraternity brothers. Part of the pledge process creates a special bond between men that sometimes lasts a lifetime. These men will always hold a special place in my heart: Marcus Greer, Dale Hamilton, John L. Colbert, Tony Childs, Jeff French, Flotille Farr, Anthony Acklin, Reginald Campbell, Harvey Hampton, Fredrick Tollette, Ronald Jordan, and of course Carney Butch Carroll.

I also became close to several women besides Chris Hinton. Overtis Hicks and Janis Kearney were in the journalism department and offered me friendships I still treasure. There were also Mellonee Carrigan, Dinah Gail Gant, Isabella Wofford, Judy Wilson, Cassandra Smith, Sharon Norwood, Mary Parker, Cathy Winfrey, Angela Mosley, Bridgette Knox, Bridgette Coleman, Carolyn Torrence, Wanda Marshall, Kim Nichols, and Dionne Harrold, my beloved cheerleader partner and little sister, who died suddenly a few years after graduating from the U of A. I also enjoyed my friendships with my cheerleader teammates Rick Farris, Michelle Reynolds, and Patti Tiffin.

Although I didn't attend the university while they were students, I became close friends with Randall Ferguson and Mike Saint, a former Razorback great whom I met when I interned at the IBM Little Rock office. Randall became my mentor and taught me more about business and data processing than any college professor could have, and Mike kept me entertained with his stories about his busy social life and playing running back for my favorite team of all time, the Arkansas Razorbacks.

To prove the adage that everything changes with time, I became great friends with Lonnie Ray Williams, an administrator at the University of Arkansas whom I didn't care for as an undergrad mainly because he was in a rival fraternity. Thank God we grow older and become wiser.

In Dallas, I formed friendships with a group of buppies-in-training and several of my fellow IBMers who lived in cities other than Dallas. Ken Hatten was the cousin of a good friend from college, Patrick Martin, and remains one of my closest friends. I'd also like to mention Ken Baker, Vernon Walker, former Notre Dame football great Clarence Ellis, and Tommy Walker. At IBM, my close buddies included Terry Brantley, Michael Keeler, T. Parker, and Paul Pecka.

When I moved to New York, I formed close friendships with two white women I met at Wang Labs. Jane Dolan and I spent long lunch hours talking about life after corporate America. She was a beautiful girl and wanted to be a model, and so I introduced her to Tracey Nash-Huntley. Lynn Offen shared intimate details of her love life with me over drinks at the Russian Tea Room, and we skipped out on sales calls to attend Broadway matinees. Once, during a performance of *Dreamgirls*, she became so emotional I thought the management was going to ask her to leave the theater. Although she was an attractive and brainy blonde, Lynn closely identified with the character of Lorrell Robinson.

Speaking of the theater, a visit to the backstage of *Smokey Joe's Café* was a moment when I realized that being a writer had made me somewhat famous. I can't tell you how many times I have stood at the stage door hoping for a glance of Broadway performers as they whisked by well-wishers. One night, I was at it again at *Smokey Joe's* when the stage manager recognized me and welcomed me in to meet the cast. I was so excited I didn't know what to do, but I went into my own private shock when I reached backstage and many of the cast were excited to meet me and wanted to take pictures with me and asked for *my* autograph. Never in a million years would I have imagined this would happen to me.

While living in New York the last three years, I have formed very strong and loving friendships with several people who call Broadway home. I have been dazzled by their talents and amazed by their kindness. Thank you: Lee Summers, B. J. Crosby, Adrian Bailey, Billy Porter, Brian Chandler, Leonard Wooldridge, Marva Hicks, Lawrence Hamilton, Charles Holt, Bobby Daye, and Terri Burrell for letting me into your world.

I am proud to be a writer today because of the wonderful people who also do what I do for a living. To be quite honest, I didn't know what to expect. When Anchor Books was preparing to publish *Invisible Life*, I asked if they were going to send the book to certain famous writers to provide quotes. I was disappointed when I was told that they weren't writers who were willing to do such a thing. I thought maybe they thought they were too good for me. Now I realize they were just busy working on their own stuff, and boy do I understand. Still, there are a number of writers, known and not so well-known, whom I cherish as friends: Tina McElroy Ansa was the first published writer to reach out and offer advice, love, and friendship. I learned to be gracious and giving to fellow writers from Tina and her husband Jonee Ansa. Pearl Cleage was the first writer to buy one of my books and offer me moral support. Pearl is a wonderful woman and writer.

I was a big fan of Terry McMillan long before *Waiting to Exhale*. I remember feeling my palms sweat the first time I was in a room with her. It didn't matter that there were at least two hundred other people and she didn't have a clue as to who I was or why I was there. She was just nice and has been throughout my career, offering me friendship and advice as I follow the path she has so brilliantly blazed. I could say the same thing about Walter Mosley, and I'm grateful for the example he has set.

There are other writers whom I admire and call friends: Frank McCourt, Eric Jerome Dickey, James Earl Hardy, Kimberla Lawson Roby, Michael Eric Dyson, Bebe Moore Campbell, R. M. Johnson, Iyanla Van Zant, Marita Golden, Jill Nelson, Tananarive Due, Brian Keith Jackson, Keith Boykin, Yolanda Joe, Wally Lamb, and Victoria Christopher Murray. I am so proud to be a part of this group of writers.

The African American gay community got the buzz going on me, and for this I will be forever grateful. There were a few special individuals, like Stanley Bennett Clay, Devere Jackson, Charlene Cothran, and Phil Wilson, who offered support and friendship. I guess you could say becoming a writer allowed me a little nerd's revenge. After *Just As I Am* had been published and was garnering a place on bestseller lists, I was in Washington, D.C., on a Sunday afternoon. After a book signing, Bruce Fuller and Tim convinced me to join them at Tracks. At first I said no as I recalled the many Sunday evenings I'd gone there only to leave alone and depressed, but something inside me said, "Go." When I walked in, you would have thought I had discovered a cure for AIDS; the boys made way for me like God was getting ready to part the Red Sea again. The reception I received was awesome. Good-looking men were lining up to shake my hand and give me a hug. After a couple of hours of this, Tim leaned over and whispered, "Damn, bitch, I think I'm going home and write me a book." I knew the words were coming out of Tim's mouth, but it sure did sound like Randy. The only bad thing was the timing of all these good-looking men showing me love. I was still on a mission for something greater, which meant I was still celibate. In the words of the TV character Florida Evans, "Damn, damn, damn."

Before I put this puppy to a close, I would like to thank and mention a few people who went out of their way to make this dream come true for me in ways both big and small. These are people I met in Atlanta, Washington, D.C., and other cities when nobody knew what an E. or a Lynn was. These people cared enough to find out: Valerie Boyd and Phyllis Perry, two wonderful women and talented authors; Keith Thomas, whose story about me in the *Atlanta Journal and Constitution* got the buzz sounding so loud that they heard it in New York; also Mingon Goode, Carl Cromwell, Larry Banks, Bruce Fuller, Jerry Gibbs, Janis Murray, and countless others who told just one person about my books, and then they in turn told someone else, and so on and so on . . .

Thank you all for making a little boy from Little Rock's dream come true.

INVISIBLE LIFE

In his last year at law school, Raymond Tyler seems to have it all, but there are secret, terrifying issues for him to confront. Being black is tough enough, but Raymond becomes increasingly conscious of conflicting sexual feelings: He is completely committed to Sela, his longtime girlfriend, but his attraction to his friend Kelvin has become more than mere friendship.

Fiction/0-385-46968-3

JUST AS I AM

Just As I Am picks up where *Invisible Life* ends. Raymond struggles to come to terms with his sexuality and with the grim reality of AIDS. Nicole, an aspiring singer/actress, experiences frustration in both her career and in her attempts to find a genuine love relationship. Both Raymond and Nicole share an eclectic group of friends who challenge them to look at the world through different eyes.

Fiction/0-385-46970-5

ABIDE WITH ME

In this masterful conclusion to the Invisible Life trilogy, E. Lynn Harris traces the evolving destinies of Nicole and Raymond and reintroduces readers to their respective lovers, best friends, and potential enemies. *Abide with Me* moves between the worlds of New York City, where Nicole has settled in order to pursue her dream of returning to the Broadway stage, and Seattle, where a late-night phone call from a U.S. Senator is about to change Raymond's life dramatically.

Fiction/0-385-48658-8

NOT A DAY GOES BY

John Basil Henderson has always played the field as a professional football player and as an equal opportunity lover. After retiring his jersey, the dashing playboy is getting married to his new love, Yancey Harrington Braxton. Yancey is a fiercely driven, emerging Broadway star who would seem his ideal companion, but she is also an insatiable opportunist, and when Yancey unearths Basil's most carefully guarded secrets, she finds more than she bargained for.

Fiction/0-385-49825-X

ANY WAY THE WIND BLOWS

When her wedding to John Basil Henderson didn't co:
planned, Yancey Harrington Braxton flew off to L.A. ar
herself as mega-diva Yancey B. And Basil started concen
his career as a high-powered sports agent. But then Yancey ̣ ̣ ̣ ̣ ̣ ̣ ̣
gle, "Any Way the Wind Blows," hit the charts, and now it threatens
to blow Basil's cover—if anyone learns who the song is really about.

Fiction/0-385-72118-8

A LOVE OF MY OWN

After Zola Norwood meets media mogul Davis McClinton on a New
York–bound flight, he makes her a couple of offers before they even
land. One is editing his hot new urban style magazine *Bling Bling*.
The other is more personal. As Zola and Raymond Tyler, Jr., *Bling
Bling*'s CEO, pursue their ambitions and search for love, secrets from
the past and events out of today's headlines keep the action moving.

Fiction/0-385-49271-5

AND THIS TOO SHALL PASS

In the locker rooms and newsrooms of Chicago, four lives are about
to intersect in romance and scandal. Zurich is a rookie quarterback
for the Chicago Cougars, and his trajectory for superstardom has
just been interrupted by a sexual assault charge from Mia. With his
career in jeopardy, he hires the high-powered attorney Tamela, while
Sean, a gay sportswriter, covers the story and uncovers his heart.

Fiction/0-385-48031-8

IF THIS WORLD WERE MINE

Four friends keep a collective journal they call "If This World Were
Mine." Yolanda, a media consultant, has a no-nonsense attitude;
Riley, a former marketing executive, has been reduced to a "kept
woman with kids." Computer engineer Dwight's anger at the world
is offset by the compassion of Leland, a gay psychiatrist. After five
years, the bonds of friendship are weakening, and the group must
face the challenges of work, love, and a stranger in their midst.

Fiction/0-385-48656-1

ANCHOR BOOKS
Available from your local bookstore, or call toll-free to order:
1-800-793-2665 (credit cards only).